Uses of the Future

HERBERT J. MULLER

Uses of the Future

INDIANA UNIVERSITY PRESS
Bloomington & London

Published in Canada by Fitzhenry & Whiteside Limited,
Don Mills, Ontario
Library of Congress catalog card number: 73–15240
ISBN: 0–253–36210–5
Manufactured in the United States of America

Library of Congress Cataloging in Publication Data

Muller, Herbert Joseph, 1905–
    Uses of the future.

    1. Civilization, Modern—1950–   2. United
States—Civilization—1970–   3. Twenty–first
century—Forecasts. I. Title.
CB428.M854   901.94   73–15240
ISBN 0–253–36210–5

To My Former Students

Contents

[v i i i]

Acknowledgments

In a few passages I substantially repeat what I wrote in an article-review of *Can We Survive Our Future?*, a symposium edited and introduced by G. R. Urban, in collaboration with Michael Glenny. This appeared in *Technology and Culture*, Winter 1973. I have also used material from "Some Problems of Meaning," published in *The Journal of Aesthetic Education*, April, 1973, and from an article, "Modern Civilization and Human Survival" in *The Philosophy Forum*, Spring, 1973, Vol. 12, issues 1/2.

Chapters III, VI, and VII are expansions of articles, somewhat revised: "Education for the Future," *American Scholar*, Summer 1972; "Reflections on B.F. Skinner," *Journal of the Otto Rank Association*, December, 1972; "The Possibilities of a Universal Faith," *Religious Humanism*, Winter 1973.

Preface

This is a book of speculation, not prophecy. While I am deeply indebted to the efforts of our systematic forecasters—efforts that seem to me clearly essential in a technological society and an era of fantastically rapid change—I stress the uncertainties and the hazards of prediction, which they themselves freely acknowledge and sometimes emphasize, because popular journals have made a fad of predicting with much hoopla new wonders or gadgets. And though my study here is fairly comprehensive, it is by no means either exhaustive or authoritative. I write as an educator in the humanities and a nonprofessional historian who has roamed all over world history, and made a broad study of modern science and technology too, but without attempting a thorough mastery of any one field or becoming an authority on any subject. In particular I am not up to systems analysis, model building, or other such features of the current vogue of "methodology," a term I am weary of; I simply don't know how to construct a model, or to "process" data by feeding computers. As for the future, I have positive enough opinions about a desirable future, but otherwise can only speculate about possibilities.

In a sense, moreover, my main concern is the extraordinary *present*. This has created the need of efforts to anticipate and control change because of the terrific drive of science and technology, and the current problems thereby created. As I write (1973), it seems highly unlikely that the most serious of these problems, such as the environmental crisis and in America the urban crisis, will be "solved" within the next generation, or by the year 2000, which is about as far ahead as most of the forecasters try to see. Although there will surely be significant changes, to a considerable extent we must anticipate more of the same. The uses of the future have become so insistent that they may obscure the more insistent claims of the present—and not merely because we have to live in it, or because it is all we have for sure. As I stress in my introductory chapter, what the future will be like is being determined to a considerable extent by what our political and business leaders are doing—or failing to do—right now. One reason why we cannot predict with assurance is that we cannot assume with confidence that they will act rationally and responsibly.

This concern with the present entails an obvious danger of provinciality. I have written under the cloud of the Cold War, the nuclear arms race, and our war in Indochina. At the moment, the great powers on the world scene are America and the Soviet Union, and to a lesser but increasing extent China. Their relations will no doubt continue to be important, but I do not assume that they will necessarily continue to dominate the world scene. Western Europe is emerging as a great power again, and if it succeeds in achieving unity it might throw off its dependence on the United States and speak as an equal in the world's councils. Japan is already more obviously a force to be reckoned with because it has become one of the greatest industrial powers in the world. Conceivably, too, a great power might emerge from the developing nations—Brazil, for example, has been considered a likely candidate, and Mexico a possible one; and though I see no immediate prospect of such a development, these nations are at least asserting themselves more. They constitute a "Third World" that even now has made archaic the old division between the Communist world and what Americans have called the "free world"; while they all want to modernize or industrialize, most of them—alike in Asia, Africa, and Latin America—do not welcome the leadership of either the United States or the Soviet Union, but want to go their own way, in keeping with their own traditional culture. And if or when any of them succeed in making their own atomic bombs, they would constitute another threat to world peace. All such possibilities accentuate the impossibility of confident prediction.

Similarly I have tried to guard against the provinciality implicit in my primary concern, the state of America. This is clearly pertinent for my present purposes because we are the most advanced technological society, and as a people the most disposed—with the possible exception of the Russians—to conform to the compulsions of modern technology, but I do not assume that we will necessarily maintain our vaunted technological leadership of the world. (Right now we might do well to bring in some Japanese to teach us how to run our railroads.) I do assume that America will not be free to determine its future just to suit itself. Given One World, its future will surely be affected to some incalculable extent by what happens in the rest of the world.

A provincial people, notoriously lacking in a sense of the past, Americans also bring up one of my major themes—the need of such a sense, even for the purposes of futurism. To begin with, we cannot fully understand the present without some knowledge of the past out of which it came, and much of which is still alive in institutions, beliefs, and popular attitudes. Problems may seem worse—or get worse—because most Americans do not see them in a historical perspective, and lack a tragic sense of life, or of the human condition as it has been all through the endless travails of man's history. Thus many people now deplore the "instant" culture of the youth, with its stress on immediate gratification, which among other things has led to the addiction to drugs; but conservatives who attack such results of "permissiveness" do not see that this is deeply rooted in the vaunted American way of life, a hedonism now promoted by an immense advertising industry, built up by the free private enterprise that they regard as the very heart of the American way. And Americans young and old, radical and conservative, typically have a passion for instant solutions of our problems, by new legislation, crash programs, or too often merely by political rhetoric, as in President Nixon's proclamation of a "new American revolution," a program that was neither new nor revolutionary. As for the future, both government and the public are disposed to consider only immediate consequences, or the short run—not to take a long view, still less a global view. Thus our federal agencies typically live from hand to mouth on an annual budget. Though the Pentagon has been able to count on living high, at the expense of domestic welfare programs, and the lavishly financed space program has demonstrated the possibilities of long-range planning, backed by sustained, coordinated effort, the federal budget makes little or no provision for such planning and sustained commitment, which would be necessary, for example, to restore the American city. As typically, our politicians look only as far ahead as the next election, not to the year 2000. In effect, they don't give a damn about the future.

Readers should be warned that if only for this reason I am not optimistic about our prospects. I should then add that because of all the notorious crises of our time, there is some disposition to use too easily and habitually the language of crisis, with notes of desperation, and to blow up every problem into a crisis. (Thus Oscar Handlin has seen a "crisis" even in the study of history, whereas his article on the subject came down to a complaint that many younger historians were no longer respecting their elders.) Nevertheless I think that the emphasis should finally be on the gravity of our most obvious problems, which is not obvious enough to most Americans. Although they now lack the confidence of their ancestors, reflected in the pioneer refrain "We don't know where we're going, but we're on our way," they still tend to be too complacent in their consumers' paradise, while having no clearer idea of where they're going, or why.

Some of the chapters in this book are based on articles I have published or public lectures I have given, as indicated in my formal acknowledgements. All have been revised and amplified, however, and though they might still stand separately, the book is not just a random collection of essays. It is necessarily selective because of the immense scope of my subject, and the impossibility of treating thoroughly in one volume all of the many problems I bring up. I have mentioned, for example, that what happens in the Third World is sure to affect us; but an adequate treatment of its problems and prospects would require at least another volume. Here I have offered only an illustrative chapter on Mexico, which I know best. Mexico is one of the most successful of the "developing" countries, exemplifying the kind of gains in welfare that explain the universal effort to industrialize; it also makes plain the costs of economic development, the new problems created by such development—basic problems that have everywhere cropped up with success in "modernizing"; and as our neighbor it illustrates most clearly as well the unfortunate influence of America on the needy countries of the world, and the costs of our own success, the American way of life. Likewise the capital of Mexico points to another subject that I periodically bring up, but that would require still another volume for adequate treatment—the problems and prospects of the modern metropolis.

Granted these reservations, however, my book is sufficiently unified and focused by not only its basic theme but by other recurrent themes, such as my concern more with our spiritual than our material resources, or with fundamental questions of human values, and my stress on the necessity of value-judgments, especially moral judgments, just because they are considered unbecoming to analysts in our positivistic climate of opinion. My freely expressed judgments are personal opinions, of course, which readers are as free to disagree with, but I would still insist that they are not therefore "merely" subjective, as positivists are wont to say.

At any rate, I am not trying to disarm criticism (as every writer knows, a hopeless task) when I add that this book does not build up to a resonant conclusion, a positive answer to the questions it raises. It is chiefly an effort to raise the right questions, not to give all the answers. In this effort my guiding principle remains a principle of ambiguity. I have come to write habitually in terms of "on the other hand" or "yes and no," to an uncertain extent: a habit that can be pretty depressing, to me too, but that at least may serve as a healthy reminder that in spite of the "knowledge explosion," which has involved a great deal of trivial knowledge, we still know too little about most basic questions, and cannot hope to know positively all we would like to know. So we might heed the antique wisdom of Socrates, who explained that he was wiser than most men because he knew that he didn't know.

Postscript: This book was completed before the revelations about the Watergate affair and other corruption in the campaign to re-elect President Nixon that discredited his administration and eroded his popularity and his great "personal triumph." The scandal gives me no reason to alter the judgments of Richard Nixon expressed in chapters toward the end. Neither do his achievements before the Watergate affair monopolized headlines and front pages. Before completing my book I at least knew of Nixon's most positive achievement, the agreements he reached with Red China and the Soviet Union, by repudiating the policies on which he had made his political fortune. But when he told the country that there is no longer an urban crisis, I could only say that this was nonsense.

Uses of the Future

I

The Vogue of Futurism

Among the endings that haunt the mind of contemporary man,
up to the possible end of our civilization, is the end of Utopia,
the old dream of an ideal society of perfect justice, or a kind of
heaven on earth. Even so I think it is possible to contemplate this
particular end calmly. The utopias conceived by thinkers from
Plato on have typically been purely "rational" societies, and as
such were not organic growths but organizations imposed on
people, ruled by an elite, at the cost of the values of freedom,
diversity, and openness to experiment and change, since these
values necessarily entail a measure of instability. (In fairness to
the utopians, let us remember that the Christian heaven is no
democracy either.) With the rise of revolutionaries in modern
times, utopias have been imposed by violence, and have been
sufficiently discredited by the example of the Soviet Union, the
tyranny that came out of Karl Marx's dream of a classless society.
Today the more naive apostles of technology offer visions of
abundance, comfort, and ease, but hold out no promise of either
a rich culture or the realization of the ideals of justice and brotherhood. When elaborated in any detail, they too often suggest
Aldous Huxley's Brave New World. And usually they are still
provincial, like Plato's Republic and most of the other utopias of
the past; B.F. Skinner's Walden Two is a conspicuous example.

[3]

The basic fact today is that utopia is impossible for America or any other country alone, no matter how great and powerful; only in a world utopia could the age-old dreams of an ideally just society be realized. Long ago H.G. Wells, one of the most indefatigable dreamers about the shape of things to come, said truly: "No less than a planet will serve the purposes of a modern Utopia."

Needless to add, the prospect of such a utopia is pretty dim. The technology that makes it theoretically possible is also making it practically impossible as it continues steadily to widen the gulf between the advanced industrial countries and the many more poor ones, aggravating their resentments and hatreds of the favored affluent peoples—above all, Americans—and raising the dread possibility of a kind of global class war. Yet for just this reason, visions of utopia may still serve as not only an inspiration but a guide to practical effort, and a necessary corrective of the typically narrow, short-sighted "realism" of professionally hard-headed men, in both government and the world of thought, who too easily take for granted as natural or unavoiable much that is simply senseless in our supposedly practical society, devoted to ideals of technical rationality and efficiency.

We have grown wary of wishful thinking, for good reasons, but now we may have an excessive fear of it, in view of the many plain absurdities in our society that people put up with. It is to my mind preposterous, for example, that life should be growing intolerable in the big cities of America, by far the richest nation on earth, in the most urbanized civilization in history, with technological resources undreamed of in past societies. These absurdities recall George Bernard Shaw's remark long ago: "I hear you say 'Why?' always 'Why?' . . . But I dream things that never were; and I say 'Why not?' " We might ask more persistently "Why not?" even of "impossible" dreams, such as providing spacious living quarters in clean, pleasant surroundings for all the residents of our cities. The question may serve realistic purposes too by leading to a fuller awareness of the "practical" reasons for the absurdities, which involve the interests of hard-headed businessmen concerned only with private profit and the avoidance of higher taxes.

Still another reason for utopian thinking is the vogue of futurism, or what is now dignified as the "science" of futurology—the systematic effort to forecast the future by specialists working in think tanks, or such organizations as The Institute for the Future and the Commission on the Year 2000.

Although men have tried to foretell the future ever since the ancients consulted the stars or the entrails of animals, and they have dreamed or speculated about it especially since the rise and spread in the eighteenth century of the historically novel faith in progress, never before have they thought about it so intensively. The obvious reason is the imperious fact of change in a technological society: continuous, often radical change, at an unprecedented rate, which has created a plain need of efforts not only to understand it but to anticipate it, if possible direct and control it. These efforts raise the basic questions of what is *probable*, what is *possible*, and above all what is *desirable*.

2. THE "SCIENCE" OF FUTUROLOGY

Some probabilities are easy to forecast because of the steady drive of science and technology, and the immense sums now being spent on research and development, which make it almost certain that anything that can be discovered or invented will be sooner or later. Thus Herman Kahn and Anthony Wiener predict confidently a hundred important technological innovations that they say are almost certain to appear by the year 2000. I for one am quite willing to take their word for it, inasmuch as scientists and technicians are already at work to realize these possibilities, including such seemingly unlikely projects as "programmed dreams." I assume that there will also be some unexpected discoveries and inventions like many in the past, such as X-rays. But as Kahn and Wiener recognize, the serious uncertainties of prediction arise with the social and cultural consequences of these innovations. (Who, if anyone, foresaw the profound, far-reaching effects of the invention of the computer?) Some of the innovations in store, such as new chemical weapons and new techniques for surveillance and control of people, are obviously alarming. But even such presumably beneficent ones as the prolongation of life by organ regeneration and transplantation raise problems of public policy, for in view of the expensiveness of the operations and the scarcity of surgeons, how are the fortunate patients to be selected? Simply by their wealth? Daniel Bell, who heads the Commission on the Year 2000, has said that the only prediction about the future that can be made with certainty is that public authorities will face more problems than ever before.

Most of the futurologists are modest men, who clearly realize the hazards of prediction. In any case they are not setting up as prophets. Their main objective is usually just to anticipate likely developments and then perhaps to suggest ways of dealing with the problems looming up, possibly of avoiding or minimizing them, or at least to provide policy makers with options, through an awareness of possible alternatives. In this effort they have the advantage of increasingly sophisticated techniques. Thus "systems analysis" has already been supplemented by "systems dynamics," in which Jay M. Forrester of M.I.T. has pioneered. Computer models enable analysts to deal with the interaction of variables in complex social systems in terms of if/then propositions, and thereby to anticipate the dynamic consequences of given assumptions, and to supplement or correct the intuitions of common sense, which usually assumes "all other things being equal," which they rarely if ever are. On "world dynamics," for example, Forrester has devised a model that interrelates population, capital investment, geographic space, natural resources, pollution, and food production. Whereas common sense seized on a birth control program as the obvious way of combating the population explosion by reducing the birth rate, which it may do for the short run, his dynamic model indicates how this rate may be affected too by the amount of food available, the extent of pollution, and improvement in the quality of life; such obviously desirable measures as increasing the food supply and improving standards of living may therefore have such unfortunate consequences as increasing the birth rate. In analyzing the dynamics of urban systems, Forrester has shown that the housing problem is due not so much to a housing shortage as to an excess of poor housing; so the government might revise accordingly its so far largely ineffective program for dealing with the problem.

In effect, the futurologists are trying to enable us to choose our future. But this laudable effort raises some questions about their qualifications. They are able to maintain that futurology is a "science" chiefly because they confine themselves to an analysis of current trends, which they then project into the future. Up to a point this seems to me clearly a sensible policy, for the basic drive of science and technology seems sure to continue, even though the power they give man is often clearly dangerous. Still, the futurologists may not be imaginative enough to foresee the possibility of counter-trends. (Bertrand de Jouvenel, who in France is directing a study of "futuribles," or possible futures, prefers the term "conjecture" to "forecasting," and has written about the "art of conjecture," declaring that "the intellectual construction of a likely future *is a work of art, in the full sense of the term."*) Among other things, cultural developments will be very important, but Daniel Bell has observed that these are the hardest to anticipate. The ruling values of the future may well be different from ours, and as he grants, what seems important to futurologists now may come to seem much less important, or what they regard as inconsequential may come to have considerable consequence. They cannot deal "scientifically" either with such imponderables as the possibilities of more revolutions, dictatorships, and wars, or the response of people to the changing conditions of life. (Although they were at work in the late 'sixties, none of them—to my knowledge—anticipated the student revolt, both at home and abroad, any more than I did.)

In general, they are not very bold thinkers. While they anticipate a future fuller of problems, they seldom suggest any radical changes in our political, economic, or educational system in order to deal with them more effectively than our institutions are dealing with the sufficiently serious problems now on our hands. Likewise they seldom stress the apparent need of more and stricter controls in order to prevent such plain evils as increasing pollution. They can be as shortsighted as the rest of us, for few of them anticipated the environmental crisis. (When the Bell Commission on the Year 2000 was formed in the late 'sixties, it included no ecologist.) And now that this world-wide crisis has been recognized, they still concentrate on forecasts of the future of our own country, with only occasional attention to the effects on us of what will be going on in the rest of the world, including the alarming possibility of some kind of explosion in the "Third World" made up of all the poor countries. With an eye to the needs of these countries, Robert McNamara has said that we do not need and cannot afford to make still more automobiles, but all the signs are that we will go on turning them out by the millions, and I have heard of little alarm from American futurologists over this probability. It is no doubt too much to expect them to anticipate the state of the world in that year 2000, inasmuch as there is no "scientific" or any other method of doing this with any assurance, but anyway we had all better try to keep in mind that America will not be able to determine its future just to suit itself, not to mention that it cannot afford more Vietnams.

As it is, the predictions of futurologists may be dangerous because of some tendency to be self-fulfilling, by inspiring more effort to exploit than to prevent the technological innovations in store, most of which offer a market for businessmen. When they

[8]

tell us that within a generation most Americans will be living in monstrous urban agglomerates like "Boswash," extending from Boston to Washington, realtors may begin planning and "developing" or wrecking accordingly, while encouraging government to build still more highways and expressways, bulldozing still more landscape. Predictions can also be self-defeating, as was Karl Marx's prediction of the inevitable doom of capitalism. This possibility adds to the uncertainties of forecasting, while also raising questions about our policy-makers, doubts that they can be trusted to act wisely on the options that the futurologists point out.

An immediate difficulty is that most leaders share the popular faith in technological "progress," with too little regard for social or human costs, exemplified by President Nixon's passion for supersonic planes. These would not only pollute the stratosphere, but create such plain nuisances on earth as sonic booms and deafening noise in the vicinity of airports; so the obvious question is—or ought to be—what are they good for? Why build them? They are less economical than jets or jumbojets, so much so that the airplane manufacturers will not build them unless the government pays the heavy costs of research and development, or subsidizes the whole program. Their only apparent use would be to enable wealthy travelers or bureaucrats to save a few hours in crossing the oceans. Nixon defended them chiefly as a matter of prestige: we had to build them in order to maintain our technological "leadership" of the world—a leadership, be it added, that we have not in fact maintained in the more basic steel and automobile industries, not to mention such desirable products as watches and cameras. Add that the discontinuance of the SST program threw engineers and other technicians out of work; this only accentuates the basic irrationality of our economy; for these men could be put to work on socially useful projects, including the badly needed one of restoring the environment.

Similar questions are raised by the most obviously practical mode of futurology—extensive planning, inaugurated by the Five Year Plans of the Soviet Union. While big corporations try to plan their future operations as a matter of course, the idea of planning by government long scared or horrified American conservatives, who thought of it as something that only Communists did and therefore a threat to free private enterprise. By now, however, it has become respectable if only because the planning has been primarily for economic or fiscal purposes, and has served the interests of business too. It has helped to promote the national goal of economic growth, as measured by the gross national product. The idolized GNP is of course a very gross measure, suited to a grossly materialistic society; it lumps together the production of all kinds of material goods, no matter how trivial, superfluous, or socially harmful, without distinguishing the material costs of combating such by-products of industry as pollution. It obscures such important considerations for a democratic society as how equitably the increased wealth has been distributed, and how much of it has been devoted to promoting the public welfare; for while economists rejoice that the GNP has more than quadrupled since the World War, and has now soared to over a trillion dollars, many appear to forget that most Americans are obviously not four times better off, many are relatively worse off—not to mention the millions of unemployed. And as a purely quantitative measure, the GNP takes no account of the quality of American life, which has plainly deteriorated during this phenomenal economic growth.

In Western Europe planners have been trying to pay more heed to such considerations. While they too have been planning primarily for economic purposes, they are trying to provide as well for social and cultural development, as in the "regional planning" by the Council of Europe. But then they run into the difficulties of futurology. Planners and forecasters alike feel most at ease when dealing with factors they can quantify, and there are no agreed measurements for the quality of life, or for the esthetic, moral, broadly spiritual values that must be considered in any judgment of the good life.

Another basic difficulty is that planners typically try to provide for what people want right now, not necessarily what we ought to want, or what people in the coming generation will want, as foreshadowed—perhaps—by our rebellious youth. This difficulty becomes more serious when we ask, Who selects the planners? The answer is usually government, which tends to take a short-sighted, provincial view of the national interest—a kind of view popular with the taxpayers.

As for the possibilities of the future, they are limited by the requirements of modern technology, which we may assume will not and cannot be simply dispensed with, like it or not. Although one might prefer a simple agricultural society, there is not the slightest chance of returning to such a society as long as our civilization endures; even apart from the fact that without our science and technology we could not sustain the billions of people now inhabiting the earth, we cannot possibly scrap them or just forget all we have learned. But by the same token the possibilities may be regarded as otherwise almost limitless. While common sense may dismiss the possibility of a heaven on earth, it might still be unwise, or even inhuman, to set sharp limits to utopian visions of an ideal society. The basic fact here is that we now have the wealth and the technological means to achieve almost anything we want, as demonstrated by our fantastic feat of putting men on the moon. Only this brings up the tragic aspect of our condition, which is more like a peculiar predicament because of the painful awareness that the ideal possibilities of our unprecedented power have been largely unrealized.

It also leads to what is for me the most important question raised by futurology—what is desirable, or what we *ought* to want. This of course involves value-judgments that are not scientifically verifiable and so are commonly tabooed by social scientists. This whole problem is a matter for educators, which I shall take up in

[11]

a later chapter. Meanwhile I should remark that many futurologists, especially those in Europe, have been much concerned about human values, other than economic ones, but that their "science" makes them liable to tendencies the rest of us should be wary of. Because they aspire to an objective analysis, they may succumb to the common fallacy of dismissing value-judgments as "merely" subjective or emotive, as if only technical specialists or "experts" were entitled to express opinions in these vital matters. As an example I have cited Ithiel Pool, a political scientist on the Bell Commission, who has granted that philosophy and literature "have their value," but declared that the knowledge by which "men of power are humanized and civilized" comes from psychology, sociology, political science, and systems analysis—civilizing influences I have failed to notice in most American technocrats, or the chiefs they advise. At any rate, I am writing on the assumption that while these alleged sciences have their value, we could do with more attention to philosophy and literature as we approach the problem of possible or desirable futures.

Still another hazard of forecasting is that while there is now talk of the future as "the cause of the present," the fact remains that our future will depend on what our leaders, in both government and business, do—or fail to do—right now, and that we cannot count on the responsibility, still less the wisdom or idealism of our policy-makers. Let us remember that a great many people anticipated World War II, with dread—and it came anyhow. As a sardonic French reviewer commented on some book about futurology, these men seemed unaware that the future may be behind us. Or as Paul Valéry said prophetically after World War I, "We are backing into the future"—which turned out to be the catastrophe of World War II, following which we backed into the Cold War and a nuclear arms race.

Then we must face the final complication, that we can no longer be sure even that man has a future. We have to reckon first of all with the problem of human survival, forced on us by our technological "progress." And on this in particular I should stress the necessity of moral judgments. We need all the knowledge that futurologists can give us, a full awareness of where current trends are leading, but we also need much more moral sensitivity, moral imagination, or simply more sense of moral responsibility, in the interests of all mankind. I am willing to say that we need more heart and soul—imprecise or unscientific though these terms are, and immeasurable the qualities they refer to. For this purpose man has never had more practical need of visions of ideal possibilities.

II

The Problem of Human Survival

The first thing to be said about the problem of human survival is a commonplace, that it is historically unprecedented. The end-of-the-world tradition come down from early Christianity, which inspired apocalyptic visions on the approach of the year 1000 A.D., affected relatively few people, and the end was not simply feared; it meant the Second Coming of our Lord, for good Christians a blessed event. Today it may serve only as a reminder that our specialists on the future offer no such apocalyptic visions about the year 2000. Myths of other great societies, such as India, foretold universal cataclysms, but in a future too remote or hazy to scare people or influence conduct.

In our day serious thinkers are for the first time viewing human survival as a real problem, and for obvious reasons. An all-out thermonuclear war might well destroy our civilization, conceivably put a melodramatic end to the human race. Short of this catastrophe there remains the environmental crisis, intensified by the population explosion; scientists tell us that if we go on living as we have been, our deteriorating earth will sooner or later become uninhabitable. Meanwhile the technological drive that has generated such crises continues to seem irresistible, as in the insanity of the nuclear arms race. So in my own study of the impact of modern technology on society and culture I raised the basic questions: Can we control this terrific technology? Can we direct the extraordinary power man has achieved to humane, civilized, or just sensible ends?[1]

As I see it, these questions are still open. No inevitable, predetermined fate awaits us. We still have a real choice in futures; what the future will be is strictly up to us. But for just this reason we can no longer afford the simple optimism of the American past, which was not as "wholesome" as it may appear in the spirit of the pioneers because it led to an increasingly naive faith in a kind of automatic progress, primarily material. We need first to take a hard look at the worst. And let us begin with a look at our own country, which prides itself on being the world leader in technology.

As the greatest power on earth, America is a major threat to hopes of human survival, to my mind even the most dangerous threat today. Immediately it forces consideration of the powers that actually direct our technology—government and big business. By government it has been directed primarily to military purposes, a huge "defense" program that continues to get the top national priority even though we have already spent more than a trillion dollars to develop a power great enough to devastate the whole world many times over. The fear of Communist aggression and expansion has obscured the plain truth that we have been by far the most expansionist power, setting up hundreds of military bases all over the world, proclaiming a vital national interest in all of what we choose to call the free world, no less because much of it is ruled by military dictators, types our military appear to have a particular affinity for. Allied with government is big business in the now notorious military-industrial complex that President Eisenhower tried vainly to warn us

1. *The Children of Frankenstein,* 1970. In what follows I cannot avoid repeating some ideas that to me seem depressingly obvious, but evidently are not obvious enough to most Americans.

[15]

against. Big business has also helped to create the "American Empire" that troubles many Europeans as well as Latin Americans. This refers not merely to the military imperialism we are often charged with, in particular because of our war in Indochina. It refers directly to our economic empire, represented by investments abroad totaling more than 100 billion dollars. The protection of our empire, both political and economic, including all our military bases, is among the excuses for the dangerous power of the military-industrial complex, and for the often sinister activities of our ubiquitous C.I.A. It also helps to explain our apparent preference for military dictators over popular liberal or Leftish governments, for such dictators can be counted on to be anti-Communist and more easily bribed by military aid. The "free world" by our definition need not be democratic but simply pro-American, hospitable to our military and our businessmen, and never so independent as to oppose our interests, or our notion of its interests. For our own hemisphere, President Kennedy laid down the doctrine that we would not tolerate any more Cubas.

Otherwise business directs our technology primarily in the interests of private profit, not the public welfare. It makes its most apparent contribution to welfare by its devotion to the popular goal of economic growth, the production of ever more material goods to satisfy private wants, even though Americans already consume many times their proportionate share of the world's dwindling natural resources, and contributes as much more to the pollution of the natural environment.

As I write, the chances of a thermonuclear war appear to have been lessened by President Nixon's agreements with China and the Soviet Union. In theory these imply the abandonment of the assumptions on which our Cold War policy has been based, as also our hot war in Vietnam. But in practice we are still operating on those assumptions. Thus we are still committed to the nuclear arms race, supposedly to protect ourselves against Communist aggression. Having announced that his arms agreement with the Russians was another historic advance toward the promise of peace for our generation, the President and his Secretary of Defense at once insisted that we must nevertheless spend still more billions on the defense program, in particular for some fancier or more destructive weapons; the race had simply shifted from the goal of quantity to the quality of arms. It is still justified as a necessity for national security, even though we are less secure than we were at the outbreak of the Cold War, and can never be secure now that the Soviet Union too has much more power than is needed to devastate our country. The basic argument remains that we cannot trust the Russians, and certainly there remain good reasons for mistrusting their intentions, but then we forget that on our record they cannot trust us either; after all, we are the only country to have dropped atomic bombs, and we have men in high places who wanted to drop them on North Vietnam, others who believe that we could "win" a thermonuclear war, as if there could be victors in such a holocaust. In any case, neither side is willing to risk the disarmament that could alone assure human survival. So the survival of our civilization depends on the "balance of terror." This may continue to work because neither side has yet dared to use its most destructive weapons, but we cannot count on a fear of retaliation to work indefinitely. Apart from the constant possibility of accident or mad impulse, we also have to face what Gunther Anders has called the "new, truly infernal innocence" that has entered history.

This is exemplified by our frightful tactics in waging war in Indochina: massive bombing that has resulted in the indiscriminate slaughter of several hundred thousands of peasants, that comes down to systematic, high-powered atrocity, but that is no longer called atrocity because it is highly organized, nor felt as atrocity by the military men who give or follow the orders. The Pentagon has made no estimates of civilian casualties before or after it orders bombing raids, nor has President Nixon ever asked for such estimates.[2] Yet the men at the top—the Chiefs of Staff, President Nixon, Lyndon Johnson before him—have given no public sign of a bad conscience; they think of themselves as only patriots combating the enemy, "saving American lives," by what modern technology has made supposedly the most efficient way of waging war. So President Truman in as good conscience authorized the dropping of the atomic bomb on Hiroshima. And so we must assume that a leader who touched off a thermonuclear war—the last word in "infernal innocence," and perhaps in the history of the human race—would still feel that he was doing his patriotic duty.

As for the environmental crisis, we have some reasons for hope in the growing alarm over it, the beginnings of measures to curb pollution, and the occasional successes of conservationists; but even most educated Americans do not realize how dangerous it still is.[3] Although a few countries, such as Japan and Sweden, have managed to stabilize their population, the many poor countries are still either unable or unwilling to do so, generally both; they continue to lead the world in the rate of population growth, which in some of them threatens mass starvation by 1980. The advanced industrial countries that can still manage to feed well enough a growing population lead the world in consumption of dwindling natural resources and pollution of the environment. America, the worst offender, is now being challenged by Japan for the distinction of having the worst air to breathe in its cities, but continues to illustrate most clearly the chief menaces to hopes of a decent environment. Champions of technology who

2. My figure of several hundred thousand is the estimate of the Kennedy committee in the Senate, necessarily rough because of the lack of either statistics or official concern. The phoney "body count" that our military boasted of for years covered only the "enemy," supposedly fighting men; though it inspired some old-fashioned atrocities by officers seeking prestige or promotion.

3. For this purpose an excellent comprehensive survey, sufficiently frightening, is Paul and Anna Ehrlich's *Population—Resources—Environment,* 1970.

assure us that it will enable the human race to sustain a population of 50 billion neglect to ponder an elementary question: What would life be like on so crowded an earth? Americans, already the most drugged people on earth, make plain that their man-made environment is bad for not only physical but mental health. If the alarm of specialists in human ecology may be excessive, the rest of us might be alarmed by how little we know, or can hope to know for a long time, of the delayed, cumulative, long-range effects of our environment on people.

Meanwhile the commonplaces about our rapidly changing world may obscure the obvious truth that change in national policy is still far from being rapid enough. "It is now or never," President Nixon rang out when he at last woke up to the problem of pollution, or at least the political advisability of expressing some concern about it; but soon it became apparent that in effect he meant, "Well, not right now—we mustn't try to go too fast or too far." Government remains reluctant to enforce severe regulations on business, the main producers of pollutants, and it is spending only a small fraction of what is needed to restore the environment; its program seems more piddling by contrast with the immense sums squandered on the so-called defense program. The national goal remains indefinite economic growth.

This brings up problems still knottier than further threats to the environment. Economic growth makes obvious sense in the poor, undeveloped countries, even though it also disrupts their traditional culture and its values by demanding more attention to economic values. At home the national goal would make better sense if the immense wealth were distributed more equitably and devoted to promoting the public welfare, including the elimination of poverty and of both the rural and the city slums—again primary considerations that are obscured by devotion to the GNP, which does not at all measure the collective welfare. As it is, we are faced with another basic absurdity, now that the GNP has soared to over a trillion dollars—wealth unimaginable in past societies, and in a way meaningless to ordinary people today.[4] Even so we are being told that we cannot afford to spend more on public welfare programs, the government is running out of money. Likewise the GNP fails to distinguish the social costs of economic growth. The most conspicuous example of such costs remains the automobile—not only the immense sums spent on highways but the traffic congestion and the pollution in and about the big cities. It would accordingly seem senseless to go on turning out cars by the millions—except for further complication. The automobile industry is vital to the economy. Limits on its production would cause widespread unemployment, which is already serious despite our booming economy. So would a halt to economic growth, a "stable" state that could also mean stagnation. One might think that a trillion dollars would be ample to provide for all public needs, but in our society economic stagnation even at this level would mean further unemployment, with still less attention to the needs of the poor and unfortunate. Growth would be needed too if by any chance Americans should remember that their country is supposedly Christian, and it assumed the moral obligation of providing adequate economic aid to all the poor countries of the world. (As it is, no government program is less popular than the foreign aid program—what Americans regard as not charity but mere give-away.)

When one looks to the future, it would seem clear that our economic growth cannot continue indefinitely because of the earth's finite natural resources. The actual question is when and how it will be stopped—by nature, or by human choice? Or can it be stopped in time, in ways not too painful or disruptive, or injurious to the poor countries?

4. Who can really grasp that string of statistical zeroes? Who but a billionaire can get a clear idea of what just a billion dollars means—not to say a thousand of them? What difference would it make to most of us if we were told that our GNP is a quadrillion dollars?

The answer is highly uncertain, or to my mind most likely No, because of another major threat to human survival: our basic problems are simply too big for us. Managing technological societies so massive and complex, and a world grown so interdependent, calls for more sensitivity, flexibility, and resourcefulness, or broadly more intelligence, than we are clearly capable of. We have much "know-how" that our technicians are proud of, but we don't have enough know-how to deal with such large-scale problems, involving immense masses of people. When we know that something must be done, we too often don't know how to do it. Thus we certainly should know by now that economic growth cannot continue indefinitely all over the world, but the problem remains how to call a halt to it.

More complications are raised by the question who is meant by "we" in such common observations. Sometimes "we" means man, or the human race. Then it may call out the common basic confidence that man will somehow have the wit and fortitude to carry on, as he has all through history in spite of many disasters. I suppose there would probably be some survivors of a thermonuclear or ecological catastrophe who might make do with what is left of our good earth, maybe start all over again from a primitive state. It is hard really to conceive the end of the human race.

More often "we" means we moderns, members of our civilization. Then it is somewhat easier to conceive of the end of this civilization, in view of the fate of all previous ones. But what is "our" civilization? It used to be called "Western" when Europe and its offshoot America dominated the world; in spite of all the national differences, it had a common cultural heritage, going back to ancient Greece, Rome, and Israel. Today I suppose we must speak rather of "modern civilization," which is no longer predominantly Western. Its common element is industrialism, or dependence on science and technology. It must include the Soviet Union and eastern Europe, and presumably Japan, with all other countries sufficiently "developed" or "modernized," now including China—or what have you? Our civilization accordingly embraces peoples with quite different cultural traditions. It is harder to feel a real kinship among us moderns, such as Europeans could feel before the World Wars. While we are all in the same boat, we have no captain, chief engineer, or pilot, but also no crew working as a unit, and no navigation charts. When we get together in the United Nations, our differences become more apparent than our common interests. Our differences, and rivalries, also accentuate our common neglect of the interests of the many poor "undeveloped" countries that need our aid, and that because of our technology are now involved in the common problem of human survival.

Or at home "we" is likely to mean we Americans, allegedly the most modern of peoples. The popular rhetoric about "this great country of ours" may obscure the truth that we have suffered from our bigness, as well as our vaunted wealth and power, and that our problems appear to be too much for our capacities. Our government has been less intelligent, enlightened, and responsible than that of the small democracies, such as Holland, Switzerland, and Denmark. While our smaller cities are still able to govern themselves tolerably well, the American metropolis or megalopolis now appears to be virtually ungovernable, unable even to make life in it decently safe. The big cities are the locus of our most serious problems—unemployment, poverty and welfare relief, crime, pollution, and in general the deterioration in the quality of life. Their continued growth and sprawl, into what are now called "metropolitan areas" (which may recall the description of Los Angeles, the self-styled city of the future, as "seven suburbs in search of a city"), is one consequence of the national passion for size, or gigantism, and for economic growth at whatever human cost. Industrialism has in all countries, capitalist or communist, led to a productive system that naturally tends to expand indefinitely, but nowhere more automatically, mindlessly, or heedlessly than in America.

Let us consider specifically the conclusion of some students of modern technology, that to deal effectively with our basic problems would require a radical reorganization of our whole system —political, economic, and social. Communist countries have demonstrated the possibility of such a reorganization, but by coercive methods almost all of us condemn. Can we bring off anything of the kind by democratic methods? I for one doubt it very much. To begin with, we have no accepted blueprints for a new system—from either planners or futurologists—and no social class ready to attempt to carry through the necessary changes. In particular Americans have become an intensely conservative people, more fearful of "radicals" in our midst than is any other people on earth, and with less reason. (So George McGovern was doomed to defeat when he was branded as a radical, even though in terms of the basic changes in the American system contemplated here he was not radical enough.) Once famed for its Revolution, which made it the great white hope of common people everywhere, America is now a world symbol of conservatism, the chief enemy of radical movements everywhere that appeal to the common people. (At home it has produced such bizarre types as the Daughters of the American Revolution, dedicated to the proposition that there must never, never be another revolution.) Any effort at a fundamental reorganization of the American system would of course meet powerful opposition from the vested interests in business and government, but also from the public. Americans are devoted to the self-indulgent American way of life, with its premise that everything should be made easy and painless as they go about discharging their economic duty of being first and last faithful, ardent consumers, buying all the latest models and gadgets.

As for economic growth, once more, the basic problem as Americans see it is to maintain this growth steadily. By the year 2000 they may at least begin to realize that it cannot continue indefinitely, but meanwhile—in the present that we must keep returning to—all the signs are that for some years to come we will go on producing a superabundance of material goods, with still more industrial waste, at the further cost of the neglect of the hundreds of millions of poor people in the world who will be fortunate if they are simply getting enough to eat in that year 2000. Many scientists, concerned about the environmental crisis, are accordingly insisting on the necessity of national austerity programs, but neither business, government, nor the public is at all prepared for any such program. All are alike devoted to the national gospel of a high material standard of living as the sovereign good and goal.

And this has become more of a menace because the rest of the world, including the Soviet Union, is aspiring to something like our standard of living, with a GNP as an index of success. The poor countries have to face up to the hard truth—made harder by their rising expectations—that the earth's limited resources will never permit them to industrialize on a scale that would enable them to approach our standard. This means that there is no prospect whatever of a universal Brave New World, such as Aldous Huxley envisaged, but it also means that Americans will be fortunate if they are permitted to go on enjoying their consumers' paradise in peace; though this paradise is so mindless that one may doubt that they are really enjoying it very much. Certainly they are not behaving like a joyous people. An immense advertising industry is forever telling them that they need to buy and consume still more to be happy.

For all such reasons Robert Hutchins has said bluntly that our technology is being directed by the wrong men, in wrong ways, to wrong ends. But this forces another question: Who, then, are the *right* men to put in charge? To whom should we look for the solutions to our problems?

One professional class that speaks with authority is made up of assorted technicians, experts of many kinds unknown to past societies. They have propagated the popular faith that tech-nology can solve all the problems it has created. This, it cannot be said too often, is a dangerous illusion. Although technology is of course an aid, today an indispensable one, it cannot replen-ish all the natural resources we have squandered, cannot repair all the damage we have done to our environment. Typically it creates new problems by its solutions, such as the grave dangers of radiation heightened by the nuclear power plants that are supposed to take care of our power problems. It also brings up the basic problems of technocracy, rule by experts devoted to technical rationality, efficiency, and system, who in the name of objectivity or realism may pride themselves on eschewing value-judgments, especially moral judgments, and whose expertise is in any case no assurance of a concern for humane, civilized pur-poses, still less a guarantee of wisdom. (One has only to consider the tragic case of ex-Secretary of Defense Robert McNamara, who realized too late that the war in Vietnam was a terrible mistake.) In particular the faith in technology as a cure-all ob-scures the need of a mighty national effort to restore a decent environment, a very costly effort that will not be made so long as the exorbitant demands of the Pentagon get top priority, and that would require some sacrifice, drastic changes in accepted poli-cies, attitudes, and values. As it is, we got President Nixon's call for a "new American revolution": a program of administrative changes that was not at all revolutionary, that made no changes in national priorities, and that called for no sacrifices by the American people; and then his fanfare over a "new prosperity," which amounted to a promise of only more of the same.

Ecologists, who have made plainest that technology cannot solve all our problems, bring up other questions about scientists, the obvious authorities on problems of human survival. Since they gave us the atomic bomb, many scientists have acquired an acute sense of social responsibility, exemplified by the admirable *Bulletin of the Atomic Scientists,* and lately by an increasing stir

[25]

among life scientists, who have been most insistently sounding the alarm, calling for national austerity. They are also more concerned than most technicians or technocrats about basic human values, no longer so devoted to their traditional assumption that science is properly neutral. They are now telling us not merely what we can do but what we ought to do, even must do, to make the world a safe and decent place to live in. And certainly we should all listen to their advice. They have much less to say, however, about how to change public policy, how to get people to do what they ought to do, how to overcome the obstacles deeply rooted in the American system of government and American way of life. There is no prospect whatever of scientists being put in control of our technology, but even if they were, the rest of us might not welcome it. Apart from the frailty and fallibility they share with all other mortals, science too does not and cannot guarantee wisdom.

Thus René Dubos, speaking as a biologist, complains that the life sciences "deliberately ignore the most important phenomena of human life." As in all the sciences, specialists concentrate on small segments and reduce phenomena to quantitative elements, such as molecules and genes. About the immediate problem of the clearly bad effects of a crowded, polluted environment on people, Dubos points out that these may be more alarming because very little is known specifically about them and little study is being made of them. He accordingly calls for a "science of humanity," including studies of the total organism in relation to the total environment. As one who would welcome such studies, I nevertheless doubt that there ever can be an adequate science of humanity, with anything like the precision and certainty of the physical sciences. As it is, I shudder at the brash confidence of too many psychologists in particular, notably B.F. Skinner. Similarly I question other public-spirited scientists who are proposing a "science of survival." I am quite sure that there is no such science: there are only a number of different sciences, with no unified view of nature, man, or society, and no prospect whatever that I can see of attaining such unity. Meanwhile, to repeat, I welcome all that scientists can tell us—so long as they do not support the popular belief that science can give us all the answers.

There remain students of the humanities, the most obviously relevant of which is history. It is clearly necessary to a proper understanding of modern civilization, immediately of the distinctive Western culture that gave birth to modern science, generated an Industrial Revolution, and now has made human survival a problem by making man the worst pest in the history of life on earth. Presently I shall consider at some length the uses of history, including the philosophy of history. But meanwhile the first thing to be said is that it too cannot give us the answers. We cannot learn from the past how to live with H-bombs, or how to deal with the ecological crisis, simply because it is only in our generation that men have faced such hazards. The hazards are greater because too many of the world's leaders are old men with old ideas, policies that were questionable even in the past, but that may be plainly obsolete today. And they bring up the conventional uses of history.

As taught in our schools, these commonly feature a nationalistic history that inculcates superficial, distorted, or even false notions about the past that are more dangerous than simple ignorance of it. Obvious though these abuses are, they need to be mentioned because they influence national policy, support arrogant claims to a right to do whatever we decide is in the national interest, with too often no decent respect for the opinions of mankind; even the childish boasts about how we have never lost a war influenced our policy in Vietnam. Otherwise the bulk of American history has been more or less parochial, typified by innumerable regional studies and especially the many thousands of books about the Civil War—an immense amount of effort devoted to the study of a bloody parochial affair, out of which has come little of real significance that I am aware of, still less of relevance to the crisis of our time (though it could be made more relevant as a study of political and moral failure). This in turn raises questions about the bulk of historical scholarship in general, all manner of specialized studies. When not trivial, most of them have little bearing on our major concerns today. Few contribute to a basic use of history that is now especially important —a better understanding of the extraordinary present, or of who we are, where we are, and how we got this way, and then, perhaps, what we might do about it.

And so with the humanities in general, about the possible values of which I shall have more to say in the next chapter. Ideally, students of them are concerned with the always relevant pursuit of truth, goodness, and beauty. Because of their essential concern with human values they should have much to say about what we *ought* to do—not merely to survive physically, but to survive as civilized human beings, in an environment fit for such beings, or to build a civilization worthy of the fabulous wealth and power created by technology. In fact many spokesmen of the humanities have displayed much concern over the vital issues of our day. A revulsion against merely academic interests has supported the common demand for more relevance, created so much stir that we now hear of a "crisis" in the humanities. Yet in spite of all the soul-searching the humanities are still dominated by conventional academic interests and practices that have little relevance, not merely to contemporary problems but to the crying need of wisdom, or for that matter the promotion of simple humanity.

In all fields it is the same story: thousands of learned articles in professional journals that will be read by few but other specialists, who write chiefly for one another rather than the educated general reader; the Ph.D. industry, accentuating the common curse of narrow specialization and fragmentation of knowledge, grinding out more candidates for the privilege of publishing or perishing; and then the annual trade conventions, at which convivial members may jest over their martinis about how dull most of the papers are, but forget how little attention the proceedings get, or deserve to get, in the public press, or in the journals of other professions either. This is a tedious story, about which one may hear many complaints, especially from the younger people, but the dreary business goes on. As a product of organization and professional technique, it appears to be as irreversible and irresistible as the drive of modern technology. So far the humanities have responded to our revolutionary age most conspicuously by producing a little knowledge explosion of their own, which has produced little noise or light either, but chiefly has obscured the philosophical question of what is important to know or to think about. Scholars will never agree, of course, on criteria of significance, inasmuch as Max Weber pointed out long ago that these cannot be determined by scientific methods either; but at a time when there is growing concern over national priorities, one might hope for more attention to priorities in research too.

In the social sciences, including political science, fundamental questions are more likely to be disregarded just because they are philosophical and cannot be handled by what are considered proper scientific methods.[5] Likewise the theoretical taboo on value-judgments confirms the accepted aim of an objective study of what *is*, from which it is said that we cannot logically derive notions about what *ought* to be—a feat I nevertheless keep on attempting myself, though without pretensions to logical certainty, on the assumption that knowledge of the social and political realities, in particular the obvious enough failings of our society, at least suggests clues or guides to judgment of what ought to be, or might be done. In effect, however, the neutrality

5. Professor W. Riker, for example, has observed that the traditional studies of government produced at best "only wisdom and neither science nor knowledge." While granting that wisdom is useful, he emphasized their "failure to live up to the promise in the name of political science."

of specialists in these sciences comes out as a basic conservatism. They are disposed to an acceptance of the *status quo* that is the immediate subject of their inquiry; their methodology does not lend itself readily to a study of revolutionary change, still less to a consideration of the possible necessity of radical social and political change for human survival.

That they nevertheless have a natural interest in our survival —a cause about which they are no more neutral than the rest of us—brings up further anomalies. In all fields of thought men who are not avowed radicals are using something of their traditional vocabulary. Thus Robert Hutchins concluded that to direct our technology intelligently, first of all to get it out of the hands of the wrong men, would call for a "revolution," political, economic, moral, and intellectual. Many others—like me—are insisting on the need of radical changes in policies, some on the need of a thorough reorganization of government and society. They do not agree on any specific program, but presumably do agree on the necessity of political action. Only government can curb the frightening power of the Pentagon, bring about disarmament, enforce measures to preserve or restore the environment, assure action to make the world safe and fit for civilized living. In America most thinkers would agree too that political action should be through democratic processes. Then the question is: To what party or movement should we look for intelligent, effective leadership?

The two major parties in America as constituted offer little or no promise of bold action. Never distinguished for firm commitment to clear or lofty principles, they have lately been making a point of staying close to the "center"—a center that is in no mood for any mighty national effort, any real sacrifice of the American way of life. It might therefore appear that hopes for an adequate program for survival must rest on radicals, especially the younger ones who in the universities have been protesting against the irrelevance of conventional scholarship and insisting on the need of political commitment and action. About Robert Hutchins' dictum that intelligent control of our technology requires a revolution, they may ask another question: How does he —a cloistered academic—propose to make such a revolution? Specifically, what does he propose to do about our government and big business, the powers in control? The many other thinkers who declare the need of basic changes may seem as ineffectual because they offer neither a comprehensive program nor specific proposals for such changes in a political and economic system that resists them. Yet radicals offer no clear hope either, even apart from their inability to agree on a program. The old Left, discredited by the brutal tyranny of Stalin, can hardly bank on the promise of the Soviet Union; it remains a despotic technocracy, and with its own military-industrial complex, another plain threat to world peace. The New Left has already been so badly splintered and disorganized that it is difficult to identify; it lacks any substantial nucleus. Most futile are the young radicals who still call for political revolution, in the name of Mao, Ho Chi Minh, Castro, or Che Guevara. They have no mass support, least of all from "the workers" many absentmindedly appeal to—in America the least revolutionary proletariat in the world.

In short, I see no one party or class—social, political, or professional—to look to for the promise of a better future. Having myself no definite program for survival to offer, I see no hope except in a sustained effort at public education, to alert more people to the threats to our civilization and enlist more public support for measures to combat them. This is an effort to which scientists and humanists, moderates and radicals, men of different faiths, professions, and parties can contribute. It is of course an uncertain business that at best takes time, perhaps more time than we can safely afford. It is more discouraging because we have long been told that the public in a mass society is a "phantom public," whose will or whim counts for little in the determination of national policy. Still, public opinion clearly does count

[31]

for something in the democracies. As the growing opposition to the war in Vietnam caused some change in national policy, so the growing alarm over the problems of the environment helped to defeat the SST program—an especially heartening change as the first successful effort to curb the technological drive to what Americans call "progress."

At any rate, some hope of education is implicit in the professional business of all of us who teach or write. I now address myself to my own immediate concern here—the uses of history.[6]

2. THE USES OF HISTORY

"You may be sure," said Henry Adams in a presidential address to the American Historical Association in 1894, "that four out of five serious students of history who are living today have, in the course of their work, felt that they stood on the brink of a great generalization that would reduce all history under a law as clear as the laws which govern the material world." In the 1960's the Association held a session devoted to the topic "What Happened to the Great Generalizations?" Offhand the answer was clear: they were *passé*. Few historians today would commit themselves to such comprehensive theories of history as were ventured by Vico, Voltaire, Hegel, Comte, Marx, Buckle, and Spengler. Although the avoidance of brinkmanship is due most obviously to specialization, historians have good reason for their caution. All the great generalizations oversimplified history. None of the laws that have been proposed, including the "iron

6. I should stress that I am writing as a nonprofessional historian, an outsider who wandered into the field some twenty-odd years ago, and since then have been roaming freely all over world history, always enjoying an unearned kind of freedom as I picked the brains of specialists who had done the hard work of basic research. Then I may add in humility that as an outsider I have enjoyed a possible advantage in perspective, breadth of interest, and detachment from the concerns of specialists, who in writing have to keep an eye on professional brethren lying in wait with their hatchets.

laws" of Karl Marx, have the certainty of scientific laws, for none can ever be strictly verified. In particular, none make possible such positive predictions of the future as Marx confidently ventured.

Yet the great generalizations of the past are by no means dead and done with. They live on at least in the background of contemporary thought, also for good reason. They have had an enduring influence on thought because they opened up new dimensions, raised new questions that are still pertinent. They called attention to the universal history of mankind, which for the first time we are now making on a global stage, our little spaceship that has become One World. They created the "philosophy of history," a term introduced by Voltaire and made much more of by Hegel. To most American historians this subject is suspect, except perhaps as an analysis of terms, concepts, and methods, comparable to the philosophy of science; even apart from the monsters of Hegelian metaphysics it conjures up, it scares off specialists who pride themselves on purely empirical studies, inquiries in which they can hope to come up with positive answers. Nevertheless empiricism itself remains a philosophy. However unconsciously, historians also operate on roughly philosophical assumptions about what is natural for man, important for man, good for man. Too often these assumptions may be unconscious because provincial, absorbed from the traditions of Western culture. A broader, more truly philosophical view of history and of mankind has become more important because the One World we have to live in is still far from being one in thought, feeling, sentiment, and aspiration, for it is made up of great societies with quite different cultural traditions.

And so with one of the most distinctively Western of the great generalizations, the theory of progress. It is of course not dead in the Communist world. Now that atomic bombs have discouraged the old Marxist slogans about a world revolution, and plainly threaten human survival, I suppose many Communist thinkers would no longer agree with the dictum of George Lukács some years ago, that Marxism offered "the final certainty . . . that the development of mankind does not and cannot finally lead to nothing and nowhere"; but short of this certainty, most presumably would defend the theory of progress. Few thinkers in the Western democracies are defending it, at least as anything like a law of history, an assurance of indefinite progress in the future; and to my mind any belief that the future is bound to be better than the past is not only groundless but as dangerous as the naïve faith in technology. Nevertheless the idea of progress survives at least as a hope, a much more live sense of potentiality than past societies had—now most obviously as potentiality for the worst, but still for the better too. One incidental sign is the recent "theology of hope," involving a religious restatement of the idea of progress. A more significant sign is the very flood of books of alarm about our crises, such as no past society in trouble ever produced; for almost all the books imply when they do not argue explicitly that we can and should do something about our desperate problems. And there can be no hope for human survival unless we retain this belief.

Hence it is important to recognize that in some respects human history has indeed been a progress. Most plainly it has been a technological progress, through a vast accumulation of arts and skills giving man more power over his environment, a power he has never voluntarily relinquished. There has also been a plain enough intellectual progress, such as Voltaire pointed to: a corresponding accumulation of positive knowledge, together with a wealth of ideas and ideals, cultural or spiritual values, incorporated in the great works of art and thought that the human race has likewise hung on to. Over the last hundred years this has included an immense stock of factual knowledge about history, and I should say a progress in historical understanding, especially through the questions raised by the great generalizations. Few thinkers today share the confident belief of James Harvey

Robinson earlier in our century that our knowledge of history is our greatest single aid in preserving us from the fate of past societies, but at least it can help; no past society had so comprehensive and trustworthy an understanding of the past, including all that remained alive, as we have grown capable of. And now that we are worrying over our science and technology we need to remember that, for better or for worse, the whole non-Western world is taking to them in its efforts to modernize—efforts signifying that it has also taken to the Western idea of the possibility of progress. It is making more meaningful Hegel's famous generalization that "the history of the world is none other than the progress of the consciousness of freedom."

A quite different idea of history, however, is represented by another of the great generalizations, the ancient theory of cycles, which in our century was revived by Spengler and Arnold Toynbee. They helped to make popular analogies between the Roman Empire and modern America, which Brooks Adams (the brother of Henry) had employed in his *Law of Civilization and Decay*. To my knowledge, their theories are taken seriously by few historians and impress many fewer intellectuals than they once did. They alike grossly oversimplified the history of civilization as they forced it into their neat cycles, no less confidently because they disagreed widely on the number of civilizations they discerned.[7] In particular their stress on analogies—the basis of their whole argument—led them to slight the fundamental differences between our civilization and all previous ones, which were always plain enough but have been accentuated by the problem of human survival.

Yet the cyclical theory continues to haunt the imagination of

7. I should add that in his *Study of History* Toynbee combined his theory of cycles with a theory of religious progress, on the grounds that some dying civilizations had given birth to the higher religions. But he substantially agreed with Spengler on the decline of the West, and expressed a low opinion of our "post-Christian" society because he saw no prospect of its producing such a birth.

men, and again for understandable reasons. Thus in an issue devoted to modern civilization and human survival the editors of the journal *The Philosophy Forum* posed a question: Is there a law of decay? Is it possible for a technological civilization to overcome or modify it? My answer is that there is no *law*, strictly speaking, but neither can we say simply that history never repeats itself. It has repeated itself, to the point of monotony, in the common story of growth and decay, rise and fall, of states, empires, whole civilizations, which gives a vivid sense of endings. As Hegel remarked, the first thing we see when we contemplate the past is ruins. Americans need to be told plainly that there are no grounds at all for their traditional belief in a unique destiny to escape the fate of all other peoples in the past. Then we may consider more profitably the essential differences between our technological civilization and all previous ones, including the reasons why we may escape the common fate of stagnation in ancient Egypt, Rome, India, Islam, and China.

In Andrew Hacker's recent book, *The End of the American Era*, for example, something of the old cyclical theory is implicit. The failure of America both to provide enlightened world leadership and to deal at all adequately with its grave domestic problems led Hacker to a bleak conclusion: "We have arrived at a plateau in our history, the years of middle age and incipient decline." I think it quite possible that we are nearing the end of the American era, but there remain questions to which the declining societies of the past suggest no answer. What would become of our most powerful military establishment? Our immense industrial establishment? Would Americans consent to allow any other power to assume our role as world leader, and then to retire and decline quietly? Though Americans look quite middle-aged, and may even be in a mood for decent stagnation, will the dynamism of their technology permit anything like the security and stability many yearn for? Meanwhile they remain dedicated to the national goal of unlimited economic growth, with its promise of a still higher standard of living.

Implicit in this aspiration is the claim of Americans to a right to consume many times their share of the world's resources. And this claim points to a major positive use of history—a guide to what to look out for, and immediately a warning against the common abuses of history.

The most obvious and dangerous of these is again a nationalistic history that buttresses the claims of all the major powers to a national sovereignty in their own interests first and last, and strengthens the inveterate tendencies to both selfishness and self-righteousness, the ageless sources of folly and evil. Historians have also grown more critical of the conventional use of history to exalt tradition, honor institutions, sanction current authority or belief—a use that may be honorable, but may be especially dangerous too in view of the apparent inability of our institutions to deal effectively with the crises of our day, and the apparent need of basic changes in attitudes and values. While in their common ignorance of history Americans could do with more reverence for the great works of the past, they need as well to escape the tyranny of the past. The anachronistic policies of leaders today come down to variations on another ageless theme, which might inspire histories of anachronism in all the great societies. With this comes another abuse of history that has grown more dangerous, the fallacy of false analogy. Because we inevitably do think by analogy, we might recall the dictum of Lord Bryce: "The chief practical use of history is to deliver us from plausible historical analogies." One example is the common appeal to Munich to justify our aggressive foreign policy, and then specifically our war in Vietnam; whereas there are obviously important differences between prewar Czechoslovakia and the dictatorial, corrupt, unpopular Saigon regimes we maintained in power.

Still another possible use of history is suggested by not only the stress on economic growth but the immense amount of money and time being devoted to research and development, representing the most deliberate effort man has ever made to shape the future. Historians might consider a novel enterprise—the history of the future. So far they have contributed little to futurology, which has been largely monopolized by assorted social or behavioral scientists. I think they could contribute much more. The studies of the futurologists are to some extent historical because the trends they extrapolate come down from the past, but they have not been trained to think historically and may know too little about the past. Historians of the modern world could supplement their work by fuller studies of deep trends, critiques of their extrapolations, perhaps a better sense of both the probable social consequences of the technological innovations coming up and the possibility of countertrends. For one thing, historians are likely to be more aware of the power of tradition—an actuality that has commonly been neglected in social science. With due recognition of the uniqueness of our situation today, they may also be more aware of the continuities and underlying uniformities of history; the predicaments of modern man have been aggravated by both old needs and old habits. And for our immediate purposes historians might help to combat the provincial obsession with modernism, the common delusion of contemporaries that we are emancipated from the past—a delusion that promotes not only a lack of reverence for its great works but the possible tyranny of the past.

I suspect, however, that most historians will shy away from the question where we may be going as an unprofitable inquiry, because it cannot be strictly empirical. Again we run into the disagreeable facts of professional life in an age of intensive specialization, in which fundamental questions are commonly ignored because the subjects of inquiry are dictated by accepted methods and professional practices instead of by what we most want or need to know, or at least to think about. Thus we may not be helped much even by the great deal of work that has been done in the history of technology, an important new field opened up in this century. The bulk of it consists of highly specialized technical studies, with relatively little reference to the impact of technology on society and culture—what seems to me the major concern for a historian. (A distinguished exception is Lewis Mumford—a nonacademic pioneer.) Similarly the stress on technological developments, how one invention led to another especially when invention became organized and systematic, may obscure the important truth that the whole drive was a distinctive product of Western culture. With closer studies of how the drive got under way and gathered such terrific momentum, we could do with more studies of the efforts of non-Western peoples to adapt modern technology to their different cultural traditions, as the Japanese did most successfully, in ways Americans might study profitably.

I am reminded, at any rate, of de Tocqueville's classic study of American democracy, made without benefit of methodology more than a century ago (1835–40). In dwelling on the popular passion for material well-being, not to him as a foreign observer simply a natural phenomenon, he got at the roots of the American way of life, which remains at the roots of our ecological problems today. In particular his study has become more relevant today than it was in his own day because he dared to speculate freely about the future, and did so shrewdly. In some respects he was remarkably prophetic, anticipating the popular fear of radicals and revolution in America, the increasing centralization of power, the growing dependence of people on government, the nature of "mass-men," and the possibility of a benevolent kind of despotism, something like Aldous Huxley's Brave New World, in which people would be relieved of the cares of thinking. On the future of America he was a far better prophet than Marx. And de Tocqueville's study remains pertinent for a fur-

[39]

ther reason, an apparent inconsistency he has been charged with.

Thus he argued that the movement toward democracy in Europe too was irresistible, in effect inevitable, thereby implying a kind of determinism. At the same time, he flatly rejected historical determinism. While dreading the consequences he anticipated of some natural democratic tendencies, he insisted that they were not inevitable; what people made of democracy was their responsibility. In all this I see no basic inconsistency. He perceived a deep trend toward democracy that was in fact to prove irresistible for a century, until the rise of totalitarianism. He also believed that within limits man was free to make his own history, as Americans had demonstrated by their novel experiment in democracy. And so today with the deep trends that have made the drive of technology seemingly irresistible. Although historians have liked to ask the question whether major occurrences, such as the American Civil War, were inevitable, and often argue that they were, they are of course unable to offer conclusive proof; and anyway my impression is that few are strict determinists. But they may still dwell on real possibilities; they may point to probabilities in terms of if/then propositions, based on current trends; and in the spirit of de Tocqueville they may suggest what might or ought to be done to lessen the dangers— not laying down a definite program for salvation, any more than he did, but maintaining his belief that in a full awareness of the dangers men are capable of doing something about them. And because we have heard so much since his time about the "vast, impersonal forces" governing history, exemplified by an unplanned Industrial Revolution, I would insist that these still result from the doings of a great many persons, and like Michael Polanyi I would stress the issues of human responsibility for history, which points to the necessity of value-judgments.

3. SOME PERSPECTIVES

Meanwhile we may get from history some helpful perspectives on our present state and our possibilities by raising strictly empirical questions, which should not scare off historians. David Hackett Fisher, for instance, has urgently raised the question: "What are the historical conditions in which social stability, social freedom, and social equality have tended to be *maximally* coexistent?" Knowing of no impressive response to his challenge, I do not know, either, of such historical conditions in past societies. Ancient India achieved the most remarkable measure of social stability by its caste system, but at the plain expense of freedom and equality. None of the great Eastern societies held up ideals of freedom and equality. Ancient Greece, on the other hand, made the farthest advance toward freedom in its little *polis*, together with a measure of equality for its citizens, but these were a small minority in a society based on the institution of slavery, which both Plato and Aristotle maintained was natural and proper; and Greece failed to achieve the stability they both prized more than freedom. Rome finally did no better under either its Republic or its Empire; the famous *Pax Romana* that brought stability to the empire for a century was accompanied by a loss of freedom that was one reason for the subsequent decline and fall. Medieval Europe—still idealized by some writers—made much of the Christian ideal of spiritual freedom and equality, but it was an authoritarian society that obviously fell far short of achieving either freedom, equality, or stability in social or political life.

Hence I venture to say that the modern Western democracies have come closest to a maximum coexistence of these ideals.[8] In

8. Primitive societies have come still closer because they have in general been basically democratic, as well as much stabler—until they were demoralized by the

[41]

spite of all the revolutionary changes and upheavals, including the strains of two world wars, they have had the stablest government for a century; the various forms of totalitarianism and dictatorship took hold in countries lacking a strong democratic tradition. Certainly they have offered their people as a whole more personal freedom than did past societies, and with it, despite the glaring economic inequalities, more political equality; in our century equal political rights have been extended to women for the first time in recorded history. Today Communist countries tacitly acknowledge the strength of democratic ideals by calling themselves "people's democracies." Altogether, I substantially adhere to the conclusions Ortega y Gasset stated in his radical critique of modern society, *The Revolt of the Masses:* "that liberal democracy based on technical knowledge is the highest type of public life hitherto known," and that although that type may not be the best imaginable, "the one we imagine as superior must preserve the essence of those two principles."

Since he wrote, however, the cause of liberal democracy has been complicated by the immense growth of "technical knowledge," with a concomitant growth of technocracy, especially in the all-important matters of war and peace. The American people knew nothing about the atomic bomb, of course, until it was dropped on Hiroshima, but they were not told either about such important decisions as to make H-bombs, wage war on North Vietnam, and invade Cambodia until after these decisions were made. Hence the calls for more participatory democracy—popular especially among young Americans—signify a growing effort to substitute democratic controls of our technology for control by a technical elite. This seems to me not only clearly essential but up to a point quite feasible. Many citi-

impact of our civilization. But our concern here is with ostensibly civilized societies, the given terms of our problems.

zens, now with the aid of more of their representatives, are combating the power elites in business and government; Ralph Nader has demonstrated brilliantly what even one citizen can accomplish. I do not think that liberal democracy is necessarily doomed by the authoritarian tendencies of modern technology. Even in the Communist world there has been growing resistance to these tendencies.

Still, the issue remains complex and uncertain. Large-scale government has always involved rule by some kind of elite, and today it must include many specialists of all kinds. A wholesome mistrust of "expertise," as in economics, foreign policy, and public administration, cannot do away with the need of many more trained specialists than ever before. The problem remains *how* to keep all the technocrats under democratic control. Political machinery alone will not do. Immediately we run into all the government agencies bent on protecting and promoting their own bureaucratic interests; a Congress devoted more to local business interests than to the national interest, and responsive to the pressures of powerful lobbies; and a most powerful Presidency, at the moment isolated from the public by the largest White House staff to date (at latest report including some twenty-odd publicity men or professional image-makers). Again I can see no better hope than sustained effort to educate the public.

Similar questions are raised by government efforts at planning the future. About these it should first be noted that planning has not only been primarily for economic purposes but has been restricted to the immediate future; even a Five Year Plan would still smack of Communism to most politicians. At best various agencies draw up programs for their own limited purposes, the most successful of which has been the space program, lavishly financed more for the sake of national prestige than of the public interest. No important government agency is engaged in long-range planning on a national scale, or efforts to coordinate policies and programs in terms of national goals.[9] Meanwhile, for lack of national policy, technological innovations keep pouring in without any prior assessment of their possible social consequences. We mustn't try to go too far or too fast, industrialists say when they are called on to stop polluting rivers and the air, but that is precisely what we go on doing in technology. Ralph Lapp, a scientist, has summed up the state of affairs in a nation that prides itself on its technological leadership of the world:

> No one—not even the most brilliant scientist today—really knows where science is taking us. We are aboard a train which is gathering speed, racing down a track on which there are an unknown number of switches leading to unknown destinations. No single scientist is in the cab and there may be demons at the switch. Most of society is in the caboose looking backward.

Despite all the to-do about futurology, our society remains unprepared for the future.

Plans for achieving national goals might well involve more government controls, however, and so bring up the old political problem ignored by the builders of the Soviet Union, as by the designers of most utopias in the past: Who is to control the controllers? Yet controls, like planning itself, need not simply limit public freedom; they may limit the freedom of the powerful few to conduct business as usual in order to promote the interests of the many, as in measures to curb pollution. More advocates of planning are now committed to something like Karl Mannheim's hope of "planning for freedom," in particular by encouraging public participation. Thus Lyndon Johnson's declared "war" on poverty—a proper democratic enterprise—might not have been

9. Antiquarians may recall that President Eisenhower once appointed a commission to set up such goals and prepare broad outlines for such coordination, and that it duly prepared a report, *Goals for Americans.* This made no impression to speak of on the public and still less on the government. At that it was a quite conservative report, suited to the temper of the Eisenhower administration. The national goals it proposed were based on traditional assumptions and called for no basic changes in the social or political system.

so sorry a skirmish if his fanfare had been accompanied by some effort at careful planning, including some consultation with the poor about their needs, and consideration of means of avoiding the humiliating treatment of them as mere objects of public charity instead of as victims of our economy. Certainly I should hope that if ever there is any real effort to set up national goals, and coordinate policies for achieving them, private citizens will be encouraged to participate and express their opinions about both means and ends. The whole enterprise would no doubt then look messy to systems analysts, social engineers, human engineers, and all the other "new utopians," and it could never hope for agreement on a set of blueprints; but so it must be if people are to have a say about the kind of future they will have to live in.

This would again involve the need of educating them about possible or desirable futures—the problem I shall return to in the next chapter. Here I should stress that another use of history is a study of the values of other civilizations. As Westerners once learned much from ancient Greece, so they might learn more from Confucian China about the possibilities of harmonious human relations, and from India about the psyche and its powers. Today non-Western peoples, with their different cultural traditions, might teach the West something by efforts to avert the tyranny of the ideals of merely technical rationality, or the goal of economic growth at any social cost. Maoism, for instance, in its ideal theory makes primary the goal not of economic but of human development—the development of *all* the people—and for this purpose plays down both economic incentives and the authority of technical experts. It has also restricted personal freedom to an extent Westerners would find intolerable, but this need not be an inevitable cost of its ideal.[10] In general, compara-

10. Although Mao of course cites Marx and Lenin as his official authorities, I have wondered how much he may owe to the humanistic tradition of Confucian China.

tive studies of the values of other societies throw light on much that Americans too readily assume is natural and normal. And here a most pertinent example is the distinctively Western idea that man has a natural mission to master or conquer nature.

Rooted in the Biblical myth of the creation, in which God gave man dominion over the earth and all other living creatures, and potentially strengthened when Christianity endowed man with an immortal soul that set him apart from other animals and devaluated the natural world, this key idea owed more to the rise of modern science, with its impersonal view of the natural world as a mere mechanism and visions of increasing power over it. When industrialism began realizing such visions, nature became something merely to be exploited. In our century modern technology has triumphantly demonstrated man's mastery of nature by the most ruthless exploitation of its resources, and by the most dangerous pollution of air, soil, and water, now including even oceans. The vaunted "conquest" of outer space accentuates another frightening truth, that in all history man has never shown less respect for the "good earth" than do Americans today. Now that DDT threatens with extinction the bald eagle, the national symbol, they might substitute the bulldozer, the billboard, or the beer can.

To be sure, man through the long ages has always sought power over his environment, by both magical and empirical means. Nevertheless the Western drive to master nature by technology is by no means simply natural. It is quite alien to the spirit of ancient China and India, it was not a driving force in ancient Greece or Rome either, and today the non-Western world is having a hard time getting on to its demands. By now many Western thinkers regard it as a major source of the alienation of modern man. René Dubos has accordingly proposed the need of a new social ethic, based on the idea of living in harmony with nature instead of forever exploiting it, or regarding land as a mere commodity. Such an ethic may seem feasible as well as

[46]

desirable since there are still many nature-lovers of sorts. It may be strengthened by the growing awareness of One World—and our only one—in the sense stated by Adlai Stevenson years ago: "We travel together, passengers on a little space ship, dependent on its vulnerable reserves of air and soil; all committed for our safety to its security and peace; preserved from annihilation only by the care, the work, and, I will say, the love we give our fragile craft."

The upshot is again necessarily uncertain. Westerners can draw on a tradition that has also included many expressions of pleasure in nature. Lynn White, Jr., has suggested that ecologists take as their patron St. Francis of Assisi, who most beautifully exemplified the sense of kinship with the rest of creation. Ecologists might remind us that science itself has helped to promote a closer, more loving study of nature than any past society produced. On the other hand, our technology is still devoted primarily to the extension of man's dominion over nature. In America its own dominion is still supported by a gospel of free private enterprise that has long insisted on a right to exploit and squander. To my knowledge, futurologists have been giving little attention to the possibility of inculcating the ideal of living in harmony with nature. They talk much more about the need of better adaptation to the man-made world created by technology, and to the innovations we must expect.

Meanwhile, to repeat, the quality of American life has been steadily deteriorating with the steady increase in the very gross national product. Any hopes of improving it must rest on much more emphasis on judgments about the good life in both the world of thought and the world of affairs. I have myself stressed the need in particular of a much stricter moral judgment of our business and political leaders, and of the technical elite who serve their interests. Such judgment is indispensable as well in decisions about national goals and priorities, which cannot be determined scientifically; in a democracy primary considerations must include social justice and the preservation of human dignity. Likewise I should stress the related importance of aesthetic judgments. Among the plainest reasons for the worsening quality of American life has been the national insensitivity to drabness, garishness, and sheer ugliness in the man-made environment. To my mind it clearly has something to do with the coarse moral sense in public life and the want of moral imagination in national policy, the blindness to an "infernal innocence" that should no longer be considered innocent. The connection is suggested by the common expression "ugly deeds."

Well, critics can and do go on indefinitely in this vein. Their apparent ineffectuality raises a final question. What are the probabilities, first of mere survival, then of a better future by humanistic standards? All along I have been saying that no man can answer with assurance. On the possible end to man's history on earth even a Herman Kahn—our leading specialist in thinking about the unthinkable—cannot calculate the odds. As for me, the most I can say is that this side of catastrophe, I think it possible that man may succeed in establishing a stabler world order by that year 2000. I am less sanguine about the chances of democratizing and humanizing our technology, instilling more respect for nature and reverence for life, introducing more grace and beauty into daily life, and in general creating a civilization worthier of our historically unparalleled wealth and power. Here the most I can say is that detachment and objectivity have become a source of deep confusion in an age dominated by science and technology that has most highly prized these ideals. They are of course honorable, up to a point clearly essential to hopes of philosophical wisdom. They have nevertheless obscured the need of commitment too, which is no less essential to wisdom, and obscured as well the actual commitment of specialists to their own professional values, or their notion of what constitutes rationality. At best their illusions of pure objectivity amount to a kind of philosophical innocence. At worst they have led to a plain neglect of

[48]

basic human values. While I take for granted that we will never agree on the good life, or need to agree, we can no longer afford to subordinate these values to economic expediency and technical efficiency, or in the world of thought to the pretensions to a "value-free" science. Else we may some day find ourselves asking the question in the heartbreaking last scene of *King Lear:* "Is this the promised end?"

III

Education for the Future

Historically, the European universities began as pioneering institutions in the Middle Ages, and then contributed to the spread of humanism in the Renaissance, but thereafter they tended to settle down as highly conservative institutions. Thus they contributed little to the rise of modern science, and outside of Germany to the study of it after it had become clearly established as a basic force in Western civilization; Oxford and Cambridge in particular remained bulwarks of the classical education established in the Renaissance. Today American colleges and universities, which are more highly diversified than European ones, reflect both historic tendencies, at the cost of a good deal of confusion over their objectives. Although essentially conservative, they have for some time been more open to experiment, in keeping with the American democratic tradition of offering a "practical" education suited to all kinds of students instead of the sons of the upper classes, the potential young gentlemen traditionally turned out by Ox-bridge. And of late they have been responding to the vogue of futurism. Dozens of universities have been offering all manner of "future-oriented" courses, as the fashionable jargon has it. Alvin Toffler, author of the best-seller *Future Shock,* has been going up and down the land addressing university audiences on the primary need of "education in the

[50]

future tense." Henceforth, he writes, "we must search for our
objectives and methods in the future, rather than the past"—the
past that has traditionally provided the subject matter of education.

Now, Toffler is so completely sold on the new vogue that he
exemplifies its most extravagant tendencies. He writes in a
breathless journalistic style that may make one wish he would
pause now and then to take a deep breath. He is fond of such
coinages as "ad-hocracy" to define a basic need of properly future-oriented people, who may then assist in the creation of the
brave new "Super-industrial" world he anticipates. In education
he reflects the popular faith in technology by welcoming the
prospect of "a whole battery of teaching techniques," including
the inevitable computerized programs. With ad-hocracy must
come provisions for "life-long education on a plug-in/plug-out
basis." And so on, through a battery of plugs.

Yet I propose to take his thesis seriously, on the assumption
that the new vogue is by no means another passing fashion.
Toffler is uncommonly well-informed about the whole subject,
having consulted all kinds of specialists. However naïve, his faith
in technology is something that educators have to reckon with,
especially since many of them too are pleased with all the new
educational hardware and techniques. Even so, he has many sensible things to say in his diagnosis of contemporary life, including
sound criticism of our schools. And even in his extravagances—
or just because of them—he forces fundamental questions that
are too often overlooked in the universities.

And so with his basic proposal that we should look to the future
rather than the past for our objectives and methods. To my mind
it is obviously not a question of "rather than," but of "as well as."
In reading Toffler I found myself adhering more firmly to some
old-fashioned notions about a liberal education, and rising to the
defense of the uses of the past, as represented not only by history,
but by literature, the arts, and philosophy. To these uses, espe-

[51]

cially for the purpose of value-judgments, I shall give the last word. At the same time, much that has come down from the past in the universities is of questionable value for contemporary needs, and has been unquestioned simply because it has long been customary, as comfortable to academics as old habits, and as mindless as the ivy on the college walls. I have myself supported the common complaints of students about the irrelevance of too much of their education, and have pointed to the need of education for the future. This need I think should get the first word.

Then we perforce begin with the commonplaces about revolutionary change and radical discontinuities that have antiquated much traditional policy and practice. Certainly our curriculum has not focused enough on the most relevant use of the past, a better understanding of the present and of ourselves. Considering specifically our radically new kind of society, with its drive to technological "progress" that has generated our major problems, one has only to ask: How many students acquire an adequate understanding of how the drive got started, how it gathered such terrific momentum and accelerated the pace of change, even though most people do not really like living in a revolutionary world, and are indeed suffering from "future shock"? And why it nevertheless seems irresistible, bound to continue?

So we perforce move into futurology. For our students, speculation about what life will be like in the year 2000 is not at all idle or academic: they will be in their prime then. To be sure, they had better understand clearly the reasons why prediction is necessarily uncertain. But on the traditional assumption that education should prepare young people for life, it should now make them aware of major developments that are not only possible but may be highly probable or even virtually certain, such as all the technological innovations predicted by Kahn and Wiener, and the problems most of them will raise.

There is accordingly a wide field for courses on the future.

[52]

Only one of the most obvious possibilities is the already popular subject of the environmental or biological crisis, aggravated by not merely the population explosion but the national goal of steady economic growth. Because of the latter I would welcome courses in economics for the future, beginning with criticism of the current idolatry of the great god GNP. I also welcome the suggestion of the late Louis Armand[1] that biology ought now to be the basic subject in our schools—biology taught as a humanistic subject, which might give students more respect for nature and life, make them more critical of the Western technological drive to "conquer" nature at any cost, or in effect to exploit it. I do not heartily welcome A. Sargent's suggestion that "biocracy" is our only hope of salvation, for this comes down to a kind of biological technology or engineering. In any case, students ought to know about the "biological revolution," both the extraordinary possibilities it is creating and the problems they raise. Because of the prospect of genetic engineering, for example, Herman Kahn has gone so far as to suggest the possible need of "an index of forbidden knowledge." I doubt very much that there will ever be an official index, and would not care to authorize one myself, or to curb the freedom of scientists to pursue their natural passion to find out everything they can; but anyway students had better know that, basically honorable though this passion is, it has become more dangerous than ever before, and that it is pretty sure to lead to new horrors as well as to new wonders.

Such considerations bring up a basic problem for educators that troubles me much more than it apparently does Toffler and most other futurists. In a course on modern technology I set students to exploring independently a wide variety of problems, and those who did the most thorough job of research uniformly reported pessimistic conclusions about our prospects. What

1. "Restoring Man's Symbiosis with Nature," in a symposium, *Can We Survive Our Future?*, edited and introduced by G.R. Urban.

[53]

troubled me was the difficult effort to maintain a nice balance: on the one hand, young people need to be clearly aware of what they are up against, the very real dangers, the good reasons for alarm about the future; on the other hand, they need to retain a hopeful spirit if there is to be any hope for the future. The most that I could say to my students was that the growing alarm was the best reason for hope.

In more familiar terms, young people have more need of being flexible, adaptable, and resourceful than any generation before them, immediately through a fuller awareness of their fast-changing world, and then by developing their powers of choice. Some of the new courses on the future, I gather, attempt to do this by games presenting possible alternatives. Although the drive of science and technology will force adaptation to much change, like it or not, students still have plenty of vital options—a point that Toffler rightly emphasizes, in view of the stereotypes about our standardized mass society. More freely than any previous generation they can set their own goals and life-styles, as many have been doing in unconventional ways. As citizens they can hope to have some say about their future by influencing policy-makers. And on both counts I am led to my particular concern—the role of the so-called humanities in education for the future.

2. THE ROLE OF THE HUMANITIES

As I have already pointed out, historians have contributed relatively little to futurology. Literary people and philosophers have contributed still less, presumably because they are not equipped with the necessary specialized knowledge and techniques. Nevertheless, I think they too have much to offer, especially when it comes to options or choices in futures. We might recall that more than a generation ago, before the vogue of futurology, Aldous Huxley offered an imaginative forecast in *Brave New World*, in which, without benefit of fancy techniques or

[54]

methodology, he was remarkably prophetic about some developments.

As for formal education, humanities departments could offer relevant courses just because of their traditional preoccupation with the past. An obvious example is a study of utopias, which have been a distinctive product of Western civilization from the Renaissance on, and as a tradition strengthened by the rise of the idea of progress, have had a growing influence on its history, most conspicuously through Karl Marx's vision of a classless society. Such studies might illuminate the revulsion against the utopian tradition, as in *Brave New World, 1984,* and much science fiction. Then they might make clear that utopianism is nevertheless by no means so dead as it is reputed to be outside the communist world. It survives not only in the apostles of technology but in such humanistic thinkers as Paul Goodman and Lewis Mumford. With this, a study of the utopian tradition might make clear the pertinence, even the practical need, of visions of ideal possibilities, however improbable their realization, in a society that could do with much more imagination or vision.

But my main concern is a more fundamental one. Toffler writes approvingly of "the people of the future," the small minority—even in the advanced industrial societies—who are well adjusted to the increasingly rapid pace of change, in a "short-order" or "instant" culture. They live faster, they regard transience and novelty as normal, they welcome change—in short, they are "the advance agents of man," who are already living the way of life of the future. Education, it follows, should concentrate on molding many more such people, with specific preparation for changes to be expected. "Even now," Toffler writes, "we should be training cadres of young people for life in submarine communities."

Here I shuddered, and the more so because some of the young people conceivably may *have* to live in such communities, or in the underground cities envisaged by other futurists. I would concentrate instead on efforts to give the young a better idea of what

[55]

civilized life has meant and can mean at its best, so that they might help to shape a future in which people would not be condemned to so unnatural a life. The "people of the future" who welcome change are not disposed to think hard enough about the fundamental questions: Is all the change really necessary? Is it *desirable*? If so, by what standards? Such questions raise the abiding issues of permanence and change, of the natural life or the good life for man, of basic human values. While Toffler recognizes the necessity of value judgments in developing powers of choice, I doubt that even whole batteries of the latest techniques can do the job well enough. My thesis is that the most important contribution the humanities could make to education for the future is a basic study of the problems of human values and value judgments—judgments that students are not trained to make in the sciences, especially the social sciences, in which the approved methodologies do not lend themselves to such purposes, but rather support the common illusion that true science is "value-free"; and judgments that call for more knowledge of the past than specialists in these up-to-date sciences usually have. Toffler's people of the future are implicitly committed to the old faith in progress, which has been most uncritical and naïve in America. Like all other students, they need to ponder the philosophical question of in what respects, and by what standards, all the obvious change has been change for the better.

These value-judgments, which have always been essential but are especially important in a society devoted primarily to economic values, and are clearly indispensable for the purposes of choosing a desirable future, raise a further problem in that they are necessarily personal, and in our positivistic age are therefore commonly branded as "merely" subjective or emotive. I object to the "merely" because they can and should be based on positive knowledge and an effort at hard, objective thought. But grant that they are ultimately subjective, incapable of strictly objective verification, and they bring up another matter of vital concern to

[56]

all students. Now that there is growing concern over national priorities (even if it is largely ineffectual because the demands of the Pentagon come first), it might remind them that personal priorities are also a problem. Inasmuch as they cannot get everything possible out of life, no matter how affluent their society or privileged their status, they have to decide what they most want to get out of it, or put into it. More broadly considered, their vital options, sprung from the historically unprecedented freedom and opportunity they enjoy, force them to decide what kind of persons they want to be or become. They need to look not only forward but inward. For such purposes the study of literature and philosophy are obviously valuable. As it is, there is already too much "ad-hocracy" in pragmatic America, in both political and personal life.

3. ON PERMANENCE AND CHANGE, AND SOME ISSUES OF RESPONSIBILITY

Now let us consider more commonplaces. Transience is plainly the order of the day, above all in America, where it has invaded all spheres of daily life. Americans have grown accustomed to impermanence in their surroundings because of their mobility and the constant demolition and new construction; few live out their life in the house in which they were born. Their economy features throw-away goods, planned obsolescence, the latest models, the latest fashions; a major purpose of the immense advertising industry is to make them dissatisfied with old possessions. In their cities their seemingly so solid new skyscrapers that keep replacing old buildings are not built proudly for keeps, as men used to build. Lewis Mumford, though a harsh critic of our technological society, has himself celebrated "the death of the monument," in which all past societies expressed their aspirations to the everlasting; to this symbol of "death and fixity" he opposed the value of a capacity for vital renewal in civic life.

Behind Mumford lay the philosophies of Becoming, from Hegel on through John Dewey, that have largely supplanted the traditional philosophies of Being, based on assumptions of fixities, immutable essences, eternal verities. For Dewey the main end of education was growth—a good word for change. And I should add that a survey of the long ages of man may give one a deeper appreciation of some important respects in which the human race has grown in its pursuit of truth, beauty, and goodness.

Yet man could not have grown aware of change, of course, except for a background of unchanging realities. Permanence remains a basic condition of his life in the natural world, including the uniform fate of mortality. As Mumford knew, a capacity for renewal itself implies biological and social constants. These have made possible the enduring values that man has wrested from his endless travails, which have likewise been a constant in his history. Today the extraordinary pace of change may obscure the underlying continuities and uniformities, the always powerful conservative tendencies, the elementary truth that change is not the only constant in our time, and that our problems are complicated by both old habits and old needs. While I happen to cherish old possessions, prefer the old cities of Europe, and admire many of the great monuments of the past, I also write as a conscientious relativist who came to conclude that, short of eternal verities or life everlasting, there are permanent values, absolute goods, which must be considered in any aspiration to the good life—and especially today, above all by "the people of the future."

These goods bring up immediately the issue of the "natural" life for man. The study of history makes plain that we cannot talk easily of such a life for a creature who moved from the cave to the life of the soil, later from the village to life in cities, and who all along developed a remarkable diversity of cultures that alike seemed natural to the people brought up in them. His record shows that man is an extraordinarily adaptable creature. So in adapting himself to an industrial society radically different from all previous ones, he learned among many other things to live by the mechanical clock instead of the natural rhythms of night and day and the seasons. I assume that most people could adapt themselves to life in submarine communities. Conceivably, too, man may in time be made still more adaptable by not only systematic conditioning, such as B.F. Skinner aspires to impose on the whole society, but such imminent possibilities as new wonder drugs, genetic surgery and engineering, and biochemical controls of the nervous system. Another eminent psychologist rejoices in the prospect that by biochemical means "we will achieve the ability to change man's emotions, desires, and thoughts."

Yet "we" would mean in practice the various specialists in social or human engineering. If I am myself too set in my ways, or too content to go on with my own thoughts and feelings, laymen in general cannot simply trust to the wisdom of these technicians. Meanwhile we have to deal with young people who have the same basic biological and psychological needs as their ancestors have had through the ages. For this reason we must consider too the plain reasons why modern life may in some respects be legitimately called unnatural. Certainly life in a noisy, congested, polluted environment is not natural for man, or good for him, even if people get used to it; quiet, sunshine, fresh air, open space, and greenery are among the elementary natural goods.[2] When René Dubos calls for a "new social ethic" based on the idea of living in harmony with nature instead of forever exploiting and "conquering" it, we might be reminded that this is a very old idea, common not only in folk cultures but in ancient Greece, Confucian China, Buddhist Japan, and much Western

2. There is indeed a well-known planner (whose name I forget) who has an animus against grass. He wants to replace lawns by green asphalt, which he points out would be much more efficient and for the long run more economical. But his animus seems to me strictly a phobia. At least most Americans still prefer natural greenery, even though it means that they have to go on mowing their lawns.

literature. In a historical view it is the technological drive to exploit and conquer, at any cost to the natural environment, that is strictly unnatural, as now its menace to human survival also suggests. So too is the American rage for endless acquisition and consumption, to satisfy "needs" created by admen, often at the plain expense of mental health. The more adventurous young people are themselves seeking more "natural" ways of living.

There remain the higher needs of the life of the mind, developed during the history of civilization, which are the special concern of the humanities. Embracing aesthetic, ethical, intellectual, broadly spiritual values, they lead us to the issues of the "good" life. Needless to say, we shall never agree on this. It would be most unfortunate if democratic educators ever did approach agreement, inasmuch as their task is to assist their students in deciding for themselves what the good life for them is. Then the young people might settle for the life of the super-industrial future as pictured by Toffler. But first I would like to widen their range of choices in possible futures, for both themselves and their society, and to develop their powers of judgment, by making them think hard about the perennial questions, how to live and what to live for—the right questions even though, or again just because, they cannot be given conclusive answers by scientific or any other methods.

Any such effort would call for some introduction to the wealth of possible answers suggested by the diverse cultures of the past, in both East and West, embodied in the great works of art and thought that the human race has hung on to. I doubt that most thoughtful, independent students would welcome Toffler's vision of a super-industrial technology that will manufacture "experience" instead of mere commodities, since so many are bent on having their own experience, doing their own thing; but for this reason too they need to be acquainted with the kind of

[60]

experience provided by Shakespeare, Rembrandt, and Beethoven, and by such rebels against the modern world as Dostoyevsky, Nietzsche, and D.H. Lawrence. With all this they might get too some tragic sense of life, a deeper sense of the abiding realities of the human condition—a spirit lacking in Toffler and most other futurists, who may therefore often seem superficial.

I think it is unnecessary to survey the many ways in which the liberal arts may obviously promote a full development of capacities for growth, self-realization, and self-determination. (I am assuming that most young people are still not ready to let B.F. Skinner determine the kind of self everybody should have.)

Now, all such old-fashioned talk may seem still more academic and ineffectual because of the facts of professional life in the so-called humanities, on which I have already dwelt wearily. (I say "so-called" because the subjects commonly so labeled lack a common purpose or clear core, such as the old classical education had, and it is not clear to me why the study of Middle English, say, is more humanistic than biology or anthropology.) Both as teachers and as scholars, engaged in the now most honored activity called "research," specialists in the humanities seldom concentrate on the basic problems of human values and value-judgments. No more, of course, do the universities as a whole, which foster above all conventional research, contributions to knowledge or learning rather than to philosophical understanding or possible wisdom. So we must wonder about the university of the future in America, and to what extent it will offer a suitable education for hopes of a better future. It will almost surely grow still bigger, and more important too in spite of its current financial difficulties; the signs are that education of all kinds will be a major enterprise in America. The universities I assume will probably offer still more kinds, in particular more "continuing" education, or re-education of adults, since scientific advance and technological innovations will antiquate some professional skills and require professionals to keep abreast.[3] One can only hope that the universities will concentrate more on fundamental problems, which would involve the social criticism that to my mind ought to be one of their major objectives today. An obvious difficulty, however, is that neither government nor business, on which they depend for financial support, is likely to welcome such criticism.

For different reasons contemporary art may make talk about permanent values seem as irrelevant. Here transience is the order of the day in the form of the fashions that keep sweeping over the arts, often with the announcement that old styles or art-forms are dead. In this welter of novelty there is indeed much imaginative work of merit, perhaps of promise for the future, but most conspicuous is the element of mere fashion, the latest "ism," the rage for novelty or superficial originality. Mostly short-lived, the fashions support Toffler's belief that the values of the future will be more ephemeral than the values of the past.

I suppose he may be right, especially because all the signs are that the pace of change will continue to accelerate. As he writes briskly that "permanence is dead," so the historian J.H. Plumb writes soberly that "the past is dead." They are not actually dead, of course; people can never escape from the permanent conditions of their mortality in the natural world, or from the past out

3. Some years ago Harry Gideonse, former president of Brooklyn College and now Chancellor of the New School for Social Research, remarked that the content of the training of engineers and doctors in particular was likely to become obsolete in five or ten years, and went on to suggest that *all* diplomas might have an expiration date on them, like drivers' licences, and not be renewed automatically, but only "unless the study is continuously refreshed." He also remarked that for teachers this raised a hard question about their cherished principle of academic tenure. Such tenure is rightly cherished as a bulwark of academic freedom, but it notoriously also protects mediocre teachers, and in the universities can be a bulwark of a trivial kind of learning, and of obsolescent policies and practices, or of vested interests grown basically irrelevant. As it is, teachers' unions (such as the American Federation of Teachers) commonly defend not only tenure but seniority rights. In practice—in both the schools and the colleges—this may mean that the rights of students are subordinated to the rights of dodoes.

of which their society came, and which therefore molded their precious selves. It is only the *sense* of permanence and of the past that is dying; and if it dies, I should still say so much the worse for the future and its ephemeral values. Meanwhile so much the worse for us too right now because of the common lack of a sense of history and tradition, and in particular what the sociologist Philip Rieff has called the "barbarism" of a systematic rejection of the past and of the constraints of the past. An ignorance of history has also promoted an obsession with novelty and our uniqueness, the common delusion that we are wholly emancipated from the past.

European students are rightly suspicious of conventional history as it is taught, and complain that their universities neglect contemporary history, regarding it as mere journalism. American students usually have ample opportunities to study contemporary history, but generally know too little about past societies to develop much historical sense; they may illustrate the old saying that if you know only your own time and place, you can't really know them. They need in particular to consider the traditional wisdom of the past, which typically involved a strong sense of natural limits and the need of inner constraints, or of self-control and self-mastery, which were taught by all the world's major religions and philosophies. Since they are all for more freedom, they might ponder as well Goethe's definition of freedom as the opportunity to substitute self-control for external controls.

All this goes as well for our many dissident students, whose "counter culture" embraces the instant culture of Toffler's people of the future. This involves a stress on immediate gratification, which has promoted the drug culture, and in general a hedonism that is akin to the self-indulgence of the American way of life that the dissidents are supposedly rebelling against. At best, an instant culture is hardly a sound basis for concerted, sustained effort to build a better society, or make civilized choices in futures.

[63]

Meanwhile, however, we also have plenty of earnest students who are not so wedded to transience and novelty as Toffler's people of the future. The actual problem for educators aware of the challenges posed by the pace of change is much more difficult than fighting a rear-guard battle in a steady retreat. It is to create a more selective, usable past by instilling more reverence for its great works of art and thought that can still speak meaningfully to us, but also by recognizing its too common tyranny, in both the world of thought and the political world, a tyranny strengthened by the fond illusion of too many scholars that its great works embody nothing but timeless truths; and by instilling an appreciation of both the enduring values it created and the values of change and growth, recognizing the inveterate unreasoned tendency of most people to resist change, but now also the too common tendency to accept it as unthinkingly. In short, a perpetual balancing act, in which educators can never be sure that their timing and emphasis are right.

They face a related problem of balance in their judgment of science and technology, in particular because of the animus of many literary intellectuals against them. It is obviously futile to treat them as simply a curse, inasmuch as we now could not possibly live without them. Quite apart from all the material benefits flowing from them, they too have inspired great imaginative works, while contributing the indispensable scientific spirit to the values developed by our civilization. Today humanists have no more effective allies than the many life scientists who are deeply concerned over the problems of not only human survival but survival in a decent environment, fit for fully human beings to live in. At the same time, humanists have to point out the limitations of science, and to contend against the popular faith that it can give us all the answers. Although they may find allies too among behavioral scientists who know better, they have to keep pointing out that too many others have an excessive faith in the latest techniques, or in a methodology that, far from answering the fundamental questions, tends to obscure them or rule them out. Toffler, an ardent pupil of the behavioral sciences, is typical when he calls for a "science of futurism," the establishment of more "scientific futurist institutes," "scientific measures" of the quality of life, social experiments with "the most rigorous, scientific analysis of the results," and so forth. He is too sophisticated to believe that all this could give us positive answers, but the magic word remains "scientific"; so it is necessary to emphasize that he is using it in a not at all rigorous sense.

Then I should add that properly taught, both the humanities and the sciences can inculcate a humility needed alike by futurists, students, and the power elites they are critical of, and with it a sense of responsibility for the maintenance of our rich heritage in both. As it is, specialists in both naturally tend to overrate the importance or value of their subject. I am not jealous when I go on to say that inasmuch as scientists have more prestige, and are more lavishly supported by our society, they in particular might reconsider the social value of their work, or of things they do just because they like to do them. Thus many justify the billions spent on the space program, while hundreds of millions of people on earth don't get enough to eat, because of its scientific by-products, such as the rocks on the moon that the astronauts brought back for them to play with.

In humility, all educators might then deplore the growing tendency to make a fetish of the college degree, and increasingly of advanced degrees, as a requirement for a good position. This creates a social problem by handicapping young people from not only poor families but the lower middle class, who cannot readily afford a degree; it is one apparent reason for the public hostility to the universities. It has also created a technical elite whose expertise is not distinguished by either humility or wisdom. And it has spread the insidious idea that only the technical expert is entitled to express opinions about social and political problems that affect all of us, often more painfully than they affect the technical elite: we may know better when and where the shoe hurts than do the experts who designed the shoes as "solutions."

Finally, however, I would again emphasize chiefly that any serious concern for the future demands first of all thoroughgoing criticism of the present state of America, to which both scientists and humanists have been contributing. The root of our trouble remains the American way of life, with business as usual, politics as usual, consumerism more than usual. I think that education for life in that year 2000 might do no better than turn out more Ralph Naders. Or at least it might concentrate on the difficult problem stated by John Gardner: "to make it possible for young people to participate in the great tasks of their time"—and to begin with an effort to single out and define these tasks.

4. POSTSCRIPT ON AESTHETIC EDUCATION

Given all the plain ugliness that industrial societies have created, and that blights the landscape and cityscape of America in particular, I should say that education for the future ought to give much more attention to aesthetic education than this usually gets in either futuristic theory or contemporary practice. Our schools all offer courses in literature, and in the early grades may teach students on the side something about drawing; our universities usually have fine arts departments; but most of our students never get a basic training in the fine arts, or more broadly in the education of the senses, the whole realm of nonverbal and non-logical meanings, including such matters as "expressive" or "significant" form—terms that are often used too loosely, but that nevertheless refer to realities of direct perception, which are important in not only painting but architecture, the most public of the arts, and to my mind the most important in education for the future.

Since I never had a basic training in the fine arts myself, and my experience as a teacher has been limited to literature, I do not know just how to educate the aesthetic sense, or to set up standards of aesthetic judgment. I do know that at some stage in the long evolution of man he developed an aesthetic sense, and that it remains part of the hereditary equipment of all people, as is most apparent in young children—before they have been schooled. If its biological value, or the reason why it was preserved by natural selection, may seem unclear, it becomes clearer when we reflect that the aesthetic sense is intimately associated with man's creative or craftsman impulse, which obviously did assist him in his struggle for survival. At any rate, we may appreciate what a priceless inheritance it is if we try to imagine a world in which nothing ever struck us as beautiful—how much poorer life would be. We do pay a price for our aesthetic sense, of course, as we do for all the values of human consciousness: a keen sense of beauty makes us more aware of all the man-made ugliness about us. (Nature can be frightening or repellent, but it is rarely if ever ugly, even in barren regions.) Then we may wonder about the many Americans whose aesthetic sensibilities appear to have been so dulled that they do not mind or even notice all the ugliness. They might be considered fortunate since they have to live with it willy-nilly; yet their lives are poorer because of their dulled sensibilities. It seems to me clearly another reason why Americans, in spite of their unprecedented material advantages, are not a particularly joyous people.

To return to aesthetic education, my point is that in a technological society whose main business is business, it is more necessary than ever before to develop sensitivity of perception, refine powers of choice, and enrich ideas of desirable futures. It could make more meaningful and effective the common complaints about "the quality of American life." Now that President Nixon has added this cliché to his stock, it is fair to remark that he is only typical of our society in that on his record he has a pretty vague or vulgar notion of the standards of excellence the phrase implies, including aesthetic standards, and has displayed little awareness of the deterioration in quality during the phenomenal economic growth of the nation. For young people the aesthetic judgment is more pertinent because it accordingly enters as well into judgment of the life styles they are experimenting with, which with some of them have involved considerable slovenliness, in not only dress but behavior.

All this brings up questions about the future of art, and its possible contributions to a desirable future. Daniel Bell has observed that artistic activity is the most unpredictable. In my own speculations I have ventured only the expectation that art in the year 2000 will be marked by as much variety, confusion, and conflict as we now enjoy, or don't enjoy. Since then the *Journal of Aesthetic Education* has devoted a special issue (January, 1970) to the topic "The Future and Aesthetic Education." Its contributors, who were not professional futurologists, ventured little or no positive prediction, but dwelt rather on ideal possibilities that they hoped might be realized, such hopes as that aesthetic interests would become much more important in the future and also would come to seem "natural" to the common man; though sometimes I thought they glided too easily from "might be" to "would be." (Alvin Toffler contributed an article on "The Art of Measuring the Arts" in which he typically argues that by "behavioral analysis" artistic quality could be measured, and that our immediate need is a "cultural data system.") Most interesting for my present purposes was an article by Harry S. Broudy in which he argued that the role of the serious artist for the future is to offer images of the good life and models of life styles. He evidently had in mind chiefly literary artists, for reasons that seem obvious to me. I assume that in the past the fine arts may indirectly have had some such effect by expressing the spirit or the ideals of their society, as Greek sculpture and architecture did, and perhaps such later artists as Vermeer, Mozart, and Wagner; but I also assume that no one would look to modern abstract art, or even to Picasso, for images of the good life or models of life

[68]

styles. Then the immediate question is: How much influence have writers actually had on life styles, and today how welcome or desirable is the influence of contemporary writers?

Considering our Western heritage as a whole, one of course has a choice of a remarkable variety of images of the good life, in Homer, the Bible, Plato, Dante, Montaigne, Rabelais, Milton, Wordsworth, Thoreau, Tolstoy, and so on *ad infinitum.* (In historic China, by contrast, the basic image was fixed by Confucianism, later tempered by some influence of Taoism, but it prevailed with remarkable consistency for some two thousand years.) The Romantics—especially Byron and the young Goethe of *The Sorrows of Werther*—had perhaps the most obvious influence on lifestyles. Coming to modern writers, Ibsen had some such influence as a rebel against bourgeois convention (the Women's Lib movement might be traced back to his *Doll's House*) as did in more recent times D.H. Lawrence and Ernest Hemingway. Otherwise the major writers of our century, who by common consent include Joyce, Proust, Yeats, and Eliot, had little direct influence on life styles that I am aware of. To Americans this might suggest the sobering thought that the most influential of their writers in this respect was probably Horatio Alger, with his endless variations on the popular theme of the poor boy who made good; his influence on the life styles of Americans was certainly more apparent than that of Emerson, Whitman, or Thoreau—a voice crying in the American wilderness.

Among contemporary writers, one of the most influential in America—at least on the youth—is Allen Ginsberg (with assists from the beatnik writers and the Beatles). There is some question, however, about the wholesomeness of his influence, or of his images of the good life, which involve a good deal of self-indulgence, and more question about his role as a prophet, whether the chants that impress our youth will impress the next generation, or enter our cultural heritage as the chants of Walt Whitman did. And so with contemporary art in general. Here

[69]

again we run into the welter of passing fashions, with pretentious manifestoes proclaiming that old art forms or styles are dead.[4] Even as fashions, however, they are at least symptomatic, and might have considerable influence in their brief day, which is our feverish day. This issue was forced by Daniel Bell in an essay "The Cultural Contradictions of Capitalism," published a few years ago in *The Journal of Aesthetic Education*, which devoted a special issue to it. Here Bell advanced the startling thesis that our society, supposedly dominated by technology, is in fact now dominated by culture. This thesis might have heartened educators in the humanities and the arts except that the dominant culture as Bell saw it is an "adversary culture," in effect the counter culture of the youth, which is not only antibourgeois but anti-intellectual; and he concluded that this "cultural crisis" is the deepest of our many crises today. The arts are contributing to it by the *avant-garde*, which provides the art of the adversary culture, and in his view is having a significant influence on "manners, morals, and ultimately politics."

Tell it to Richard Nixon, I have suggested—or to any of the leaders of the power establishments, in government and business, which more plainly continue to dominate our society. To my mind, Bell fantastically exaggerated the social influence of *avant-garde* art. Still, it is popular among the youth and might well be having some influence on their manners and morals, and I

4. It may be salutary to recall the movement in painting called Futurism, headed by Marinetti, before World War I. Its manifestoes proclaimed that traditional values had to be destroyed, and they glorified modernity, specifically speed, power, the dynamism of technology, but also—more prophetically—absurdity, violence, and war, which they welcomed as "the world's only hygiene," together with "the beautiful ideas that are death-bringing." In this spirit the Futurists hailed "the magnificent radiance of the future." Although I am not qualified to judge the artistic merits of their paintings, of which I have seen only a few reproductions, their manifestoes now seem sillier because this movement is long since dead; it did not survive the hygiene of World War I. Today it serves only as a warning against the pretentiousness of the many artists and art-critics who take too solemnly the latest fashion or ism.

[70]

gather that it is now considered chic in suburbia or among the more sophisticated bourgeois, whom its devotees once delighted in shocking. Bell cited no names or examples of it, and I have only a limited acquaintance with it; but from what I know about it, or hear from its devotees, I judge that most of it holds little promise for the future, and meanwhile is scarcely a trustworthy guide to the good life.

In literature one current vogue is the "new novel" in France, with the usual manifestoes about how and why it is now impossible for serious writers to write novels in traditional ways.[5] But more pertinent for my present purposes are such fashions as the theater of the absurd, "black comedy," and in general the literature of negation, with antiheroes, nondrama, and stress on utter futility, as most strikingly exemplified by Samuel Beckett's *Waiting for Godot.* These may be considered a legitimate expression of the predicament of modern man, which is surely a proper subject for serious writers, but they scarcely offer images of the good life or models for a satisfying life style. At best they warn readers about what they are up against in any quest of the good life today.

By all this I do not mean to say that contemporary art holds out no promise for the future. There remain countertendencies in the welter of fashions, in literature the many serious writers (such as Saul Bellow) who may sound the fashionable themes of alienation and frustration, and thereby attract a large enough audience, but who remain deeply concerned about the issues of the good life and offer suggestions, if not models, for satisfying life styles. In any case, we are dealing with very real and important possibilities for the art of the future, opportunities for artists in a techno-

5. I should confess that I have managed only to skim through a novel or so of Robbe-Grillet, the herald of the vogue, for I find in the new novel only some possibly interesting experiments in technique, or stunts, but no moving drama such as I still enjoy in the great novels of the past; when I made out the identity of the main characters (with some difficulty), I simply didn't give a damn what happened to them.

logical mass society in which their sensitivity and their natural concern with basic human values, including aesthetic values, have become more needed than ever before, and may make them better qualified than behavioral scientists who trust to new techniques—not to mention the professional image-makers in government and business, who like admen and publicity men are specialists in phoniness. Whether or how artists will rise to this challenge remains to be seen. But meanwhile they may at least be trusted to carry on their long tradition of criticism of conventional life styles, by which they help to set standards of judgment of the quality of life. In America going back to Emerson and Thoreau, this tradition has included such once influential writers as the Sinclair Lewis of *Main Street* and *Babbitt*. He might remind us that satirists in particular can be socially effective. There are still Babbitts among us, some in high places, but they are not so common and popular as they once were, nor quite so brash, even in Rotarian small-town America.

Today serious artists have to contend against the popular stereotypes mass-produced by the mass media, including the vulgar images of the good life in television commercials—the happy, happy young people prancing along beaches, full of zest because they use the right kind of shampoo, smoke the right kind of cigarette, drink coca cola, or what have you. Herein, however, also lies the opportunity of serious artists. They have a potentially large audience, especially among the growing number of young people who know better than this banal way of life. Their opportunities are enhanced as well by the very confusion of values and life styles in America, the differences between classes, professions, and localities, and between men and women, young and old, white and black, in a "standardized" mass society that is also the most heterogeneous in history. Artists will of course not speak the last word about the good way of life, nor lay down the law, but their word will remain pertinent just because they naturally tend to be aware that there is no one good or right way nor uniform law.

The mass media may also serve to remind us of the commonplace that beauty is not skin deep, as it appears to be in the glamor girls featured by television. I would finally stress the deep connections between truth, beauty, and goodness that the ancient Greeks felt but that are obscured by the modern tendency sharply to separate major interests, making truth the province of science, beauty the province of art, while only the Lord or the Devil knows who are the authorities on goodness, now that the churches have lost much of their traditional authority. Truth and beauty are of course not identical, as Keats declared, in stating all we know or need to know on earth, but we still need to know that they are not wholly separate either. The study of the natural sciences has an aesthetic value that is often stressed by leading biologists, astronomers, and theoretical physicists in particular. Of the latter, Murray Gellman has remarked that their choice between conflicting theories when the evidence is insufficient is often determined by aesthetic criteria, which have as often proved trustworthy, he thinks because nature at bottom really is beautiful; while Werner Heisenberg has stressed the significance of a remark of an eminent mathematician, that there is no place in the world for ugly mathematics. As for the arts, literature is among other things plainly an effort to render the truth of human experience and offer a "criticism of life," which may be no less valid because it is not strictly verifiable. *Hamlet,* written before the rise of modern science, remains a pertinent as well as eloquent comment on the human condition. And now that people talk less of good and evil than of right and wrong, issues dramatized in literature, we should note that these terms more clearly imply the idea of truth, however relative or fallible such ideas may be. "Truth" is not the word for the symbolical meanings—nonverbal and nonlogical—expressed by the other arts, but these meanings are nevertheless a significant enough form of experience and mode of communication to warrant the title *Philosophy in a New Key* that Suzanne Langer gave to her study of them, and to make necessary efforts to distinguish pretentious or superficial from honest, serious, possibly profound art.

Most important in America today, I think, are the connections between the aesthetic sense and the moral sense. They are never so simple as to assure that a love of beauty will lead to a love of goodness. It is a commonplace that artists can be selfish, callous, even heartless in their human relations, and their private lives make poor models for a life style. I am more concerned about the connection between aesthetic and moral insensitivity, which seems to me plain enough even if it is impossible to demonstrate conclusively. Let us consider D.H. Lawrence's impassioned indictment of early industrial society:

> The great crime which the moneyed classes and promoters of industry committed in the palmy Victorian days was the condemning of workers to ugliness, ugliness, ugliness . . . formless and ugly surroundings, ugly ideals, ugly religion, ugly hope, ugly love, ugly clothes, ugly furniture, ugly houses, ugly relationships between workers and employers.

Who would deny that "ugly" can be the appropriate word for not only houses and surroundings but human relations, hopes, fears, ideals, even religion? Today American workers are better off, and though they may work and live in a foul industrial environment, they are not so utterly condemned to ugliness as workers were in early Victorian England; but there remains plenty of ugliness in America, both physical and spiritual. Granted that an aesthetic education alone could never assure the elimination of the black ghettos and the ugly racism of Americans, or the prevention of the barbarous ways in which our military now wage war, my point remains that the national insensitivity to ugliness has something to do with the moral coarseness of too many Americans (now

[74]

including their President) and the lack of moral imagination in our foreign policy, including our dealings with the Third World. Not to mention the ugly self-righteousness of a Mammon-worshipping people who will go on singing "God bless America." To this I am always inclined to say "sweet Jesus!"—and now to add that sweetness too may have some connection with the aesthetic sense. Although an unbeliever myself, I think that most of the teachings of Jesus deserve to be called sublime too. "Sublime" is not the word for any contemporary art I know of, still less for the sermons of Billy Graham, the self-proclaimed "warrior for Christ"; but it embraces the related ideas of grandeur and beauty, and recalls the deep connections in man's loftier aspirations. In preaching goodness, Jesus thought that he was preaching truth too, and though presumably not a conscious artist, he had some evident feeling for the beauty of nature, and in his use of language was a poet too. Unbelievers can still appreciate the magnificent poetry of the Bible—a book that as a teacher I have learned is now virtually unknown to most young Americans except by hearsay. The artist for the future might do no better than recall them to the richness of our cultural heritage, specifically its rich variety of images of the good life.

IV

The State of Ignorance

All the talk about the "knowledge explosion," the "knowledge industry" as the biggest industry in the country, and the many revolutionary discoveries of "breakthroughs" in science has obscured our frightening ignorance about some vital matters. I am not thinking primarily of popular ignorance, deplorable though that is in a country that has had an "education explosion" too. Neither am I thinking of the common myopia in an age of ultra-sophisticated techniques that failed to anticipate such obvious problems as pollution, which engineers surely ought to have seen coming. My concern here is an ignorance shared by our presumed authorities. It has become frightening most obviously because its issues involve the very survival of the human race, or of life itself, now that modern technology has made man by far the most dangerous pest in the history of life on earth. It has flourished on an explosion of trivial knowledge, together with a standardized professional neglect of fundamental questions by our thriving knowledge industry. It is immediately more dangerous because it is not only displayed by our business and political leaders but often exploited by them for their own purposes, with the help of technologists who support the popular illusion that technology can solve all our problems. And it is not pure ignorance, but frightening as well because of an awareness of it due

[76]

precisely to our new knowledge, in particular to such new sciences as ecology and geophysics.

An obvious example is the much publicized environmental or biological crisis. Ecology is an infant science dealing with extremely complex environmental systems, now often being disrupted by man more than ever before; but while we have learned enough to know that unless we change our ways we face alarming possibilities, we cannot be certain just how alarming they are, given the current tendency to blow up every new problem into a candidate for being viewed with alarm; crisis has become fashionable. Specifically, we don't know enough to judge with assurance between the different estimates, all of them necessarily rough, about how much more abuse our earth can stand, or how many billions of people it could support. Similarly with the fears of geophysicists about what we have been doing to our planet. Some say it may heat up enough to make life difficult, if not intolerable, by the next century; others say that the ice cap at the poles may slide into the oceans, set off devastating tidal waves, and start another ice age; and again we simply don't know the probabilities.

2. SOME IMMEDIATE PROBLEMS

Since such possibilities of universal catastrophe are always likely to seem too remote to be real, let us stay closer to home. Right now we live in an increasingly noisy, congested, polluted environment that is clearly bad for both physical and mental health. How bad? How serious is the danger of the current trends? Once more we don't know. In my own study of modern technology I was dismayed to learn how little is known of the specific effects, still less the total effects, of our environment on people, how relatively little study is being made of them, and how long it would take to acquire an adequate knowledge of them, since they include cumulative, delayed effects. René Dubos pointed to another difficulty when he called on his fellow biologists to begin studying the total organism in relation to the total environment. To my knowledge there has been little response to his challenge, for understandable reasons. Like all scientists, biologists are specialists, and such a study would require a knowledge of not only physiology, ecology, and demography but psychology, sociology, anthropology, and I suppose all the other behavioral sciences; it might require the services of a whole think tank.

Meanwhile our severely limited knowledge is an aid to the vested interests obstructing efforts to deal with even the most obvious problems of the environment. A standard defense of industries polluting air, water, and soil, or rushing still more chemicals into profitable production, is that there is no conclusive evidence of really serious harm (just as the cigarette industry attacked even the strong evidence about lung cancer). A particular difficulty is that an adequate program to do away with pollution would cost many billions of dollars, maybe as much as the Pentagon keeps spending on obsolescent weapons systems; and it would also call for drastic regulation of business, some sacrifice of the private profits that are the life-blood of the American economy. As the appointed guardian of business interests, ex-Secretary of Commerce Maurice Stans called first for studies to determine "which elements classified as pollutants really cause harm to health," and also called for directives to all federal agencies "to balance known environmental damage against known economic factors." Economic factors naturally come first in America, but anyway they are much better known; big corporations can come up with estimates of how many millions it would cost them to stop polluting the environment, and how many workers they would have to lay off meanwhile. Although environmental damage is plain enough, it cannot be assessed so readily, and as usual we don't know just how much harm it does to health.

Now, the problem is complicated because economic factors of

course have to be considered—we are not dealing with simple wickedness. In a rational economy, workers laid off in polluting plants could be put to work on the immense job of cleaning up and restoring the environment, but as it is, the government would have to pay the bills. Given our system, a thorough-going environmental program would cause severe economic dislocations.

For my purposes here, however, more pertinent are the complications raised by DDT—now the popular villain in the environmental drama. The commercial interests backing it earned its evil reputation by their efforts to discredit the clear evidence of the harm it was doing to wild life. At the same time, it has been a real boon to farmers as a pesticide, and it has also saved countless hundreds of thousands of lives in malarial and vermin-infested regions all over the world. Hence Dr. Martin Borlaug, winner of a Nobel Prize for his contribution to the "green revolution," has protested against the growing movement to ban its use, on behalf of all the poor, undeveloped countries; he argues that these countries badly need DDT, as their leaders are saying too. On the other hand, we now know that it has not only killed many birds but got into vegetable and animal life the world over, and so into the tissues of all of us as well. Some scientist has cheerfully assured Americans that they don't need to fear cannibals any more because we are all inedible: we have more DDT in us than the Food and Drug Administration permits in meat. If most of the world keeps on using it, we will surely accumulate still more of it in us. In order to make a humane decision, we must therefore ask: Just how much harm does it do? How much of it can people stand in them? And readers may guess the answer: We don't know.

Insecticides also bring up another natural form of ignorance—long-range effects. As has been pointed out by Edward Goldsmith, founder and editor of *The Ecologist* magazine, they disrupt the ecological balance to an incalculable extent, but including the destruction of birds and other animals that are very important as predators; so in killing some pests, we are creating others, as insects that were once controlled by their natural predators are multiplying and becoming a plague. Our short-term expedients "simply succeed in putting off the day of reckoning, and the more you put it off, the worse it will be"—unless we somehow take long-term measures too. Likewise the elimination of malaria in some regions has weakened or destroyed people's natural immunity to the disease, making them more liable to death if an epidemic comes in from outside. When in 1969 Ceylon stopped using DDT, a million of its people suddenly came down with malaria; the government had to send in a rush order for tons of DDT. This points to another penalty of our dependence on technology. Natural controls in ecological systems are self-regulating, but when men substitute artificial controls they have to do the regulating, and in practice they perforce go on using their technological controls, which they usually do without an eye to the long run. Our vaunted "mastery" of nature emphasizes that we do not really know how to control it, except for some of our immediate, short-sighted purposes.

The needs of the poor countries bring up again the national goal of indefinite economic growth, and the short-sightedness of Americans in particular, who pride themselves on being a "practical" people. Their leaders seem to be practically ignorant of the truth that such growth cannot continue indefinitely because of the earth's limited natural resources, even if we learn to make do with rocks instead of minerals. Meanwhile the American passion for growth brings up other forms of ignorance. In the past men had a sense of natural limits, in growth, size, and power, and therefore of the need of inner constraints. If this sense of natural limits was most clearly due to their still limited "mastery" of nature, and the abiding problems of scarcity, it has become more essential because of the modern tendency to gigantism—the growth of giant corporations, cities, nations, and of late multinational corporations. As it is, the sociologist Philip Rieff has re-marked that "the one science we do not have is the science of limits." As usual, I am inclined to doubt that there can be such a "science," in any strict sense, but at least the various sciences could contribute more to an awareness of the need of a sense of limits, and the need of inner constraints.

Some futurologists have dwelt on an immediate problem raised by our giant organizations: that we do not know how to manage them. Corporations seem able to manage well enough for their limited economic purposes, of private profit, but the social and political problem remains how to manage them in the public interest, or specifically how to control or limit their natural tendency to promote economic growth and technological "pro-gress," without regard to social costs. Some economists are say-ing that we need to calculate properly both the social benefits and the social costs of economic growth, as, once more, in the big automobile industry that turns out the millions of cars that peo-ple want, provides employment vital to the economy, but also increases congestion and pollution; only economists do not agree on how to calculate these benefits and costs, any more than how to measure the quality of life, or the extent of its deteriora-tion in America during our stupendous economic growth.

Most of them, like our national leaders, remain content with our growing GNP. They assume that economic growth, even so grossly measured, is a sign of a "healthy" economy. As "scien-tists," supposedly "objective," they generally accept our eco-nomic system as it is, despite its obvious irrationalities, and do not press the fundamental question: What is a healthy economy for social purposes? Or specifically the purposes of a democratic society ostensibly devoted to ideals of equality and social justice? These are philosophical questions, of course, involving value-judgments. Presumably they cannot be answered by the new analytical techniques, such as model-building and mathematical-econometric methods, that economists have proudly elaborated.

Still, a layman might ask: What ought we to know in order to tackle such important questions? How possible is it to get by model-building and systems analysis some idea of how alternative systems might work? To design a more rational economy, suited to the needs of an age of revolutionary change, in One World? While I have no idea, I venture to ask because some economists have begun to call for new methods of analysis that would permit the incorporation of human values, or such considerations as social health and the quality of life, into a "measured system." But apparently we do not yet have satisfactory measured systems of non-economic values. And though I suppose that "social health" cannot be defined, measured, or secured with scientific certainty, laymen might be content if social scientists attended more to the plain enough indices suggested by the present state of America. Despite its GNP of a trillion dollars, it is obviously not a healthy society in view of the extent of poverty, malnutrition, slums, alcoholism, drug addiction, violence, and crime, which we all might agree are deplorable, and which can be "measured" at least roughly by the statistics on which social scientists thrive.

Our seeming inability to do much about these problems suggests again that we do not know either how to manage or deal properly with the huge numbers of people in our massive societies. Hitler and Stalin managed after a fashion by propaganda, coercion, and ruthless suppression of dissent, but most of us naturally don't approve of their methods. Today the apparent need of more social controls raises the question of how to make them effective while keeping them democratic and humane. How do we put a stop, for example, to the dangerous population explosion? We are trying to do this by birth control, but without making it compulsory—and with least success in lands swarming with people.

In American cities the tendency to gigantism has resulted in the growth of megalopolis, which now often appears to be ungovernable, but also brings up other basic questions. Lewis Mumford has complained endlessly that we have forgotten to build to a human scale, as men used to build in ancient Greece and the medieval towns of Europe. While this makes sense in general, what specifically is a human scale? The scale of Gothic cathedrals was quite different from that of Greek temples, and was it more or less human than that of a New England parish church? The medieval builders of these cathedrals sometimes competed as to the height of their spires, more obviously out of human pride than love of God, and how was this different from the competition among modern builders of skyscrapers? Similarly with the basic complaints about all the dehumanizing tendencies in our technological society. Dehumanizing by what standards? Even Jacques Ellul, who has dealt most thoroughly and severely with these tendencies, now confesses to a basic difficulty. "The problem is: to make a moral judgment, to say that the technical system is inhuman, I would have to have an exact idea of what *is* human, I would have to have a reliable reading of what is man. Now I have no definition of man that I'm sure about."

Hence we often hear now that we need a science of man, or of humanity. We need to know much more about "human nature," which has long been the subject of loose talk; if we repeat the old saying "You can't change human nature," implying that it is always and everywhere the same, even though cultures have obviously molded people in countless different ways, we need to specify in what basic respects it is invariable and uniform. Now, I repeat my doubts that there can be or will be *a* science of man, at least one comparable in precision and certainty to the physical sciences. As it is, we have various sciences of man, notably biology, psychology, and anthropology, and I see no prospect of an agreement among them on a unified conception of man or human nature. I for one am not dismayed by this thought, and am content to put up with the different insights and perspectives offered by these sciences, just as I welcome the even more diverse

[83]

views offered by the humanities, or literature alone. Still, we should realize that there is no one science of man that can settle controversies over his nature. If we say that our environment today is in some respects unnatural or inhuman, as I think we can legitimately say (since I have kept saying it), we must keep in mind that it is a man-made environment, just as science and technology were human creations and continue to serve some important interests of "man."

In other words, we do not know enough about ourselves, including our self-hood, or how to achieve the self-mastery that we so obviously need. We must keep aware of not only the extent of our ignorance, but the overconfidence of many scientists that has tended to obscure it. By its positivistic tendencies, science has contributed to what Alan Watts called, in a book so titled, "The Taboo Against Knowing Who You Really Are." In *Facing Reality*, John Eccles (an authority on the brain and the nervous system) raises this issue. He exclaims over the "marvelous mysteries" of the brain and of the most common experiences we take for granted, such as perception, memory, and the basic fact of consciousness; and while he is excited by how much we have learned in recent years, he stresses how much we have yet to learn: "All this progress serves only to give an immensely wider and deeper vision of the fantastic problems that lie ahead." Then he adds that "the materialistic, mechanistic, behaviouristic, and cybernetic concepts of man, which at present dominate research," flourish on "a quite inadequate and primitive concept of the brain." In America behaviorist psychologists (headed by the now famous B.F. Skinner) have most obviously flourished on ignorance. The useful knowledge they have acquired about conditioned behavior, or the mechanical aspects of human behavior, has led them to propagate an absurdly inadequate conception of the human mind (a term Skinner wants to taboo as a useless fiction), and as inadequate a treatment of the most distinctively human kinds of behavior, such as the workings of the mysterious

[84]

but obviously real faculty known as creative imagination.

This subject I shall return to in a later chapter. Meanwhile, to come back to the world of affairs, let us consider a problem of immediate concern, a plainer reason for alarm—mental illness.

3. THE PROBLEM OF MENTAL ILLNESS

Among the apparent signs that America is not a healthy society today is the high rate of mental illness. Just how high it is, or how much higher than the rate in other societies, we cannot say with assurance even though we have a lot of statistics. We have more statistics than most societies because most middle-class Americans have taken to the habit of seeking help when they feel seriously troubled, or suffer from anxieties that people in other societies—especially poor people—regard as natural or normal, or take care of in the home, as Americans used to do with queer relatives. Mental illness is often plain or plainly serious, but up to some unknown point it is a luxury restricted to affluent societies.

Even so it is clearly a serious problem in America, and the problem has typically been aggravated by ignorance. We have many mental hospitals, on which we have spent millions of dollars, but Harley Shands, himself a psychiatrist, observes that they have been "strikingly inefficient at making their inmates mentally healthy." One apparent reason for their failure is the notorious disagreements of psychiatrists over their diagnoses and methods of treatment, and their inability to devise controlled experiments to decide between conflicting theories; as it is, all methods may often seem to work—or alike may fail to work. Karl Menninger of the famous Menninger Foundation (the largest psychiatric establishment in the world) has also complained of their too confident classification of their patients, slapping labels on them that may sometimes doom them. He insists that we simply don't know enough yet to place people with assurance on the various scales and degrees of mental disorder.

Let us consider specifically schizophrenia, the most common form of mental illness, which may fill up to half the hospital beds in the country. In 1970 the National Institute of Mental Health issued a report, based on a review of twenty years of research into schizophrenia, which states that at least 2 per cent and perhaps as many as 6 per cent of those born in 1960 will come down with it at some time. Harley Shands remarks that this appearance of statistical exactness was stranger because the report confessed to our basic ignorance: we don't know how to treat it if only because we don't know what it is, what its basic causes are, or how it develops. Shands added that the report also indicated that American psychiatrists diagnosed schizophrenia 13 times more frequently than Dutch psychiatrists did, and that British psychiatrists tended to classify it with "mood disorders." I suppose that Americans might be more disposed to suffer from "it" (whatever it is) because of the irrationalities considered normal in our society and culture, but its commonness at home is more obviously due to our ignorance. I used to hear that it was almost always incurable—patients labeled "schizophrenics" were virtually doomed; but as possibly no more than a "mood disorder," it presumably might be less fatal. Only, who knows?

Another clearly serious problem in America is the increasing addiction to drugs, which I assume is a symptom of something like mental illness, and more obviously of a national illness. It brings up more uncertainties in our knowledge, but in particular the less pardonable ignorance of our national leaders, notably President Nixon. To begin with, drugs are an old story: for centuries men have taken to them, in the East especially to opium, just as they took to beer, wine, and other stimulants at the dawn of history. Yet drug addiction is a new problem in America because so many more people, especially young people, have recently taken to drugs, including such dangerous ones as heroin. With the usual fanfare President Nixon accordingly announced a "war" on drugs, by the usual dependence on law and punishment, or cracking down on offenders, which on the record has long failed to work, just as it has failed with prostitution. The tough language and the method of force he is characteristically fond of concealed his failure to get at the causes of the problem, or even to ask the root question: *Why* are so many Americans now taking to drugs? Drug-pushers didn't cause the problem, any more than whores caused prostitution—they are simply cashing in on it.

Nixon has further obscured the basic causes by announcing, on the high moral grounds where he likes to pose, his firm opposition to the legalization of marijuana. Thereby he confirmed the popular illusion that marijuana is the chief source of evil, starting young people on the way to heroin—an assumption belied by what evidence we have from heroin addicts. It may well have some bad effects on people—getting stoned is presumably not good for them; but on the face of it marijuana is less dangerous than alcohol, in a land that has millions of alcoholics, not to mention the countless victims of drunken drivers. The popular horror of it, which has led to savage punishment for the mere possession of it (an injustice that does not trouble President Nixon on his moral high-horse or rocking-horse), is more irrational considering that Americans are more addicted to pills for all kinds of purposes, from tranquilizers to pep pills, than are any other people on earth.

What, then, are the basic causes of the drug problem? As might be expected, sociologists and psychiatrists who have studied it give different answers. To my mind one of the most sensitive and sensible is Leon Wurmser, who speaks out of his experience in psychotherapy.[1] He sees the immediate cause in feelings of bore-

1. See "Drug Abuse, Nemesis of Psychiatry," in the Summer 1972 issue of *The American Scholar.* Wurmser points to another admitted uncertainty, however, when he supports the use of the drug methadone as a cure for addiction. Other psychiatrists who question its use remind us that morphine was introduced to

dom, anxiety, and rage. Behind these he looks to the family, and then to the whole society and culture, the American way of life. He points to the common feelings of emptiness and meaninglessness in a society lacking any purpose beyond affluence and ease, feelings that lead to boredom and then perhaps to rage, or the rebellion of the youth. He also points to the prevalence of hypocrisy, fraud, and routine dishonesty, one sign of which is the deceptive if not false claims made by admen for their magic pills; the common lack of personal integrity leads naturally to a lack of self-discipline. Through Spiro Agnew, Nixon has attacked the "permissiveness" of the youth, especially the malcontents and "radical agitators" Agnew blamed for the unrest on the campus, including the disrespect for our President. Nixon cannot see that permissiveness is at the heart of the American way of life, in the self-indulgence systematically encouraged by admen, the voice of the free private enterprise that he regards as the heart of the American Way.

Then one might ask, what could the President do about such basic causes of the drug problem? Not much directly, of course; he could not make over the values and life styles of the American people. But he might be expected at least to show more understanding of the problem, with less ballyhoo over the few smugglers his Justice Department manages to catch or the quantities of marijuana it seizes. He might even be expected to provide some moral leadership, since he likes to flaunt his moral and spiritual values, including his alleged devotion to the Protestant

cure opium addiction, and then heroin was introduced as a cure for morphine addiction. Harley Shands adds that an immense increase in the production of methadone in recent years has been matched by a comparable increase in reported deaths of young men from this drug.

But I should add that Wurmser argues for methadone treatment only as a lesser evil, and at best an *assistance*, which must be combined with psychotherapy, family counseling and rehabilitation, and other services. In particular, he insists, it should not be allowed to obscure the urgent need of dealing with the basic causes of the drug problem, such as the ghettos.

ethic. As it is, he apparently cannot see either the basic inconsistencies between this ethic, with its traditional virtues of integrity, sobriety, and frugality, and the self-indulgent American way of life both exploited and promoted by the free, private advertising industry. Chiefly he confirms the popular ignorance about the drug problem. And though he apparently shares this ignorance, he exploits it for his political purposes by his fanfare about the vigorous, high-minded campaign he is waging against drugs and drug-pushers.

4. THE BASIC ISSUES OF PRIORITIES AND BALANCE

There remains the obvious question raised by the larger problem of the extent of ignorance among learned people too: What do we do about it? First of all we of course go on trying to learn more, with the help of scientists who have tried to alert us to the problems it raises. Some of them (like René Dubos) are combating the curse of narrow specialization that produces learned ignorance about fundamentals, and are questioning the accepted methodologies that dictate the subjects of inquiry. In effect, they are calling for more attention to priorities in research, to what we most need to know, even if we cannot hope to know with scientific certainty all we would like to know.

As for laymen, they can assist in such efforts, with more emphasis on neglected human values. In particular they may combat the popular tendency—still supported by too many scientists—to emphasize only the dazzling achievements of science and technology. On the levels of popular discourse this means combating the publicity given to such sensational stunts as heart transplants, which benefit very few people at a great expense of medical effort, while the elementary medical needs of millions are neglected.

But finally the problem calls for efforts to maintain another difficult, delicate balance: of justifiable pride in the remarkable gains in our knowledge, such as the breakthroughs in genetics that have raised hopes of controlling or guiding human evolution; of humility in an awareness of how much more we need to know, or with geneticists the vast deal they would have to learn before such hopes could be realized; and of alarm over the possible abuses of such powers, but meanwhile especially over the business and political leaders who exploit both our knowledge and our ignorance for their selfish purposes. In America above all it then calls for public policy guided by sober estimates provided by disinterested scientists and other authorities, based on what knowledge we do have, instead of a blind devotion to economic growth and technological "progress" that flourishes on unknowns.

V

The Future of Mind

Among the basic anxieties of literary or humanistic intellectuals today is what might be called an "intellectual crisis," to go with all the other crises—specifically a loss of confidence in the powers of mind that makes them worry over the future of mind, fear that the future belongs to its enemies. To begin with, the shaking of this confidence is another old story, reviewed by Albert Levi in *Philosophy and the Modern World,* which in modern thought may be dated from the radical critiques of reason by Hume and Kant. Such criticism became a major enterprise of philosophy, notably in Schopenhauer's doctrine of the primacy of will and Nietzsche's celebration of the will to power, coupled with his attack on the worship of intellect. With the rise of sociology and psychology, science contributed impressive demonstrations that man does not behave like a rational animal. Freud above all made modern man acutely conscious of the powers of the unconscious or irrational. And especially in America, democracy engendered a tradition of anti-intellectualism, typified by the popular suspicion of "highbrows"—a characteristically American coinage. Thus Adlai Stevenson, though not strictly an intellectual, was branded as an "egghead" just because he talked with style and wit. He responded gaily, saying "Eggheads of the world, unite! You have nothing to lose but your yolks." The fact remained that he was badly defeated by General Eisenhower, who in lieu of style or wit had only an engaging grin.

Yet the main source of anxiety, or of fears for the future of mind, is not just an old story. Although all history may be viewed as a record of the failures of mind, such failures have been most appalling in the history made in our own century. World War I, with its senseless slaughter, was a terrific shock to European intellectuals. Paul Valéry in particular wrote most eloquently about what a cruel blow this catastrophe was to belief in the freedom, power, and dignity of the mind, which "doubts itself profoundly." The failure of the war to achieve any lasting good was then accentuated by the rise of Hitler, a triumph of barbarism that brought on the still more murderous, indiscriminate slaughter of World War II, with such horrors as Auschwitz and Hiroshima, which shocked American intellectuals too; they realized more clearly and fully that America was involved in the fate of Western civilization, and that history was big enough to swallow us up too. And even since we have had to live with the Cold War, the insanity of a nuclear arms race that might prove to be literally the last word in human folly by putting an end to human history. Offhand, the mind has never had better reason to doubt its power.

These appalling developments, however, force us to consider the usual ambiguities of history, which are now more troublesome than ever before. It was mind that created the atomic bomb, and that is still busy devising more efficient or dreadful weapons. (Among the recent reports from the Pentagon was that its scientists are working on lasers to produce death rays—an old staple of science fiction.) Scientists, engineers, and technocrats retain ample faith in the powers of mind—for their own professional purposes. The ultimate source of anxiety is the abuses of the terrific power that man has achieved through science and technology, abuses that are more frightening because they are not mindless but systematic, efficient, even "rational"—for the purposes of the political, military, and business leaders who exercise these powers. Similarly the big bureaucracies in government and business that worry thinkers were creations of mind. Valéry was prophetic when he saw modern men "staggering between two abysses," the constant dangers of both disorder and excessive order.

At the same time, intellectuals who attack the abuses of mind are of course exercising their minds, in their official role as custodians of mind, which itself produced the radical critiques of reason and now the painful awareness of its limitations. And so we are brought to an elementary question, the kind that sophisticates may not ask often enough: What do we mean by "mind"?

2. THE PROBLEM OF MEANINGS

In psychology, according to my dictionary, the term refers to "the totality of conscious and unconscious mental processes." "Mental," however, is defined as "pertaining to the mind," so we are back where we started. The question remains: What do psychologists mean by mind? Long ago William James, a pioneer in the field, noted that there was "a strong prejudice that we have states of mind," and that "our brain conditions them." Since then behavioral psychologists have dismissed this prejudice as a mere fiction—as useless, B.F. Skinner tells us, as the term the "human mind"; but the brain remains an unquestioned physiological reality. There is no question either that it conditions what the rest of us persist in calling our mind, or that it is the seat of consciousness—another term the early behaviorists tried as vainly to get rid of, but that John Eccles, as an authority in the study of the brain, insists is the primary reality for man. Otherwise psychology does not answer our question. James concluded that it was no science, "only the hope of a science," and although by now the hope has generated a large assortment of men who call themselves psychologists, they still do not agree in their conceptions of mind or psyche, the subject matter of their alleged science. Nor does this put them in the same boat with physicists, the specialists in "matter," which at the dawn of modern science Descartes sharply separated from "mind," but which in theoretical physics today is no longer the substantial stuff known to common sense. Physicists tell us that they do not know or need to know what matter "is," but they can and do agree on concepts, methods, and formulas for dealing with the goings-on in the so-called material or physical world.

At any rate, they may help us to take calmly the news that we cannot give "mind" a precise, scientific definition, for this does not mean that we must surrender the assumption that there are indeed mental processes, goings-on in the brain that we call perceiving, feeling, thinking, willing, desiring, imagining, etc. Then we may also hope to deal sensibly with the many idiomatic meanings in popular usage—to be of two minds, to make up one's mind, to have a good mind to do something, to keep in mind, to mind one's own business, to mind the children, don't mind him or never mind, and so on; for these call attention to the important idea of mind as a *totality* of mental processes, with constant bearings on ordinary behavior. By intellectuals it is usually equated with intelligence, intellect, powers of thought and understanding, or reason, my own major concern here.

At a time when we have to deal at once with the excesses of a purely technical, often inhuman rationality that is concerned only with efficient means, to ends that may be foolish or barbarous, as well as with the dangerous tendencies to celebrate the irrational, I think it is especially important to find room for the claims of the nonrational, as in feeling, sentiment, intuition, and imagination; I repeat that to my mind it makes good sense to say that in order to deal effectively with our grave crises we need more moral imagination, or "heart" and "soul," imprecise as these terms are. Then we may add that "reason" must finally judge these claims, and distinguish between the nonrational and the positively irrational, as in the claims of Hitler for his racial mythology, or the less harmful but still foolish recent revival among the youth of the ancient superstition of astrology. Granted the limitations of reason or logical thought, and the good reasons for doubting that outside of mathematics it is ever as "pure" as its champions often claimed, from Plato on, we still can and must appeal to it; just as we must distinguish between vulgar unreasoned prejudice, as against Jews and Negroes, and opinion based on knowledge and honest thought, even though it is often biased and always fallible.

I would also stress the importance of the verb "to mind," in the sense of "to care." Upon caring enough will depend the future of mind in the intellectual sense of the word. Then we may put in a good word on behalf of our dissident youth. While we must hope that they will mind their elders' warnings against their tendencies to excess, at least most of them do care about the flagrant inequities in America today, the prevalence of hypocrisy and fraud, and such barbarities as our war in Vietnam—care much more than do the power establishments in government and business. Or for that matter in the universities as well, the main centers of intellectual training, which have been too willing to serve uncritically the interests of business and government, while also subordinating the liberal education of the mind to professional training, or stressing know-how more than know-what and know-why. We may then say more for traditional culture, or specifically the humanities and fine arts. While history is a record of the failures of mind, it is as well a record of the triumphs of mind in the great works of art and thought—the reasons for cherishing our heritage, paying gladly the price we have to pay for consciousness, and caring about the future of what Mark Twain called the very human or damned human race.

It is a reminder, too, that up to a point mind is certain to carry on its traditional work in the future, so long as there is any future for the human race. It is mind that finds and reports meanings in our experience, through both science and literature, not to mention philosophy. The complications begin because mind must also judge how valid are the meanings reported by writers and thinkers. A particular problem, or another reason for anxiety, is raised when they ask: What is the meaning of man's life, or of his whole history on earth? Logical positivists declare that this is a "meaningless" question, in the sense that we cannot give it a positive, verifiable answer worthy of the name of knowledge or truth, any more than we can to the question: Is there a God? Yet it is obviously meaningful because thoughtful people naturally do ask it, and historically have given answers to it that influenced conduct, of both individuals and whole societies. Inasmuch as positivists want precision in language, they might better drop the term "meaningless" and substitute some such term as scientifically unanswerable. For these questions involve the perennial philosophical questions of how then shall we live and what shall we live for?—questions that science cannot answer positively either, but that are nonetheless very practical, since we all have to answer them for ourselves.

3. THE BASIC UNCERTAINTIES

I am myself untroubled by the thought that mind or reason cannot give conclusive answers to these extraordinary first and last questions. I can say calmly what existentialists have insisted on rather desperately, that (in my opinion) man's life on earth is ultimately meaningless, in the sense that death is the end, for him as for all other creatures, and that the possible end of his history will make no difference to an apparently soulless universe; on earth it would mean only that other creatures would be better off for the disappearance of this pest. With me, however, this attitude is a matter of temperament, not a hard-earned philosophical wisdom or resignation. I can understand why many thoughtful men are deeply troubled by ultimate uncertainty, the inability of mind to give certain, logically valid answers to questions that in the past men answered confidently by religious faith. But meanwhile life on earth remains rich in possible meanings that men have given it, and still can give it for their living purposes, no less when they assume that death is the end.

As for the future of mind, I cannot be sure about this either, nor can anyone; not to mention that none of us could collect bets on it anyhow. I suppose that what should be emphasized most is the reasons for anxiety. Mind as I conceive it has dangerous enemies in men in power, "practical" men whose realism remains distinguished by its shortsightedness, when not by its callousness or inhumanity. In America it is threatened as well by a mindless way of life devoted to endless getting and spending in a not so brave new world, and based on what has been called the "pig philosophy"—the assumption that if anything is good, more is always better (a way of life, incidentally, that actual pigs are too intelligent to adopt—they know what they really need, and when they've had enough). The American way may remind us of the simple but subversive, historically revolutionary statement of Socrates in the *Apology:* "The unexamined life is not worth living." Then we may add that most men have always lived such a life in all societies, as apparently they did even in the brilliant Athens of his day—he was condemned to death by a jury of his fellow citizens, not simply put to death by evil men in power. Nevertheless the Greeks, and Western civilization after them, hung on to the memory of Socrates as a great pioneer in the quest of wisdom—another imprecise term that refers to a real, distinctive, indispensable possibility of the human mind. So the human race has preserved all the great creations of mind. For all the uncertainties about its powers and its future, I am disposed to think that human beings are bound to go on exercising their minds, and that many of them will continue to cherish its great creations.

All this leaves plenty of room for the disagreement on which intellectuals thrive, and which education should properly encourage. Substitute for rationalism the ideal of reasonableness, as I like to because it respects the claims of the non-rational, and calls attention to the common limitations and excesses of intellectuals too, it leaves open the question of what is the most reasonable attitude to assume or policy to adopt in dealing with any given problem. But at least a conscious effort at reasonableness may help us in the difficult job of trying to keep our heads amid all the basic confusions, contradictions, and uncertainties of our day.

Let us remember that despite his radical critique of reason, Kant remained a champion of the Enlightenment, with its basic faith in reason. He subscribed to what he called its motto: "Have the courage to use one's own intelligence!" In an article "The Enlightenment Is Dead" Michael Novak seemed pleased to think that it was dead, and declared that Kant's sentiment has become "obviously naïve." I should say that his motto is by no means naïve, but has only become more difficult to be true to because of all the confusions and the uncertainties about truth, beauty, and goodness. By the same token it seems to be more obviously necessary. Novak himself went on to argue that the most important questions are now theological (as the Enlightenment failed to realize), but in developing his thesis he of course used his own intelligence—and perhaps with some courage, because theology is unfashionable. Although no devotee of it myself, I thought he had some reasonable things to say.

Among them was a warning to other intellectuals against their tendency to be simply contemptuous of conventional Americans. Recognizing some such tendency in myself, I should add that in attacking the complacence of Americans—a job I nevertheless still consider necessary—they need to be aware of the danger that they may undermine the faith of Americans in themselves and their democratic institutions, the confidence they need to deal effectively with the many serious problems besetting the country, and with their own personal problems as well. At the same time intellectuals need to guard against their tendency to excessive self-pity or anxiety because of the common hostility to them, for among the contradictions of American society is that it supports them more lavishly, in particular by grants from foundations, than did any past society, or than does any other society today. With the help of paperbacks, moreover, they have a larger audience than they did in the past, and can still express freely enough their criticism and dissent—as writers cannot in the Communist world.

And though they now tend to be angry with one another, or more querulous, we may at least all respect the dictum of Pascal, that in thought lies the dignity of man, and we should therefore endeavor to think well—that is the basic morality. That the endeavor has never been harder makes it all the more necessary. The future of mind will also depend on how well the custodians of mind succeed in this endeavor right now.

VI

Reflections on B. F. Skinner
as Symbol and Portent:
In Defense of My Self

Now that B.F. Skinner is getting so much popular attention, let us take him even more seriously than he takes himself. For his name is legion. He speaks for not only the many behaviorists in psychology but the many more assorted specialists in "behavioral technology," ranging from well-intentioned scientists and social or human "engineers" to the admen, publicity men, and politicians who in cruder ways are bent on manipulating people, in effect denying human dignity. The difference is that in his recent best-seller *Beyond Freedom and Dignity* Skinner says more comprehensively, consistently, and openly what is often implicit in their theory, and especially their practice; he explicitly denies human freedom, the essential basis for claims of human dignity. And as all this suggests, there is considerable truth in what he says. We are not by any means dealing here with just another superficial fashion, but with very real, increasing powers to predict, condition, and control human behavior. Above all, Skinner forces fundamental questions. The objections to his thesis are therefore ultimately philosophical, which is to say incapable of absolute proof. But let us begin informally, in concrete, personal terms.

In attacking the ancient "fiction" of an inner man, Skinner

argues that behavioral science has made it unnecessary for us to believe any longer in "something going on inside the individual, states of mind, feelings, purposes, expectancies and all of that." Well, all of that is the fellow I've been living with all my life. Even as a child I began to realize that he was not always a joy to live with, and such intimations of frail mortality became much clearer as I matured, by now are often oppressive. Still, he is the fellow I know most intimately: while fond of him at his best, I am always concerned about his welfare; he has been the ultimate source of all my pleasures in life, including my enjoyment of what I continue to assume is my personal freedom; and I would not like to think that he is a mere fiction, or that all my life I have clung to an outworn illusion. Yet I know that like all other people I am capable of illusions. I am in trouble even when I say that I have lived with this fellow, for who is this "I"—the somebody or something apart from "all of that" going on inside me? In any case, the question is not what I would like to think. It is the question that science above all has forced on modern man: What is the truth? All of us who wish to hang on to a belief in our freedom and dignity had better do it the hard way, by facing up to the kind of realities emphasized by Skinner.

Thus I did not simply grow up as a child—I was "brought up" by my parents. In other words, they manipulated and conditioned me, telling me what I should and should not do, fortifying their training by rewards and punishments; I was never free to do just what I pleased. In Skinner's terms, I was also a product of my environment, as a twentieth-century American; this had much to do with my "states of mind," especially my "purposes" and "expectancies." Among many other things, my environment provided my schooling, another important mode of conditioning. For such reasons the kind of "self" I became was largely determined before I reached maturity, became more consciously devoted to the purposes of self-expression and self-determination, and to the ideals of personal freedom also fostered by my environment. I take for granted that I would have become a quite different person had I grown up in an illiterate, primitive or peasant community, or had I been brought up systematically by a B.F. Skinner, beginning with babyhood in a box.

And of course I am never wholly free, any more than any man has ever been or ever can be. As a twentieth-century American, I was blessedly spared a belief in predestination (a belief that follows quite logically from the traditional Christian assumption of an all-powerful, all-knowing God); but by the same token I am aware of scientific determinism, based on positive knowledge. We have learned a great deal about the actual determinants of human behavior—physical, biological, psychological, social, cultural. To such knowledge behavioral psychologists have contributed much by their studies of conditioned reflexes, or more broadly of habit formation. Like all other people, I am a creature of habit—habits that I still like to think I to some extent chose for myself, but that I know were socially conditioned too, and that involve compulsions restricting my alleged freedom. Or when "I" make up "my" mind, as the saying goes, again implying that the self and the mind are separate entities, both are in any case products of my whole past history, and it may be said that this determines the choice I make.

But enough for the time being of the mysteries of the mind as suggested—or concealed—by our daily loose talk. Let us now take a harder look at the practical problems raised by the truism that people are molded by their society and culture. In America today this means not only that they have been conditioned to certain ways of life, but that they are subject to systematic manipulation for commercial and political purposes, to an extent they are mostly unaware of. If many, like me, may pride themselves on not being taken in by the admen and image-makers, or by the habitually corny rhetoric of Richard Nixon, they may feel superior just because on the record you can fool most of the people most of the time. Then it may be added that they owe their sophistication to their culture, specifically a fuller awareness of how people are conditioned and manipulated, and now a growing criticism of the whole American way of life that conditions popular purposes and expectancies. And then, too, we are brought to the humane purposes of Dr. Skinner as a scientist dedicated to the service of mankind, in the loftiest tradition of science.

Most of us, I suppose, can accept his thesis of the need of "vast changes in human behavior" if we are to remove the dangers of pollution and overpopulation, violence and modern war—dangers, I have said more emphatically, that now threaten the very survival of the human race. Though I for one cannot trust to his method of removing them, let us first give him a chance. Certainly we have no reason for complacence over our schools. About the best thing to be said for our whole educational system is that it has provoked a widespread revolt against its mechanical routines, and its service of the conventional American way of life. The excesses of the rebellious youth, in particular the prevalence of mere self-indulgence, then bring up Skinner's sound criticism of the "fetish" of individual freedom and dignity. Above all in America, this has promoted a tradition of a selfish kind of individualism, exemplified by the gospel of free private enterprise with its sanctification of a profit system. Those who wish to cling to the values of private enterprise had better dwell first on the too common abuses of its freedom, and its consistent subordination of the public welfare to private profit. Because the business of America remains business, or profit-making, we all now have to live in a polluted environment. It is scant comfort that pollution has become democratic because of its extensiveness, so that wealthy businessmen too have to breathe foul air.

By contrast Skinner puts first the communal interest, the duties rather than the rights of individuals. At that "duty" is not the word for his purposes because of its connotations of a Puritanical discipline, or a sacrifice of personal interests. He maintains that

[103]

proper conditioning can make people *want* to do what is best for the community, and do it automatically, not because it is a disagreeable duty; they will be "wise and good without trying, without 'having to be' "; and so they will be much happier too. Likewise his method of conditioning is humane in that it stresses rewards, not punishments. Virtuous behavior becomes habitual because it is consistently "reinforced" by rewards, in this sense learned by heart. Punishment is avoided because it is wasteful and inefficient; it may make people learn to avoid it, but it fails to make them positively want to do good, or fails to get at the roots of the social trouble. (Page the champions of Law and Order.) *Walden Two*, Skinner's fictional account of a properly conditioned community in which all the people are cooperative, affectionate, virtuous, productive, creative, and "truly happy, " was attractive enough to become a best-seller. And it is a reminder that he comes out of the long utopian tradition in the Western world: visions of an ideal society that reflected generous hopes for mankind, hopes that the powers of modern science made men believe were real possibilities, and that became a real force in Western history, most obviously in Karl Marx's vision of a classless society.

But now it gives us pause. Although the Soviet Union that came out of Marx may be considered a betrayal of his ideal, it is faithful to utopian tradition as an authoritarian society ruled by an elite. From Plato on, utopias have almost always been so ruled, for logical reasons: the well-planned, well-organized, rational society cannot permit anything so messy and unpredictable as popular government, with freedom to dissent from the judgment of the authorities who know best what is good for people. And Skinner is squarely in this utopian tradition. Walden Two is no democracy. Its members do not elect the men who condition their children, and they are permitted no dissent from their judgment, no argument even about the code of the community. Enough that they "feel free," so that "the question of freedom never arises."

Now that Skinner proposes to recondition the whole American society, the key decisions would presumably be made by behavioral scientists like himself, a scientific elite. Their purposes would be benevolent, of course—they always are with the rulers of utopia. But so were the purposes of Lenin in creating the Soviet Union, and so are the purposes of the controllers of Aldous Huxley's Brave New World.

Now, I do not think we need to worry about Skinner's having his way. I see no prospect of a society so thoroughly conditioned as he thinks possible; though behavioral scientists have been multiplying like rabbits, I cannot believe that even he—the most ingenious, skillful, and resourceful of them—could make over people so completely to suit himself, or overcome the resistance especially of the more intelligent, gifted ones. Yet we cannot dismiss him lightly, for he is an influential advocate of actual tendencies that hold dangerous possibilities. People can be conditioned and manipulated to an alarming extent, as Hitler demonstrated; and we can never rule out the possibility of another Hitler, with more effective means of breaking down psychological defenses. Other psychologists have expressed alarm over the powers man is achieving to control behavior and transform personality—powers not generally known to the public—through new knowledge, new techniques, drugs, and imminent possibilities of biochemical controls of the nervous system; and we can be sure of more powers to come, given the irresistible drive to acquire ever more knowledge and put it to use. They are dangerous powers because we can never take for granted either that they will be exercised for benevolent purposes in our highly commercialized society, in which too many specialists in "motivational research" and other forms of behavioral technology have been willing to sell their skills to businessmen and politicians exploiting the gullibility of the public, or the American way of brainwashing (just as John B. Watson, who sold Skinner on behaviorism, ended in advertising). But even if we assume good

[105]

intentions, there remains the question of the wisdom of the men who may exercise these powers, and who meanwhile have considerable influence on thought.

With Skinner this question centers in his claims for his "science of human behavior." In invoking the magical word "science," he goes on to parade with naïve arrogance what he calls "the scientific view of man," as if there were only one, and he sounds more bumptious when he insists that pre-scientific views have got us nowhere and today it is "science or nothing;" for "science" is not at all a precise term today, and he could never define it to the satisfaction of the whole scientific community. Neither, obviously, is "wisdom" a precise term. Logically there would seem to be no clear place for it in the vocabulary of behaviorism, which prides itself on having ruled out such other pre-scientific terms as "thought," "imagination," and the "human mind." Yet Skinner obviously believes he is wiser than most men, wise enough to be entrusted with the reconditioning of our whole society and its educational system; so we must look into the "science" that gives him this assurance. We must consider as well his actual influence on education, which raises fundamental questions about what the ends of education ought to be. And finally there remains the question he forces explicitly by his denial of human freedom, in which he could claim the support of many other modern thinkers—a freedom that most of us nevertheless assume we have, or ought to have.

To begin with, it could be said that Skinner has been too thoroughly conditioned by the rats he has worked with for so many years. They have given him an illusion of powers comparable to God's—a "curious similarity" recognized by his spokesman in *Walden Two* (though with a modest admission that "perhaps I must yield to God in point of seniority"). In particular they have sold him the idea that human behavior is basically like that of rats, coming down to the same kind of mechanical reactions to stimuli from the environment. I can understand how he got this idea, since there are plain similarities that have made possible the "science" of behaviorism, but I say flatly there are plainer differences, beginning with the fact that I am now writing a chapter criticizing Skinner. Although I have no idea what it feels like to be a rat, or to what extent they have something like what I persist in calling "consciousness" (another pre-scientific term), I am quite sure that they do not speculate over what he is doing to them, or why. Say that my notion of an inner life is an illusion, it is strange how men ever developed this illusion; but anyway I am confident that rats do not puzzle over it, or brood over any other mystery. For Skinner's purposes they are much better behaved than I. And these purposes themselves point to another plain difference, that he is their lord and master. They will never talk back to him, or protest on behalf of their freedom and dignity. Neither will they ever design ingenious experiments to teach pigeons to play ping pong, or conjure up rat-utopias in which all rats will be "wise and good."

Let us now put the argument in technical terms, such as again no rat could ever conceive. Skinner's behaviorism is at best a superficial science, which in its negations can be simply silly. It has thrown light on behavior as far as it goes, but it never goes far enough to give an adequate account of human psychology. It is a woefully impoverished psychology in particular because it stops short of precisely what is most distinctively human—all that can make it worth being a human being, despite man's capacity for intense suffering and his unique consciousness of mortality, and that makes his nature and history worth studying. (Rats, incidentally, don't study their history either.) Skinner's loose talk about "the scientific view of man" may seem shockingly inhuman when one recalls that we are dealing with a creature who was capable of writing *Hamlet*—a pre-scientific fiction that gives a truer as well as infinitely richer account of the workings of the human mind. For when Skinner dismisses "states of mind" as outmoded fictions, he is harking back to the elementary fallacy of reductionism of his mentor John B. Watson, who first popularized behaviorism. There is really no such thing as "consciousness," Watson proclaimed—there are only motions in the brain or the nervous system. Although we may assume that states of mind are caused by such motions, they are nevertheless quite real and important, and obviously *not* the same thing; motions are not sad, self-satisfied, or joyous, as men know very well they can be —and as Skinner himself assumes when he wants to make them all "truly happy." He is not quite so crude as Watson, but he is still maintaining the "is nothing but" fallacy. Constantly he insists that the truth is "*not* this, *but* that," usually "simply" or "really" that. Thus he writes that what we call good and bad are "only" positive and negative "reinforcers."

Similarly with such terms as "thought" and "imagination" that behaviorists rule out on principle, or reduce to mere reactions to the environment. Granted that they too are imprecise terms, they still refer to very real and important mental processes. The point is that Skinner's "science" throws little light on them, only on the initial stimuli that get them started; then they may take many possible courses, leading far away from their beginning, following the dictates of logic, association, fancy, whim, or what have you. And so with the "human mind," another tabooed term, which he insists explains nothing. The all-important fact remains that human beings do have something we call a mind, that in the course of their cultural evolution it developed language, literature, logic, science, and all the other unique products of human consciousness, and that it differs in these fundamental respects from whatever Skinner chooses to call what goes on in the heads of his rats.

Elementary as such observations are, they need to be made because of a common tendency in all the sciences that behaviorism only carries to a naïve extreme. Scientists naturally tackle questions that they can hope to answer by their accepted methods. It is a sensible policy—so long as they and their students do not disparage questions they cannot handle by their methods, and remain aware that these commonly include the most fundamental questions, such as what it means to be "wise and good." As it is, the rest of us have to keep on pointing out wearily the limitations of their science, the too common superficiality and triviality of their research especially in the social or behavioral sciences, and the important questions they not only ignore but tend to obscure, or in their positivistic moods to dismiss as "meaningless." So the behaviorists begin by confining psychology to behavior that can be strictly observed, in the laboratory experimented on with verifiable results, and then they carry on proudly by denying the reality of what they cannot handle by their inadequate methods.

Let us consider more specifically what is called "creative imagination." Psychologists have had little to say about it, and behaviorists to my knowledge nothing helpful, for an obvious reason: it refers to a faculty or mental process that does not lend itself readily to study by scientific methods. I would like to know much more about it than I suppose we can hope to know with assurance. Meanwhile we do know at least that it is another distinctive power of human beings, which somehow evolved and became apparent in the works of prehistoric man. Now most people wish they had more of it, since it is of course not merely something displayed by poets or artists. It appears in the many works of man, all the inventions, discoveries, and new theories, including the works of B.F. Skinner. Though it might appear to be another illusion of an "inner life," he himself found room for it in Walden Two, whose members he was pleased to describe as creative. But then he overlooks or denies the obvious implications of human creativity—again because of his conditioning by those rats.

Thus with his insistence that we are all products of our environment, our behavior is only responses to it, and all causes of behavior "lie *outside* the individual." Having freely granted that I am a product of American society and culture, I may now add that I am also an individual, strictly different from all the other products, as are my responses to the same environment. Though I may prize my individuality too highly, it is a plain fact, recognized by Skinner, which scientists too often regard as an incidental nuisance because they are happier when dealing with uniformities or statistical averages. I assume the genes I inherited had something to do with it—a factor neglected by John B. Watson, who boasted that he could take infants at birth and make them into whatever kind of people he wanted. (Skinner casually admits that people have a genetic endowment, but is typically vague about it and the difference it may make in conditioning them). But let us stick to the environment, where behaviorists feel much more at home. In his characteristic "not-but" style, Skinner writes: "A person does not act upon the world, the world acts upon him." This I should say is plain nonsense. While the environment acts upon people, they do act upon it—and especially creative people, now, above all, scientists.

As Skinner also recognizes, man's environment is not merely a physical but most significantly a social, cultural environment— it is man-made. Historically man developed an amazing diversity of cultures, many of them in much the same kind of physical environment. We may be confident that he did not develop them so deliberately and systematically as Skinner creates artificial environments for his rats, but certainly much conscious effort went into them, including works of creative imagination. The history of culture, or more strictly of the wealth of unique cultures, does not at all look like an automatic, predictable process, or merely the result of the world's acting upon man. Once he learned to write—one of the countless inventions of creative individuals— and developed what we call civilization, it involved still more conscious effort, and in time increasing criticism of his handiwork. Today Skinner attributes the grievous shortcomings of Americans to a defective social environment, so he proposes to create a proper one, ideally like Walden Two. I agree wholeheartedly that our society is seriously defective in many ways; but since he too is a product of it, I wonder how, on his behavioristic terms, he got his power to act upon it so radically and dream up an ideal environment, such as never was. I can better understand the apparent brashness of his confidence in his ability to make over people to suit himself—that is typically American.

In any case, his hopes bring up the practical problems of education. Here he has contributed to the vogue of programmed learning and teaching machines, the beginning of what enthusiasts hail as a "technological revolution in education." The machines "reward" the student by telling him when he has got the right answer and enabling him to proceed at his own pace. They are accordingly useful in teaching basic knowledge, handling problems to which there are "right" answers; and like all the programmed materials and new hardware coming in, they are popular with the many educators who confine themselves to the kind of knowledge and technical proficiency that can be tested "objectively," now with the help of grading machines too. But these machine methods are much less helpful in teaching such subjects as literature and philosophy, or more broadly in achieving what I conceive to be the fundamental purposes of a liberal education—developing powers of expressiveness, imaginativeness, and creativity, of discrimination and evaluation, and especially of independent, critical judgment in matters in which answers are not just right or wrong. These are precisely the most important matters in both personal development and preparation for responsible citizenship. As a teacher myself, I especially deplore Skinner's emphasis on proper conditioning, which in Walden Two meant that people were not trained to make their own choices or develop their powers of self-determination—he taught them all the right answers about how to live and what to live for. In a society already so full of manipulators and would-be conditioners, and a bureaucratic school system dominated by authoritarians, both lavish enough in promises of rewards for conventional behavior, I think it most important to develop students' powers of resistance to unthinking acceptance by encouraging them to think for themselves and seek their own answers.

All this implies, however, that people do have such autonomous powers—what Skinner denies. So let us look again at man's creativity, to my mind one of the plainest proofs of his actual freedom. Skinner attacks the "mistaken" belief that man initiates, originates and creates"; it is always the environment that determines his seemingly autonomous activities. Apart from the fact that man somehow created his environment, I might remark that I believe that Skinner himself wrote *Beyond Freedom and Dignity,* on his own initiative and by his own powers; he was entitled to the seeming illogic of signing his name to it because it was neither preordained nor dictated by his society. But here let me appeal again to my own experience.

I am not a creative writer in the popular sense, being neither a poet nor a story-teller; I am not a born writer either, having no talent that would be death to hide; most likely I never would have become one had not my society afforded me a higher education; and for many years now writing has been a habit, to which I might be called a slave. Still, I began writing simply because I enjoyed it—there was no compulsion whatever, nor promise of sure rewards. While my society provided my materials, it also gave me a very wide range of choice, and I freely chose my various subjects, again with an eye to my own pleasure first and last. I enjoy writing because it is a creative activity, for me a primary means to self-expression and self-realization, not at all a mechanical process, automatic reaction, or mere habit. It is with me never a free activity in the sense of fancy on the loose, but it can give a fuller sense of freedom just because of the discipline it involves, the difficulties overcome, the satisfaction of the right word found. And it always involves an element of the autonomous, to my mind the essentially unpredictable. Anyone who knows me may predict that I will go on writing, and might guess where my interests will lead me; but I would insist that no psychologist, with the fullest possible knowledge of me and my environment, could predict— any more than I can—just how the next page will turn out, much less the whole book. Still less could behaviorists do so with the great original works of the creative imagination, or what we call genius.

Then Skinner may repeat that all this is nevertheless illusion, I don't know myself well enough, my whole past history has made me what I am, and from the outset this history was determined by my environment. I cannot prove he is wrong, if only because I cannot pretend to understand everything that goes on inside me. But neither, of course, can he prove he is right. What he is arguing for is not demonstrable truth but a scientific theory, and a highly questionable one, disputed by many other scientists. Given such basic uncertainties, and the apparent impossibility of resolving them conclusively, it is reasonable for all of us to con-sult our experience, that "inner life" that necessarily seems real to us, and that is in any case the source of our notions about the outer world and the behavior of other people. On this ground I cling to a belief in a margin of personal autonomy in human behavior. Granted the obvious influence of my whole past his-tory, I am still confident that when problems come up I have a real choice, my decision is not absolutely predetermined by this history, and if I make a foolish choice I can't blame it wholly on my environment, especially because I am critical of this environ-ment. In other words, I believe that within limits I am a free, responsible agent—as Skinner's better behaved rats are not.

To be sure, human freedom is a metaphysical mystery if we assume a lawful universe with uniform causes for everything that happens in it. It looks more mysterious when one consults the many philosophers and scientists who are still arguing that man is or is not free—a debate that I assume will go on indefinitely. It is less baffling, however, if we stick to the fact that in the course of his evolution man developed intelligence or brain-power, which has plainly enabled him to do all kinds of things that no other animal can do. Our experience tells us that this is a power of conscious choice, the choices we as plainly can and do make every day. However mysterious, it is easier to understand than are the elaborate efforts of determinists to explain in some kind of mechanistic terms how men can invent things, produce all kinds of original works—always including the works of Skinner himself. Call this power of free choice an illusion, as he does, it is one he shares in his own practice. Give him his way and he would condition people to become like the members of Walden Two—not like the creatures in Huxley's Brave New World; but this is strictly a free personal choice, not dictated by any scientific or logical necessity. Huxley's thoroughly conditioned people are as well-behaved in that they give their rulers no trouble, since they too "feel free" and are "happy"; Skinner's different notion of "true" happiness is not a scientific truth. As for me, I much prefer the admittedly personal choice of Carl Rogers, who on the basis of his professional experience maintains that psycho-therapy—another kind of "scientific" control of behavior—makes it possible to promote personal growth, self-direction, self-realization, freer and more spontaneous behavior; or in other words, that we can predictably assure more unpredictable behavior. If this sounds paradoxical, it is no more so than the God-like powers Skinner lays claims to while denying human freedom and initiative.

Then we may add that if human freedom is an illusion, it is at least not just a fond illusion, or a form of human conceit. As a free, responsible agent, I can claim credit for my good deeds and my achievements, but I must also assume responsibility for my moral and intellectual failures. I must live with "all of that" inside me—that fellow whom I may not know well enough, but often know too damned well. I must repeat what as a writer I have been saying for many years: that because man has a power of conscious choice he can make foolish or even fatal choices; that he is capable of biologically unnatural or even preposterous behavior, ranging from chastity and asceticism to suicide and sadism; that no other animal is as wicked as a human scoundrel, or as stupid as a human fool; and that now man has the power to destroy his environment, devastate the whole earth, put an end to the human race.

Finally, however, I would also repeat other commonplaces of Western humanistic tradition, especially the tradition of freedom that has produced rebels—types rigorously excluded from Walden Two. It is only by exercising his powers of conscious choice, developing a mind of his own, that a man can fully realize both his humanity and his individuality. It is only as in some measure a free, morally responsible agent that he can lay claim to human dignity. Skinner manifests that dignity in his deep concern over the state of our world, his high-minded efforts to assure the survival of our culture. His concern would be merely a naïve human conceit if man were in fact basically no different from his rats, no more capable of being wise and good in any meaningful sense; for why all this to-do about preserving a species that all the other species could get along without, or for that matter do better without? The reason for attacking Skinner, once more, is that he undermines the essential basis of human dignity, that if he ever did have his authoritarian way he would discourage the already difficult effort to help Americans to develop minds and characters of their own, and that in the name of science he lends support to the strong tendencies today that menace both freedom and dignity. For he will surely survive my criticism—even apart from his "curious similarity" to God, and to Richard M. Nixon.

VII

The Possibilities
of a Universal Faith

It is symptomatic of our secular age that our futurologists mostly
ignore religion, with all its traditional dreams, hopes, and fears.
While they naturally cannot trust it as a source of prophecy, or
offer apocalyptic visions about the year 2000, they appear to
assume that it is no longer a vital social influence and holds out
no promise of a better future. Nevertheless I assume that it remains a force to be reckoned with, and that it is reasonable to
speculate about the possibilities of a universal faith that might
make for a better future, as many men have in fact been speculating—both churchmen and laymen. Some foresee a unitary faith,
based on a common world culture. More anticipate or aspire to
a pluralistic faith with an underlying agreement on some basic
principles, perhaps in a consensus of the world's major religions,
perhaps in a new humanistic religion of "mankind."

While always assuming that we cannot prophesy with any assurance, I should say at once that despite the extraordinary pace
of change I see no prospects of a truly universal faith, at least for
a long time to come—much longer than the year 2000. Yet one
can make out some approaches to it, and again I think it would
be unwise or maybe inhuman to rule out flatly any such long-

[116]

range possibilities. There is some point in trying to look farther ahead than the next generation, which may confine us to our own provincial hopes and fears. For futurists religion is perhaps most helpful because of its visions of ideal possibilities, a tendency to utopianism that in Christianity was clouded by the doctrine of Original Sin, coupled with emphasis on eternal damnation, but has also been sustained by aspirations to holiness and dreams of a heavenly city. Christianity—the most ambiguous of the world's religions—has always provided grounds for a belief in human dignity by its teaching that man had been created in the image of God, and that the whole world had been created for his sake.

The most obvious reasons for all the speculation are the interdependence of peoples on One World, the approaches to world government in the United Nations, and the growing awareness of a common fate on our one and only earth, a little spaceship made visible in pictures taken by astronauts. Other reasons include the very decline of orthodox dogmatic, exclusive religion in the West; the growth of religious openness, as in the efforts at communication among the world's religions; the spiritual quest of the youth for a living faith, this side of paradise; and lately all the talk about the emergence of a "new man," presumably the advance agent of the future, who might be disposed to welcome new gods or new visions. All such developments provide grounds for hope in a spreading faith, or set of faiths, that might help to unify mankind. The very fact of a revolutionary age, from which orthodoxy has suffered, is a possible advantage for religion as a challenge, an opportunity to develop a new faith that might provide the conviction and commitment that are sorely needed, especially in America. And at least speculation about possible or desirable faiths of the future may contribute something to a better understanding of the present, a fuller awareness of how extraordinary our age is.

Now for my premises, I am assuming that in spite of much loose talk about the "spiritual needs" of man, these are very real needs. They are not necessarily religious in the traditional sense, involving a belief in the supernatural, inasmuch as an increasing number of people feel no need of such a belief; though we should remember that people the world over still seem, in Santayana's words, afraid of a universe that leaves man alone. In any case, we cannot dismiss "spiritul" as a meaningless term because of its imprecision, for it refers to a plain reality, the spirit in man that seeks truth, beauty, and goodness, and sometimes holiness. The platitudinous truth remains that man cannot live on bread alone (not to mention the flavorless kind manufactured in America). He needs a living faith to give his life meaning: if not a transcendental meaning, at least some kind of supra-personal meaning, a sense of belonging to a community that will survive his death, and a "calling," with a commitment to values or ideals he is willing to make some sacrifice for. And this need is most apparent in the affluent societies, above all America, where many people suffer —more than they may realize—from feelings of emptiness or meaninglessness.

Here one plain reason is that our fabulous technology, the national idol, cannot itself satisfy spiritual needs, but has tended to obscure them by all the material goods and mechanical entertainment it produces, which have trivialized the inner life of man. Lacking a spiritual foundation, modern technology has laid only the material foundations of One World; as the interdependence of mankind it brought about is primarily economic, so in the "underdeveloped" countries it has made economic development the main goal; and in the advanced industrial countries its champions promise chiefly still more material abundance, through still more economic growth, which has failed to make Americans either a tranquil or a joyous people, or to give them the "peace of mind" that many now yearn for and fail to get from tranquillizers. And modern technology, once more, has also accentuated the actual disunity in a world that is still far from being one in thought, feeling, and sentiment. In the past it led to an imperialism that eventually provoked the revolt of the whole non-Western world. Today it is steadily widening the gulf between the advanced or over-developed countries—again America above all —and the many more poor countries that comprise most of the world's population.

This I repeat because it calls for another serious reservation concerning the possibilities of a universal faith. Although the speculation about such a faith reflects a generous concern for the interests of mankind, much of it is provincial, in America reflecting both our spiritual and material advantages. When we consider, for example, the possibilities of a religion without God, which can satisfy many of us (as it does me), we must keep in mind that it cannot clearly satisfy the insecure, undernourished, largely illiterate majority of mankind, whose immediate prospects for a better life on earth are pretty poor.

These masses of poor people make especially provincial most of the talk about the "new man" who is emerging. We have a choice of a lot of different visions of what this new man will be like, but almost all of them are types emerging from Western industrial society. Thus we get "technological man," who in some views looks like a computerized biped or robot, in others is a multi-dimensional man with a new holistic philosophy that will make him the master instead of the slave of his technology. A variant is Alvin Toffler's "post-industrial" man, who has already shown up in his "people of the future." Others have the new man coming out of the laboratory, as by B.F. Skinner's method of conditioning, by genetic surgery and engineering, or by bio-chemical controls of the nervous system. Still others see him as the product of a revulsion against a mechanized, regimented technological society. These include Charles Reich's man of "consciousness III," Norman Brown's genital or hipster man, and Gerald Heard's "post-individual" man, grown conscious of the vast resources of "nonself-consciousness."

Still, I assume that all these visions represent real possibilities.

Significant changes have unquestionably been going on in people, especially among young people experimenting in new life styles, and we may expect further changes as they try to cope with the changing conditions of man's life. New possibilities as yet largely confined to the West are in time pretty sure to have some influence on the rest of the world as it continues its efforts to modernize. We may expect a growing convergence too because the "new" modes of consciousness proclaimed in the West include modes that are old in the East. In general, the main trend appears to be toward something like Lewis Mumford's "One World man" of the future: not, I think, a radically transformed man, still less a single type with a uniform faith, but one who will be more open to some kind of universal faith than most men now are because his thought and feeling will be more attuned to the realities of life in One World.

2. THE PROSPECTS OF THE ESTABLISHED RELIGIONS

In any case, we must first consider at some length the prospects of the world's established religions, since they still command the allegiance of most of mankind. Even so the first thing to be said about them is that none has any apparent chance whatever of winning the whole world. This goes as well for Christianity, the only religion that has launched a great missionary effort. While some of its spokesmen proclaimed the hope that our century would be the "Christian century," its many different churches have in our time at most made some progress toward achieving a measure of unity among themselves. Otherwise Christianity has provided the leading example of the decline of traditional religion. It has lost a great many adherents in the Soviet Union and its satellites in East Europe, but many too in western Europe and America. Although most Americans are still pleased to call themselves Christians, and we continue to inscribe "In God we trust" on our coins and dollar bills (as foreigners have remarked, our most cherished national document), popular religion here too often appears as a vague, comfortable belief in believing because it makes you feel better, with little deep conviction or commitment—except among Fundamentalists, and these hold out the least promise of a universal faith.

Now that science has taken over much of the work that God used to do for men, I suppose there might be a purer religion, with more effort to know and commune with God instead of begging him for special favors. But most simple worshippers the world over, who are ignorant of science, still want chiefly special favors from their gods. In America too, popular religion maintains the traditional Christian belief in the magical efficacy of prayer, and otherwise serves as an assurance that God is always on our side, God blesses or serves America, without demanding first and last that Americans serve him. It inspires little reverence and less humility. Ideally religion is a way of life, as it was in early Christianity, and later in early Puritanism; but popular Christianity in America is scarcely a way of life. In effect it supports the national conviction that one *can* worship both God and mammon.[1] And at that I doubt that popular religion in America creates a strong sense of religious *community,* such as enabled Judaism to survive, through centuries of persecution, without any promise of personal immortality or special favors for the individual worshipper.

In particular it fails to stress the crying need for inner restraints, or for self-control and self-mastery, which has been

1. Among the plainest give-aways of its vulgarity was President Nixon's Thanksgiving Message of 1972. In exalting the American tradition of giving thanks to the Father, he remarked that the blessings of our history demonstrated the "practicality" of this custom, and he added that if we continued to worship the Father we could expect still more blessings. In other words, religion pays.

I might add that on my campus some years ago an inquiring reporter asked a number of students what Thanksgiving meant to them. With one exception, none gave the historic answer; to most it meant only a holiday from school or an opportunity to eat a big turkey dinner. The exception was a student from India.

taught by all the world's major religions, or for that matter its major philosophies too. Rather it tends to support the living religion of America, the blend of self-righteousness nationalism and materialism celebrated as the American Way of Life. This has a spiritual aspect noted by Santayana in his description of Americans as idealists working on matter—working to realize dreams of plenty, a better life for common people. But in practice it comes out as a devotion to a high material standard of living, with pretty low conceptions of the good life, and too little concern about all the poverty persisting in a land of plenty; and on the record of a troubled or sick society it has failed to satisfy the spiritual needs that I think are still real needs of materialistic Americans too.

Popular religion in America might also support the cynical principle of the priest in Kafka's novel *The Trial:* "It is not necessary to accept everything as true," he said, "one must only accept it as necessary." As it is, the beliefs that orthodox Christianity has declared necessary are the plainest reason for its failure to convert the world. It has also confused the whole religious issue by its provincial assumption that such beliefs as a personal God and a personal immortality are a clear need of the religious spirit itself. (Hindus have remarked that the idea of personal immortality—John Smith living forever as John Smith in a heaven full of Smiths—is as illogical as conceited.)

Yet by the same token skeptics are as provincial when they say that "God is dead," implying that religion itself is dying or dead. Conceivably it might die out in the distant future, just as the idea of the "sacred" as a real power may be doomed in a world desacralized by science and technology; but the possible disappearance of the age-old beliefs in supernatural beings or powers seems to me too remote either to rejoice or to brood over right now. As an unbeliever myself, I would add that too many thoughtful, enlightened people cling to some sort of traditional religion for it to be dismissed as a mere superstition or relic of a primitive past—the view of Freud. Among other things it has offered a unified view of the world that thoughtful people naturally seek, and that "science" does not offer, since in practice science means a large, not too happy family of diverse sciences that lack a unified view alike of the universe, man, and society. And at least we should now know that psychiatry is no adequate substitute for religion.

So I would now stress chiefly the changes that have come over Christianity in our century, especially in the last generation, making it distinctly more liberal and open to the possibilities of a truly universal faith. These changes have been most striking—and startling—in the Roman Catholic Church, beginning with Vatican II under the saintly Pope John, and surviving the reactionary regime of Pope Paul, who has been constantly on the defensive against open opposition from both churchmen and laymen, on a scale almost unprecedented since the Protestant Reformation. Father Daniel Berrigan has gone so far as to say that "the church as we know it is doomed." As for Protestantism, it can communicate more readily with other world religions because of its historic principle of refusing to accept the absolute claims of any human authority. Its theologians, notably Paul Tillich, have been most responsive to the challenges of the spiritual crisis today. And even on the lower spiritual levels one may note some growth in tolerance. I am not heartened by the knowledge that Billy Graham, with his crude, primitive version of Christianity, is the most popular preacher in America today, and the spiritual mentor of Richard Nixon; but at least he is no fanatic, and is less bigoted than the revivalists of yore. In general, I take it that for thoughtful people there is no possibility of going back to the old-time religion, but there is a real possibility that most Christian churches will at last take to heart the ceremonial Christian message of peace on earth to all men of good will.

Since the Eastern religions have always been more tolerant, and neither Christianity nor Islam is addicted any longer to crusades or holy wars, it is reasonable to anticipate that there will be less stress on religious differences in the future, more on the common elements in the world's religions. These include an aspiration to get men into some kind of harmonious relation to the cosmic order. If their conceptions of this order make plainer the basic differences between them, in a long view of their history they are alike as a quest for more adequate conceptions of it, which Werner Heisenberg, speaking as a physicist, says may now be reconciled with the conceptions of modern science. The common elements also include ethical principles of brotherhood, love, and justice that facilitate communication among them, or what it is now fashionable to call "dialogue." Positive efforts at cooperation were exemplified by the First Spiritual Summit Conference, held in Calcutta in 1968, in which spokesmen of religions representing some two and a half billion people expounded the relevance of their faith in the modern world. What came out of the conference, reported the late Thomas Merton, was not merely communication but "communion"—a brotherhood in learning more about the spiritual values of other faiths. The proposals on which the conference unanimously agreed included the need of active effort by all the religions to speak together to all mankind, and of the formation of a "strong international, inter-religious world body."

Such a body would not be a World Church—an outcome that to me is still unthinkable. Although some prophets foresee such a possibility, I think that the most—or even the best—that religious leaders can hope for is the coexistence of religions that would retain their traditional myths, rituals, symbols, and pieties, but with a full respect for those of other faiths, ideally in an awareness that they are all only symbolic, not literal representations of truth. As Paul Tillich wrote, the way to universal spiritual truth "is not to relinquish one's religious tradition for the sake of a universal concept which could be only a concept," but "to penetrate into the depths of one's own religion, in devotion, thought and action," for in its depths its particularity ceases to be important. So Christians could continue to revere Jesus Christ —but ideally with a difference. So long as they insist that he was literally the Son of God come to earth, and that faith in him is essential to salvation, the rest of the world will not worship him. But insofar as they learn to regard him as only a sublime teacher, or in Tillich's terms as a "perfect symbol" of man's religious aspirations, he can be revered by men of other faiths, as he has been in the East.

At this point I feel obliged to pause because of some obvious, disagreeable questions. Since Christianity has typically insisted on the absolute truth of its historical myths and its dogmas, and based its claims on the resurrection of Christ, how many Christians can regard it as at most true only in some symbolical sense? How many people have ever heard of the First Spiritual Summit Conference, much less read the papers delivered at it?[2] Can ordinary people everywhere—the 2½ billion supposedly represented by the speakers at the conference—really think, feel, and behave as their high-minded spiritual leaders appeared to assume? To what extent are their traditional faiths actually relevant to the modern world? In most religious India, for example—the land of sacred cows? I am not disposed to give optimistic answers to such questions. Defenders of the established religions may argue that they must be conservative, as they have always tended to be, in order to offer simple worshippers the spiritual security and certainty they yearn for. Sophisticates may add that the lofty talk about the need and the value of religious "dialogue" too often comes down to what Thomas Merton called *"interminable empty chatter"*—"the inexhaustible chatter with which modern man tries to convince himself that he is in touch with his fellow men and with reality."

2. They appear in a book called *The World Religions Speak*—published in Holland, not America, in 1970.

Well, all of us who are not monks have to go on talking anyway (not to mention that I was paid for chattering in a public lecture on which this chapter is based). We have a good excuse in the significant changes in the attitudes of many religious leaders, who because of mass communication, especially radio and television, may hope to have a wider, more direct influence than ever before. It may be said that the world's higher religions, which alike claimed universality, are at last approaching maturity, seeking to transcend their cultural provinciality and become truly universal or catholic (more so than a *Roman* Catholic Church). To me the changes look like a clear spiritual progress, as did originally the appearance of religions that I think deserved to be called "higher"—a point overlooked by some Christian thinkers who have scorned the whole idea of progress on earth, or by Pope Pius IX in the last century when he included the faith in progress among the many "heresies" he damned in his famous or infamous *Syllabus of Errors*.

Science itself has opened up other religious possibilities. It has been said that if God created man in his own image, man proceeded to return the favor. (And Samuel Butler was not simply irreverent when he remarked that an honest God was the noblest work of man.) Because of modern science, at any rate, man now has to create God in a new image, as the author, or the soul, of an evolving, unfinished world in which there *are* new things under the sun. It is therefore a more uncertain world too, and its uncertainties have been magnified by modern technology, together with the risks they entail. From the outset Christian theology kept changing, of course, no less because theologians typically insisted on the absolute truth of their interpretations of Scripture, but it has now become clearer that theology is necessarily an unfinished business, the last word about God can never be said. That many, if not most contemporary theologians freely admit this seems to me another clear sign of religious progress. For the uncertainties also mean new possibilities, in religion as well as all other major interests. For one thing, Christianity might bring God back into the natural world it devaluated, even though it was his creation, and so it might help to restore more respect for the good earth that Americans in particular need.

There remains, however, a fundamental difference of opinion about the proper role of religion. Many of its spokesmen fear that the demand for "relevance" in the modern world may obscure the deeper relevance of traditional religion in its transcendence of temporal affairs, its concern with the ultimate, the eternal, the unworldly or other-worldly. Many others, like Paul Tillich, fear the traditional tendencies simply to oppose the spiritual or the sacred to the secular, and to keep aloof from the "profane" secular world, which is now a world in crisis. These men tend to focus the issues of relevance on ethics, but this brings up another fundamental question. The principles of love, brotherhood, and justice common to the world's higher religions have in practice constituted primarily a personal ethic, a Golden Rule governing the relations of individuals in private life; so there is now a call for more emphasis on *social* ethics. The spokesmen of the various religions can all point to elements of such ethics in their traditional teachings, but not to a vigorous, sustained effort to apply them. The holy men of the East in particular have not until modern times led any efforts at social or political reform on behalf of its poverty-stricken masses. In India, which prides itself on its spirituality, Nehru found Hinduism a major obstacle to his efforts to improve the earthly lot of its hundreds of millions of wretchedly poor people.

In this respect Judaeo-Christianity has a clear advantage over other religions, rooted in the teachings of the great prophets of Israel. Despite the historical alliance of its major churches with the ruling classes, it has long inspired more indignation over the lot of the poor, and in our century it has preached more insistently a "social gospel." So far as I know, Mohammedanism, Hinduism, and Buddhism are not yet inflamed by a passion for the cause of social justice. In view of the imperious problems confronting mankind, I think that if religion is to become a more vital influence, its leaders will have to translate their principles of brotherhood into a social ethic and strive more actively to realize it, in political practice too. I also think that the trend will probably be toward this kind of secular relevance, as it certainly has been among Christian theologians, notably Dietrich Bonhoeffer's "holy worldliness."[3] In America the criticism that our materialistic society so plainly calls for might then make possible a measure of spiritual detachment, or a happy mean between the too worldly and the unworldly. Only I have some doubts about this apparent trend toward social relevance—in particular because of my concern with the youth, who will provide an answer of sorts in the future. Those in America who are showing more interest in religion, especially in Zen Buddhism and Hinduism, generally appear to be looking to it for a kind of personal psychotherapy, rather than a means to social regeneration. The religion of the future might serve chiefly its traditional function as a haven from worldly cares.

Meanwhile the extraordinary history we have been making raises another basic question about religious possibilities. Even Paul Tillich was provincial when he insisted that "only" the Eternal can suffice for man, who needs an assurance that human history on earth has an ultimate meaning. Not only do many people feel no such imperious need, but whole societies in the past, notably ancient Greece and Confucian China, managed to make a reputable history (as history goes) without believing that man's life on earth had an ultimate, transcendent meaning, while Hindus declared that history was as unimportant or ultimately

3. Kristin Stendhal of the Commission on the Year 2000—one of the very few theologians who have contributed to organized futurology—has observed that in contemporary theology there is a "striking uneasiness about the neat distinction between the 'spiritual' versus the 'material.'" Among the examples is Harvey Cox's best-seller *The Secular City.*

unreal as time itself. Christian tradition created the need that Tillich felt, as many other thoughtful people do; but since he himself did not pretend to know what the ultimate meaning of man's history was, I suppose the most that religion can offer the thoughtful today on this score is the hope that it *may* have some such meaning.

Writing in the heyday of existentialism, Tillich could also welcome even its insistence that man's life is ultimately meaningless, because he saw in it the "courage of despair," a meaningful, positive self-affirmation—a spirit that he believed was rooted in the being of God, and might lead men back to God; but here we come upon an apparent anomaly. My impression is that *Angst* is going out of fashion. Even the appalling destruction of the world wars, and now the possibility of universal catastrophe, the literal end of man's world, have not been leading many men back to God in Kierkegaard's "fear and trembling." Particularly in the West, men have a vivid sense of the wondrous potentialities of the human mind, and though only the naïve can be simply proud of all that science and technology have wrought, it appears that the most sober cannot feel abject either, or prostrate themselves like Job, just as Christian theologians are no longer harping on Original Sin as Reinhold Neibuhr once did, but are turning more toward a "theology of hope." Come catastrophe, or hell on earth, they might feel differently; but then religious faith would offer only an escape from history. Since Heaven too is no more for sophisticates, I assume that supernatural religion will at best provide a salvation of sorts for very mortal souls.

3. THE POSSIBILITIES OF A HUMANISTIC FAITH

My own particular concern as an unbeliever—one of a growing number, especially among the youth—is the prospects of a purely humanistic faith. In America this has been preached by people who call themselves Humanists, and a generation ago issued a

[129]

Humanist Manifesto, which announced that humanism was a "new philosophy." As a lower-case humanist, I would say that although it is new in its common rejection of any belief in God, it has deep roots in a long tradition going back to ancient Greece, and in Western civilization embracing such thinkers as Montaigne, no less because he was a professed Christian. I believe that humanism can—and should—find room for the varieties of religious experience as studied by William James in his classic work on the subject, including the self-transcendent mystical experience—so long as it does not lead (as it did with Pascal) to a dogmatic insistence on the absolute necessity of belief in God. I want to respect the possible values of this experience, or what Jung referred to as the "oceanic sense"—another actual and distinctive possibility of the human mind or spirit. I think that humanists can and should respect the undogmatic faith of James himself, based on a recognition that there is no conclusive evidence to support a belief in God, but coupled with an insistence that in the absence of such evidence faith is a vital option, inasmuch as people are forced to commit themselves one way or the other; though a contented agnostic myself, I freely grant that agnosticism is not merely a suspension of belief, but amounts to a positive commitment to doing without whatever good religious belief may afford. And as James wisely added, there is no scientific or any other method for steering safely between the dangers of believing too much or too little. He recognized that most people always tend to believe too much, too easily, but that there is a tendency for modern sophisticates to believe too little, out of an excessive fear of being taken in. Such skepticism may corrode as well a humanistic faith, or specifically a belief in the reality of the spiritual values of man, the source of human dignity.

At any rate, humanists—whether upper or lower case—must first reckon with the dogmatic ideologies that have sprung from a purely humanistic faith, the secular, messianic religions—above all Marxism—that led to the establishment of totalitarian states,

[130]

demanded something like a total commitment, and in return promised something like a total solution of worldly problems— as democracy cannot. In recent years liberal democrats have been pleased to talk of "the end of ideology" in this sense, but I think their complacence may be premature. Such ideology is still very much alive in Maoism, for instance, giving China a more vital, inspiring faith than the Western democracies appear to have, and that America most conspicuously lacks today.[4]

Yet there is no question that once influential ideologies have lost much of their appeal, and no longer look like "the wave of the future" that many people saw in them. Fascism was discredited by the bloody failure of Hitler, but it had nothing to offer the world anyway except a ramshackle political philosophy to support a gospel of nationalism and racism that could only antagonize most peoples. Today the many semi-fascist dictators who rule much of what our leaders have been pleased to call the "free world" are a pretty sorry lot, and none of them arouse anything like the popular fervor that Mussolini and Hitler once did. I should add, however, that the appearance of more Hitlers seems

4. Readers should be warned that the distinctively modern term *ideology*, which entered the lexicon in the last century, has grown so fashionable, I suppose because as another -ology it has an aura of sophistication or ultra-modernity, that its meaning has grown unclear. Often it appears to denote almost any system of ideas or body of doctrine, usually—though not always—one involving a program of action. Thus in a recent book on nutrition the eating habits of Americans were described as their "food ideology."

I raise the question because it is commonly said that America has no ideology. This may mean that in spite of its traditional fear of "radicals" in our midst the country has never been so attracted by Marxism as European countries have been. Or it may mean that the loose collection of vague, largely unreasoned beliefs labeled "Americanism" is intellectually unworthy of being called an ideology. So too conservatism in America, under the aegis of the Republican Party, has never been as philosophical as the conservatism of Edmund Burke, or of such Federalists as John Adams.

My concern here, at any rate, is only with the isms that have served as secular religions. To some extent "Americanism" has done so in the guise of the American Way of Life, but this has hardly demanded a total commitment, or any commitment to ideals demanding personal sacrifice. Nor is it clearly a positive faith.

to me quite possible, or even likely—not necessarily as ideologues (since his "national socialism" was an ideology only in the loosest sense), but as the common historical type of "the man on horseback." With the help of the mass media, and modern propaganda techniques, such types might readily exploit the tendencies to mass irrationality induced by a revolt against the compulsions of technical rationality, and by the many problems that are too technical for ordinary people to understand.

Communism, on the other hand, remains a force to reckon with because it does offer the world a universal faith, a promise for all peoples of an ideal classless society. But it has as obviously been discredited by the example of the Soviet Union, first the brutal tyranny of Stalin, then the crushing of popular opposition in Hungary and Czechoslovakia, and today still the repressive tendencies of its leaders; it has lost many followers or potential radicals in non-Communist countries as they belatedly realized that workers in the alleged dictatorship of the proletariat in fact enjoy less freedom and equality than American workers, who can at least openly dissent from their government and go on strike. Moreover, the Soviet Union has obviously failed to produce the new man with a new consciousness that Marx anticipated, for it is not actually a classless society, of course, and with prosperity its people look more like bourgeois. There has been a marked decline in revolutionary fervor alike in the Soviets, East Europe, and the large Communist parties in Italy and France, all of which no longer call for the world revolution that Lenin banked on, and seem bent chiefly on holding their own.[5] In America Communism is of course a negligible influence, except as an excuse to ignore the Bill of Rights. It still scares our right-wingers—always panicky types—but it has not in fact infected the cam-

5. One may wonder in particular about the spiritual prospects of Russian youth, who have been weaned away from Christianity and are no longer inspired by either religion or the old-time ideology, but are not free to rebel either.

puses with "radical agitators," the bogies they need to thrive on.

As for China, where there is still plenty of revolutionary fervor and continued talk of world revolution, I suppose the secular religion of Maoism conceivably might become the ideology of the future; but I doubt it. It appears to be too much a national religion, not for export, and certainly it has so far made little progress in converting the rest of the world, even Indochina. So too with Castroism, which appeals to many Latin Americans because of their fear of Yankee imperialism, but as an ideology is hardly impressive enough to have world appeal. (Castro himself remains a kind of Robin Hood hero, whose appeal is more romantic than Marxist.) In view of our experience with totalitarian ideologies, I doubt, too, that any new brand will sweep the world. It has become clear that in a technological civilization the state is not going to "wither away," as Marx and Lenin fondly believed. In all the advanced industrial societies fervent ideologies have been discouraged by the steady growth of bureaucracy, today more specifically of technocracy. Bureaucrats and technicians can serve any kind of political system, as they are now doing; and though they may serve conscientiously, loyally, by their nature they are not given to either political or religious passion. Their primary faith is in organization and technique, or "system" for whatever purpose, and while they are presumably working in the public interest, they typically identify this with their professional interest, which in common practice comes first. Under capitalism, which is fervently defended by American conservatives, the huge bureaucracies known as corporations are the least likely to satisfy spiritual needs or provide a vital suprapersonal cause. One has only to ask: Who would fight and die for General Motors or I.T. & T?

Otherwise there remains the appeal of democratic socialism, especially in western Europe. This has inspired some promising "dialogue" between Marxists and Christians, the followers of the intellectually most impressive of the ideologies and of a religious faith that was once revolutionary and still could be, inasmuch as the teachings of Jesus are essentially incompatible with a capitalistic system based on a profit motive.[6]

An admirably fair-minded report on the current dialogue was offered by Giulio Girardi, an Italian priest, in "Toward a New Humanism" (*The Center Magazine*, March 1970). While he naturally recognizes the basic divergences between atheistic Marxism and Christianity, Father Girardi dwells on their growing convergence in their humanistic tendencies, their common concern with a social gospel, a social ethic, and secular values that historic Christianity neglected but the modern world rediscovered, the recent rediscovery by Marxists of the individual and his value and autonomy, and the growing criticism of the capitalist system by Christians. He observes that profitable dialogue has been made possible by self-criticism on both sides, but calls for still franker and more courageous self-criticism. He hopes for more collaboration in the establishment of democratic socialism, specifically in efforts to deal with the problem of how, in an age of increasing specialization, to assure the genuine participation of the masses in political and economic power.

The need of such participation has been emphasized still more by Roger Garaudy, a French socialist, writing in particular on behalf of the rebellious youth (who Father Girardi recognizes

6. Although most American conservatives still regard the idea of a classless society, with equality for all, as dangerously un-American, especially when it involves a measure of economic equality, it is of course essentially both a Christian and a democratic ideal. Early in the century tendencies toward a reconciliation of Marxism and Christianity were strong enough to call out a violent condemnation by Lenin. In a letter to Maxim Gorky, in 1913, he wrote: "Every religious idea, every idea of god, even any flirtation with god, is unutterable vileness." The vileness was more dangerous, he added, because it was often welcomed by the "*democratic* bourgeois," and so was "contagion of the most abominable kind." As the founding father of the Soviet Union, Lenin of course avoided contagion by democratic principles too.

In fairness let us add that American conservatives devoted primarily to the interests of big business and the wealthy class have as successfully avoided infection by Christian principles.

[154]

view the dialogue between Christians and Marxists as "merely a verbal exercise.") He insists that socialism should never be regarded as solely an economic system, another way of satisfying the needs that capitalism created—a job that the leaders of the Soviet Union have boasted that they are better at. "Capitalist society," he notes, "is the first in history not to be based on a concept of civilization"; so he concludes that socialism "must be built on an entirely new concept of civilization." Among other things, it should develop more concern with aesthetic values, and with the non-logical kinds of knowledge that the youth are seeking, in their revolt against a civilization dominated by technical efficiency and emphasis on economic rather than human "development." In effect, Garaudy argues that ideally socialism should mean a whole new way of life.

In the common practice of socialist parties in the democracies, however, it means considerably less than that. It comes down to a political and economic program, which has not solved the problems of bureaucracy or assured the participation of the masses in their government. At best the parties show more concern for social justice, and may make some effort to approach the ideal goal proposed by Marx—the full and free development of every individual. If only because democratic socialism has surrendered the promise of utopia, together with the illusion that Marx as prophet spoke with "scientific" certainty, it is not a secular religion. While it may arouse fervor in elections, it is as yet hardly a basic living faith, any more than is allegiance to the Republican Party in America, even when this is blessed by Billy Graham.

4. THE FOCAL IDEA OF MANKIND

In any case, socialism clears the ground for a consideration of the claims of a purely humanistic faith to satisfy the spiritual needs of man. Granted that many educated people find life meaningful enough without religious assurances of ultimate, transcendental meanings, and believe they can manage to live well enough by the kind of values that man can realize on earth by his own unaided efforts, the question remains whether such a faith can have something like a religious quality. It clearly does for those who call themselves "religious humanists," as it did for Einstein, who wrote that he was a "deeply religious unbeliever"; but what about the rest of mankind? I think its prospects can be sized up best by concentrating on the concept of mankind, specifically the growing interest in it as a possible focus for a universal faith—with or without God. As Father Girardi observed, historic Christianity was centered on God, but it is now being centered on man.

Now, "mankind" is a very old idea, found in all the higher religions. It is found as well in such philosophies as Greek Stoicism with its ideal of "cosmopolis," or "one Great City of gods and men," that came down in the tradition bequeathed the West by the Roman Empire. Long obscured by the provinciality and the bigotry of orthodox Christianity, it began flourishing in secular terms in the eighteenth century Age of Enlightenment. It was then promoted by the growth of science too, and by the rise of the philosophy of history, in time the efforts to write universal history, which by now have produced many volumes. And today the idea has grown more meaningful because of the obvious interdependence of mankind. It is enshrined in the Charter of Human Rights of the United Nations; it is a theme of many international conferences; it has inspired such foundations as the Council for the Study of Mankind, Inc.; it has inspired as well calls for a Declaration of Interdependence, which ideally America might proclaim during its bicentennial ceremonies in 1976. In particular it is promoted by the growing awareness that our most imperious problems are universal problems, from social inequity and poverty amidst plenty to war and peace, the population explosion, and the environmental crisis. Professor Warren Wagar, editor of a volume *History and the Idea of Mankind*, has therefore concluded that this idea must now be a spiritual commitment—a commitment to it as an absolute good, an ultimate concern, or a "supreme value." In his words, the central question of our time is: "Who is for mankind—unconditionally? Who is not?"

As usual I think we must first face up to a disagreeable truth, that the very great majority of people are not yet for mankind—unconditionally. Apart from their own selfish interests, they put first the interests of their tribe, their country, sometimes their race. If our national policy of "America first" is especially obnoxious to the rest of mankind because we are already the richest and most powerful country on earth, it is in this respect basically no different from the policy of the Soviet Union, China, and the major European powers, or for that matter of Indians, Arabs, Africans, and all other peoples. The ineffectuality of the United Nations in times of crisis is only another sign that our "little" spaceship is still much too big to be a real community. And it is crowded with too many hundreds of millions of poor, uneducated people who are too much oppressed by their own crying needs to realize that their basic problems are universal problems, or to have a vivid sense of the interests of mankind. Much less can they understand the gospel of evolutionary humanism preached by Julian Huxley, and now supported by the biological revolution, which has stirred hopes of guiding or controlling human evolution.[7] And we must remember that the long evolution of man has also meant endless struggle, a vast deal of misery—suffering for which the supernatural religions provided some explanation with means of enduring it or transcending it, com-

7. I recall a Unitarian dinner meeting I was asked to preside over way back in the Eisenhower era. The occasion was a talk by Huxley on his gospel, after which I passed him questions handed up from the audience. When this had gone on for an hour or so, I thought it would be only decent to spare him a tough question that read to this effect: Your evolutionary humanism may satisfy well-educated people, but can it satisfy the needs of the great majority of ordinary people, or for that matter of President Eisenhower? But as I stood up to call the meeting to a close and express our thanks, Huxley leaned over and whispered that I had neglected to pass him one question, and I then gathered that he himself had

pensations for it, or hopes of an after life: compensations that may seem pathetic to us, but that in humanity we cannot simply scorn in view of the multitude of ignorant sufferers.

Yet we may also find some comfort in a long view of man's history, beginning with the enduring spiritual values that have come out of his endless travails. In what has been called the "Axial period," centered about the sixth century B.C., there appeared independently, in widely scattered lands, such spiritual leaders as Buddha, Confucius, Zoroaster, and the greatest prophets of Israel; and some historians have seen in the apparent coincidence a response to an underlying spiritual crisis in the state of civilization at that time. So there might be another such response to the much more apparent world crisis today, or specifically to the spiritual emptiness of the affluent industrial societies. If so, I should think it would most likely focus on the idea of mankind, since both science and the world's religions are making much more of this idea. Then the central question would be how to make it more than a concept, transform it into something like a vital religion, with a spiritual commitment to mankind as a sovereign value.

To begin with, this would obviously call for a great educational effort. My guess is that in order to become the core of anything like a popular religion, the concept would also require some of the trappings of traditional religion—symbols, myths, rituals, temples, with the services of art. It might be aided too by some Dionysian element of fantasy and festivity, such as young people are now responding to in joyous jazz and rock liturgies, with the blessing of Harvey Cox—a kind of worship that humanism has generally been too rational and Apollonian to foster, and that can

---

written this one. He proceeded to answer it fervently, saying that his gospel was just what people everywhere really wanted, just what Ike wanted. Well, this seems to me the pathetic fallacy of intellectuals. Evolutionary humanism can offer exciting and heartening vistas, but it is obviously too esoteric a gospel for most people, including most ordinary Americans, or for that matter the likes of Eisenhower.

[138]

be dangerous, supporting the too popular cult of the irrational among the young, but that I find appealing, in particular because it might foster more respect for the natural world that Christian tradition devaluated and Americans have so grievously abused. And first of all, perhaps, it would need a great prophet, a spiritual leader who would speak with charismatic authority as a modern Son of Man—speak necessarily to his own people in his own tongue, as Gandhi did, but in terms more meaningful to people of different faiths than were Gandhi's Hindu terms. Even so he would presumably have to be a great simplifier, as Jesus was, but I think we can better afford to risk some simplifications in spiritual than in political matters, at least provided that he would not offer himself as a literal Savior. The prospects of such a prophet's appearing may seem pretty dim in a land whose most popular preacher is Billy Graham; yet I think many people would respond to a really great spiritual leader. At least there is an apparent hunger in the land for an inspiring leader, devoted to high ideals—what many young people thought they saw in President Kennedy, and what made so many people all over the world sincerely mourn his death.

Or let us come still closer to earth and consider specifically the idea of the "sanctity" of human life, which would be essential to a vital spiritual commitment to the interests of mankind. It sounded ludicrous, if not obscene, when President Nixon announced his opposition to legalized abortion because of his "personal belief" in this sanctity, even to the rights of the unborn— this after he had personally authorized a more massive bombardment of Indochina, which had already taken the lives of countless thousands of peasants. He might remind us of all the callous inhumanity, to the point of atrocity, that has marked Christian history. Still, I do not think that his proclaimed belief was simple hypocrisy. He was at least paying lip service to a Christian teaching that I assume he thinks he really believes, that is in any case backed by a living humanitarian tradition, that inspired such modern gospels as Albert Schweitzer's "reverence for life," and that contributed to the widespread revulsion against our barbarous war in Vietnam. More significantly, the idea of the sanctity of human life is rooted in the natural sympathy or fellow-feeling in man that Confucius made the basis of his ethical teaching, and that in all the higher religions engendered the ideal of brotherhood. And as a simple, natural feeling it appears daily in emergencies, such as the efforts to rescue miners entrapped in a mine. Again our One World is still much too big and strange to be a brotherly community; Americans who are moved when they read in their papers of some local disaster may feel only a casual, fleeting concern over the news of disasters that killed a million Bengalis. But again there is at least far more widespread concern over remote disasters than there was before the growth of One World, and more effort to aid the victims.

At any rate, I have been speculating here about distant possibilities, which I would not venture to call probabilities. At best it would naturally take a long time to make over our civilization and its ruling values, still longer to make over the whole world; and I would not expect America to provide the spiritual leadership of the world. Yet I would not absolutely rule out this possibility either. Democracy originally offered itself as a universal faith, proclaiming the rights of man, or of common people everywhere; in World War II it was a fighting faith, as it still is with peoples oppressed by military dictators; and at home its idealism is still alive in many men of good will. When some years ago the American Congress officially put the nation "under God," it in effect suggested that the Christian God was really dead, for a truly Christian country would know that it couldn't be anywhere else; but anyway democracy remains an essentially humanistic faith (as it was when it first appeared in ancient Greece), which can be adopted by people under different gods, or under none. And there remain the other approaches, both religious and secular, to a universal faith. Because our century has been so busy rehearsing on a grand scale the age-old story of the inhumanity of man to man, we may forget that it has also engendered much more concern than ever before over the interests of humanity. More people today call "inhumanity" by that name, even though on the historic record it might also be called all too human.

Given this record, I do not think that we can—or should—make mankind an object of worship. But short of idolatry, we can nurture a decent respect for our common humanity and exalt the best of its common elements, such as a capacity for idealism, or for devotion to suprapersonal causes or spiritual values.

VIII

How Sick Are We?

First and last, I take it that America today is a really sick society, sick enough to menace hopes of a desirable future. Among the obvious symptoms are the extent of disorder, the commonness of violence and, in our big cities, of crime, because of which it is no longer safe to walk the streets at night, and people live in fear even in the daytime. (Our greatest city of New York is the most conspicuous example.) Another set of symptoms includes the prevalence of nervous breakdowns, mental illness, alcoholism, and drug addiction. More ominous to my mind is the revolt of the blacks, and especially of the youth. This has led among other things to a violence in language—in invective and obscenity—that called out the violent rhetoric of Spiro Agnew and other politicians; simple civility has grown rarer and more difficult. And the many drop-outs from our society—not merely the hippies—are only an extreme example of the widespread loss of faith in our democratic institutions, or in America as a whole, that has led to much concern over the "American crisis." This has involved a distrust of our political leaders, a disbelief in their moral authority or the legitimacy of their power, which has been aggravated by their common response to demonstrations and disorders—a monotonous, sanctimonious insistence on the necessity of respect for Law and Order, with much emphasis on the use of force to maintain an order that supports flagrant inequities, together with little concern for either civil liberties or social justice. The upshot of all this has been a loss of the self-confidence for which Americans were once famous. Recalling the pioneer refrain "We don't know where we're going, but we're on our way," we must now add that Americans still don't know where we're going, but many feel—as never before—that we have somehow lost our way.

As usual, however, our state grows complicated when one looks at it more closely and tries to ask searching questions. How did we get this way? Just how sick are we? Are we suffering from a fever or a mortal illness? Might it not be that much of the sickness is in its critics, the many querulous intellectuals? What are the indices of social illness? Or of social health? What societies today are clearly healthy? In view of the common disorders in all past societies, and the common fate of ultimate failure, most obviously in the "great" societies, such as ancient Athens, were any of them really healthy?

Although some social scientists have talked of the need of social indicators and measures, to supplement the grossly inadequate and deceptive GNP, the trouble remains that as yet there is no agreement on a set of such indicators, still less on measurements of social health, or means of taking the public pulse. We don't know enough about what is going on in the present to size up our society as a whole. I have implied that social injustice is a source of sickness, as it plainly appeared to be in the revolt of the blacks; but many social scientists say that they don't know what "justice" means, and in their positivistic moods they may imply that it is a meaningless term, at least for any "scientific" purposes. And though I have elsewhere suggested that most of us might agree on some rough social indicators, these raise further questions.

The extent of poverty, for instance. While it led to peasant revolts and uprisings of city workers in medieval Europe—signs of "alienation" overlooked by literary people who assume that this is a plight peculiar to modern man, or who still tend to romanticize past societies, especially the Middle Ages—poverty

[143]

was basically natural or "normal" through the long ages of scarcity, when there was never enough to go around; people took for granted that "the poor will always be with us." But poverty in an age of plenty can be considered both unnecessary and unjust. Most affluent America, ostensibly devoted to democratic principles of equality and social justice, cannot in my opinion be considered a truly healthy society so long as it has so many millions of poor people, many of them so poor that their children suffer from malnutrition. Yet is it therefore positively sick, seriously sick? Although its black ghettos are a plain source of *malaise,* what about all its poor whites in both rural and urban slums? Do they feel alienated from our society? Evidently not enough so to be rebellious; they appear to be more prone to feelings of hopelessness. Still, these may be regarded as signs of sickness in America, which has never been given to the kind of fatalistic resignation common in the peasants of the past. While America has always had millions of poor people even as it prospered, their ranks being steadily swollen by immigrants during the immense industrial growth of the country, these poor workers generally lived in a hopeful spirit, believing at least that in this land of opportunity, with free public schools, their children would have a better chance.

Other questions are raised by the white Americans today who are most obviously prone to resentments—the working people of the lower middle class. Although they are much better off than the majority of people in the rest of the world, most of them owning a television set and a car, they might thereby remind us that human needs are not merely the needs of subsistence. Once people can be sure of getting enough to eat, their needs are determined by social standards and expectations, and these Americans can rightly complain that they have not been getting their share in the national affluence; unlike the vaunted GNP, their income has far from quadrupled since the World War—they have been getting relatively worse off. Among other things they cannot readily afford to give their children the college education that has become more essential to financial success, hopes of better jobs than they themselves can hope for. They pride themselves on being hard-working people, but it appears that generally they do not live in a hopeful spirit either.

Even so "alienation" is not clearly the word for them, inasmuch as they also pride themselves on being good loyal Americans. Needless to say, they are not at all a revolutionary class. Rather, they share the traditional American fear of "radicals." They have been contributing to the national *malaise* by their racism taking out their resentments on the black people. And also on "welfare loafers," on college students, on peace demonstrators and "trouble-makers" generally—except irresponsible politicians or demagogues. They belong to the "middle America" that Spiro Agnew flatters, or the "center" that both Democrats and Republicans have been appealing to.

No doubt we must all hope that the center will hold, not fall apart, but what is it holding to? In *Things to Come*, dealing with our immediate prospects, Herman Kahn and B. Bruce-Briggs of the Hudson Institute stake their hopes on the "Responsible Center," contrasted with the "Humanist Left." The implication that humanists tend to be somehow irresponsible forces the pertinent question: How responsible is the actual center in America today? In general, it is too poorly informed to take what I would call an enlightened view of the national interest. In particular its conservatism has been strengthened by an indifference to the failures of America to live up to its avowed ideals of freedom, equality, and social justice—to my mind a basic source of its sickness. So even with the flagrant inequities of its tax system, the many favors granted the wealthy. George Wallace appealed to lower middle-class Americans by exploiting their resentment of these inequities as well as their racism; but then most of his supporters went on to support President Nixon, who had shown no interest at all in tax reform, much more concern for the interests of the wealthy contributors to his campaign. Altogether, if the center represents our best hope for the future, I cannot be optimistic.

It also reminds me of Abraham Lincoln's description of the American people as "destitute of faith but terrified of skepticism." Likewise the conventional patriotism of middle Americans, so often unreasoned that it might be called unprincipled, suggests how little real devotion America now inspires, especially among the youth, because of its lack of devotion to any lofty cause or ideal. In particular middle Americans also point to the deeper sources of sickness by their approval of the use of force against demonstrators and trouble-makers, their indifference to the common brutality of the police, and their own addiction to violence, exemplified most obviously by the hard hats. Whence all the violence in America? It comes out of a long tradition, to be sure, stemming from the beginning of our history, the ruthless extermination of Indians who got in our way (and who were thereupon called "savages"); but in recent times it has looked more neurotic. It brings up the ambiguities that complicate the state of America.

On the surface Americans appear complacent, sure of the rightness of their beliefs and their ways. At the same time, they are prone to feelings of frustration, insecurity, and anxiety that may naturally lead to rage and violence. In *Power and Innocence* Rollo May traces the violence in particular to widespread feelings of impotence and personal insignificance. "I cannot recall a time during the last four decades," he remarks, "when there was so *much* talk about the individual's capacities and potentialities and so *little* confidence on the part of the individual about his power to make a difference psychologically or politically." Too many people feel that they simply don't count. As a psychotherapist, Dr. May sees in this feeling of powerlessness a major source of mental illness and drug addiction. He cites Edgar A. Friedenberg: "All weakness tends to corrupt, and impotence corrupts absolutely." But he dwells especially on its relation to violence,

[146]

agreeing with Hannah Arendt that violence is the expression of impotence. "Deeds of violence in our society," he observes, "are performed largely by those trying to establish their self-esteem, to defend their self-image, and to demonstrate that they, too, are significant." While this is most obviously true of the revolt of the long oppressed black people, it seems to me plain enough in the attitudes and behavior of the lower middle class. I would add that the superficial complacence of ordinary Americans tends to make them more impotent, for they go on supporting leaders who do not really respect them or their potential dignity, but exploit their prejudices and their anxieties, in effect treat them like dopes or suckers.

In this view President Nixon's landslide victory in his campaign for re-election had various depressing implications. He appealed mainly to the worst in the American people—their materialism, their selfishness, their racism, their lack of compassion for the unfortunate, their fears—while making easy promises that required no sacrifice by them, such as had been required by "the spirit of '76" that he is supposedly trying to revive. His campaign was perhaps best summed up by a *New Yorker* cartoon in which one hard hat is telling another in a bar, "Nixon's no dope. If the public really wanted moral leadership, he'd give them moral leadership." In spite of their discontents, most Americans are plainly in no mood for any major reform, any real change in the irresponsible American Way. Our society may be sicker because most of them don't realize it is sick—any more than Americans did in the 'twenties, the "boom days" that ended in a crash and led to the Great Depression. Voters were evidently untroubled by the evidence of corruption in Nixon's administration, or even by the shocking Watergate affair, criminal behavior that set a new low in American politics. Apparently they shrugged it off as just politics, in the apathy, boredom, or cynical indifference suggested by the popular saying "I couldn't care less"—itself a symptom of spiritual illness. By the same token, however, one may doubt that

[147]

they really trust Richard Nixon. Certainly they don't love him as they once loved President Eisenhower; he is notoriously not a lovable man. In any case, the "new majority" that he boasts of lacks a clear or firm commitment to any lofty principle. As the Congressional elections indicated, it does not share even his own plainest commitment, to the interests of the Republican Party and big business. He succeeded more obviously in confirming the mistrust of a large minority who believe that he remains basically as unprincipled as the "old" Nixon, or "tricky Dick."

No doubt the President would really like to achieve his avowed desire to pull the country together, and not merely for his immediate political purposes; his most apparent motive now is to go down in history as a great President, or to create another "public image" for posterity. But despite his overwhelming victory in the polls, or apparently clear mandate, it remains most doubtful that he can really unite the country. Or rekindle a devotion to it. As I see it, this would require a rededication to its professed democratic ideals, and immediately an inspiring moral leadership that on his record Nixon is clearly incapable of—and the more clearly because of his fondness for parading his moral values, in his addiction to corny rhetoric.

Although the succession of "new" Nixons, or carefully tailored public images, makes it hard to be sure what the "real" Nixon is like, my guess is that he probably believes much of this habitual rhetoric in his addresses to "my fellow Americans," or that he is being "sincere" in his fashion, which is shallow and coarse.[1] Nevertheless his rhetoric rings hollow enough to recall the complaint of Walt Whitman in "Democratic Vistas" a century ago. The most ardent champion of American democracy, Whitman wrote that all the popular talk in his day about our freedom was

1. His ineffable banalities more obviously spring from his heart or his "true" self. Thus his expensive staff of publicity men carefully preserved for posterity his comment on the Great Wall of China: "I think that you would have to conclude that this is a great wall."

hollow; it only emphasized that "we live in an atmosphere of hypocrisy throughout." Such hollowness and hypocrisy seem to me more conspicuous today, though with one qualification—that it is not simple or sheer hypocrisy, any more than it was in Whitman's day.

Thus I assume that in spite of his political record Richard Nixon, like most Americans, believes that he is a good Christian, not to say a true patriot. In my judgment he is simply incapable of being honest with himself. His self-deception is more dangerous than conscious hypocrisy, for while he feels free to use unscrupulous or ruthless means, he can also feel self-righteous—as America has always tended to be, of late about its nasty war in Vietnam (which President Nixon once called "our finest hour"). Offhand, one might think that the national self-righteousness would bolster the self-confidence of Americans. But the self-deception it involves points to deep confusions that both obscure and aggravate the sickness of America, and to the lack of a clear commitment to our professed democratic ideals, which troubles many Americans and provoked the revolt of our young people in particular.

In Rollo May's terms, the self-deception is the kind of "innocence" he dwells on in *Power and Innocence*—a spurious kind, or "pseudoinnocence," that is not childlike but childish, that makes things seem not bright and clear but "simple and easy," and that serves as a defense against impotence by relieving Americans of feelings of responsibility for the common abuses of our power (just as Richard Nixon disclaims any responsibility for our war in Vietnam, even though he vigorously supported it from the outset —until 1968, when it was so obviously unpopular that as a politician he campaigned on a promise to end it, by a highly publicized but unspecified "secret plan"). May points to the cherished national myth of our innocence in our New World, and of our moral superiority over the corrupt inhabitants of the Old World, which has fortified our self-righteousness as a chosen people. This myth

[149]

has flourished on an ignorance of history and the absence of a tragic sense of life, but in particular on an ignorance of American history, with its long tradition of corruption in both government and business, to a much greater extent than in Great Britain or most of the European democracies, which could not afford so much irresponsibility. Such "pseudoinnocence" also bolsters the superficial complacence of Americans that helps to make them more impotent in fact, and more disposed to violence when somehow their virtue is not rewarded.

As Walt Whitman saw it, the root trouble in America was its devotion to business—"this all-devouring modern word"—in which the sole object was money-making by any means, however degraded. With the immense industrial growth since he wrote, the main business of America became more obviously business, in which profit-making was glorified as free private enterprise, regarded as the very heart of the American Way—as Richard Nixon still conceives it. In cruder terms, the country grew more devoted to the Bitch-Goddess Success. One result is that we are now the most highly commercialized society on earth, with ad-men to exploit—or corrupt—all sentiment and desire. Thus we have made commercial rackets of Christmas, Mother's Day, and all ritual occasions down to funerals (which may recall the immortal words of a president of the funeral directors' association, who proudly announced that funerals have become part of the American way of life). While Madison Avenue helps to keep Americans buying faithfully to the end of their days (in a costly casket), and therefore helps to keep our economy "healthy," it scarcely contributes to social health.

All this would imply, however, that America has been sick for a century. I think it was not in fact as healthy as it seemed because of its vigorous growth and its confidence in its future, for it was fashioning a way of life that begot contemporary America, which represents that future. But there remain the specific reasons why only in recent years have some thinkers begun to worry over our sickness, and over the "American crisis"—as Whitman did not, since he was still confident that American democracy would realize its ideal potentialities in the future.

One plain reason was that the country was grievously split by our war in Vietnam, the most unpopular and futile war in our history, and in the opinion of many, the most dishonorable. With most Americans the war grew unpopular simply because it was costly, and in spite of the fatuous boasts of our generals we obviously weren't winning it. Many other Americans, however, were outraged by our frightful tactics in devastating and "defoliating" Vietnam, dropping bombs and napalm on its villages, killing countless thousands of innocent peasants and making wretched refugees of the survivors. Our failure to win by such barbarity gave them some inkling of the impotence of violence too. They still felt outraged when President Nixon started "winding down" the war and reducing American casualties by killing more Asians, in particular by a merciless bombardment of all Indochina. They represented the conscience of America, its traditional idealism, and were more truly patriotic and public-spirited than the majority of unthinking patriots (who displayed their loyalty and their pseudoinnocence by putting stickers with patriotic slogans on the bumpers of their cars); so the country suffered more when their faith and their pride in it were shaken. And they might still feel ashamed of it when President Nixon finally began settling for what he called "peace with honor" and without defeat, and then induced the North Vietnamese to negotiate on his terms by a ferocious bombardment of their cities that outraged the civilized world. They knew that while we had not been technically defeated, as the French had been, we had lost the war in terms of our declared lofty objectives, as of our honor in any ideal sense (beyond saving face), and in the eyes of the rest of the world, including our democratic European allies. Unlike all the

[151]

"innocent," irresponsible patriots, they might remember too that "the spirit of '76" had inspired a declaration of decent respect for the opinions of mankind.

The costs of the war, moreover, were much greater than the many billions of dollars squandered on it, and the thousands of American lives lost in it (casualties that, after all, did not equal those in the annual slaughter on our highways by that monster with excessive power known as the American automobile). One most pertinent result was the loss of confidence in our government. The Johnson administration became notorious for its "credibility gap," a polite way of saying that the President was not being honest with the American people. The Pentagon Papers then made plainer not only the poor judgment but the duplicity of the leaders who got us so deeply involved in the war. The Nixon administration, which fought these disclosures as a threat to "national security," continued the policy of suppressing or misrepresenting the news, in order to deceive and manipulate the public, only doing it more systematically and sanctimoniously. Informed Americans knew that they could not trust the word from either the Pentagon or the White House. And the official communiqués have involved a corruption of language by euphemism that is more insidious than the violence of invective. As the devastation of South Vietnam was called "pacification," so the bombing of Laos and North Vietnam was disguised as "interdiction" or "protective reactions." One may be reminded of the saying of Confucius, that when words lose their meaning the people lose their liberties. For my present purposes I should say that when the leaders of a society systematically corrupt its language, and get away with such devaluation of it, that society is likely to suffer more than it does from the devaluation of its dollar. Because the corruption is a means of disguising the national addiction to violence, it may well provoke more violence.

The apparent insensitivity of most Americans to such abuses of language, even to such flagrant ones as the explanation by an

American officer that we had to destroy some town in South Vietnam in order to "save" it (which ought to go down in the annals of infamy), brings up a kind of moral coarseness or callousness that was abetted by the war. Although we have never been a gentle or especially sensitive people, Americans used to show more capacity for moral indignation. In this war most did not get at all indignant over our frightful tactics, apparently shrugging them off more easily because our victims were just "gooks." So many of them sprang to the defense of Lt. Calley when he was convicted of old-fashioned atrocities, feeling only that he was one of "our boys," that President Nixon thought it politically advisable to prevent his imprisonment. Today they are applauding Nixon's refusal to grant amnesty to draft evaders— men who recognized, as he did not, that the war was at best a terrible mistake, not a cause worth fighting and dying for. Like stupidity, coarseness is often equated with health in individuals —it is assumed that sensitive people are more prone to both physical and mental illness. But when moral coarseness runs through a whole society, I assume that that society is basically unhealthy—as ancient Rome was in its decline, keeping its people distracted by gladiatorial spectacles.[2] A coarse people is a poor bet to create a desirable future.

At home the costs of the war, fought to defend a "national

2. A blood-curdling example of the attitudes of "our brave boys" in Vietnam was an interview held by CBS with pilots of our B52 bombers, staged among their impressive batteries of computers. Flying in relative safety at high altitudes, beyond the range of ordinary anti-aircraft fire, the airmen have an easy time of it; their computers select the targets and release the bombs. They do not even see their targets, and know only that their bombs scatter over a wide range, perhaps up to a mile. They are therefore bound to kill some civilians, including women and children, but when asked how they felt about this, the airmen replied that they had no feelings about it—they were just doing a job. Like their President, most Americans would presumably add that this job was a patriotic duty. But at least some viewers of the program wrote in to express their horror at the callousness bred by our military. They spoke for the conscience of a society that is still pleased to call itself Christian, but thereby they raise the question of how live this conscience is, and how healthy this society.

interest" in Indochina that was not at all clear or clearly vital, included sharp inflation, the sacrifice of domestic welfare programs, the reduction of the alleged "war" on poverty to a pitiful skirmish, and the dashing of any hopes of adequate efforts to deal with such urgent and grave problems as the urban crisis; so our cities keep getting in still worse shape, more intolerable to live in. Another plain reason for the "American crisis" is the evident failures in political leadership. The ordinary American cannot answer the technical question (any more than I can) whether it is possible in our kind of economy to have full employment without inflation, but he can recognize that the government failed to solve either problem: he has had to keep paying more for food while a lot of people remained out of work—and this while he was told that the economy was flourishing again. So too with all our other problems, such as crime on our streets: somehow we appear unable to solve them. Our government too seems impotent.

And what about the future of America? Americans still tend to express optimism about it, but mechanically, absent-mindedly, "innocently," because this is how they are supposed to feel as good Americans. The traditional assumption that the future was necessarily bright—a national article of faith that most Americans once felt in their bones—only makes plainer the loss of real faith; they are much less confident and buoyant than they used to be. The change becomes plainer when one looks back a generation to Henry Luce of *Time* and *Life,* who during the World War assured his vast audience that this was to be the "American century." How many journalists and popular writers today are echoing this promise? To a receptive audience? Politicians may still talk this way in campaigns, of course, but even "middle Americans" are unlikely to feel a glow over the national destiny. They are more aware of their frustrations and resentments. As for serious thinkers, Herbert Croly could still write early in the century of "the promise of American life," but who today is celebrating it?

It is only superficially paradoxical that still another plain reason for the sickness of America is its affluence, or its "success" by popular standards. This aggravates the resentments of the millions who enjoy a relatively meager share of the affluence; TV commercials constantly remind them of all that they don't own, or need to have in order to be "happy." In so far as they are able to enjoy the American way of life, they are susceptible to its unhealthy tendencies. As the most spoiled people on earth, Americans suffer from their limited sense of the need of inner constraints, of discipline, self-control, and self-mastery—needed for the sake of self-realization and personal happiness as well as social responsibility, a live sense of duties. (To realize the living truth in this platitude, one has only to remember that spoiled children are not the happiest, but the most disposed to whine.) Among the simple but noble words rarely used by Americans today are "personal honor," "integrity," and "fidelity"—words referring to ideals that again are essential to full self-realization too. Spiro Agnew's attacks on "permissiveness" are legitimate to the extent that young people are given to hedonism, a demand for immediate gratification, as in their drug culture. He and Nixon are shallow, once more, because they fail to see that permissiveness or self-indulgence is at the heart of the American way of life, systematically promoted by free, private, enterprising admen. They exemplify the deep confusions and basic inconsistencies of the American way that both obscure and aggravate our sickness.

Thus the Protestant ethic preached by Nixon is still alive in middle America, where people resent all the "welfare loafers." What is dying is the Horatio Alger myth, the belief that poor boys who work hard are pretty sure to make good; although Nixon apparently still believes this, less favored Americans know bet-

[1 5 5]

ter.[3] Also moribund are the Puritan virtues of frugality and sobriety, once exalted by hard-working Americans. They may still talk absent-mindedly of "thrift," but their economy would collapse if they became really thrifty; as it is, the advertising industry manages to keep them buying on the installment plan, or to keep them forever in debt. Most Americans appear to be as smug as their President about their values, but I suppose that many may suffer from anomie or a kind of crisis of values. It is much harder for them to be consistently smug.

The upshot of all this, I conclude, is that the sickness of our society is basically a moral sickness, the "American crisis" a moral crisis. Behind all our political failures lie moral failings. My excuse for my many topical references to Richard Nixon, which may suggest an obsession, is that his fondness for playing up moral values in his habitual rhetoric accentuates not merely the obvious moral shortcomings of his administration but its lack of moral purpose, most conspicuously in its indifference to the cause of social justice. (Nixon betrayed his indifference to the traditional ideals of America, not to mention "the spirit of '76," by calling President Thieu—a corrupt little dictator—the George Washington of Vietnam.) The President could remain popular because most Americans are no more concerned about social justice, or the ideals to which the nation was once dedicated. Likewise our society as a whole has no moral purpose. Even Henry Kissinger, a professional amoral realist like his hero Metternich, remarked a few years ago that one reason for the revolt of our youth was a "spiritual void" in our state, and "an almost metaphysical boredom with a political environment that increas-

3. He himself made a fortune in only a few years as a corporation lawyer, but his success was not clearly due to either hard work or brilliance as a lawyer, of which I have heard no reports. A plainer reason was the political connections that got him his job and fat fees. In any case, poorer Americans know that boys with access to political power and privilege have a much better chance of making good, and that people with a lot of money can make a lot more without hard work.

ingly emphasizes bureaucratic challenges and is dedicated to no deeper purpose than material comfort." Since then the President he diligently serves has offered more bureaucratic challenges, but no moral or spiritual ones, only promises of a "new" prosperity, or still more material comfort.

I am therefore reminded of an eloquent address that Adlai Stevenson gave to Unitarians in 1959 on "Our Broken Mainspring." It is seldom quoted, I suppose because it is the most somber of his addresses, and in it he did not reaffirm his faith in the American people, as he did after his crushing defeats by General Eisenhower. He had been much impressed by the revolutionary fervor he had observed in a visit to the Soviet Union shortly before, the dynamic tempo and the scale of dedication to the cause of communism. By contrast Americans were displaying no such dedication to the noble ideals of freedom proclaimed by the founders of their country; their tempo was sluggish, their national purpose was dimmed by a devotion to "easy options." Our mainspring had clearly run down. But was it broken? he asked. Broken beyond repair? As for what had gone wrong with us, one trouble was the perversion of the idea of freedom, as merely a by-product of a particular kind of economy. Another was "the cluttering, clattering tyranny of internal aimlessness and fuss" in a "chaotic, selfish, indifferent, commercial society." In view of the "iron discipline" in the Communist world, Stevenson wondered whether "outer tyranny with a purpose" might not triumph over "the inner, purposeless tyranny of a confused and aimless way of life." He did not answer his question about a broken mainspring. He merely insisted that our system of free government was not easy to maintain but demanded dedication and selflessness, that it finally depended—as George Washington had declared—on the virtue of its citizens, and that the challenge to America was accordingly a moral challenge. "An examination of what you might call our collective conscience," he concluded, "is to my mind far more important than particular projects or programs." Or in the now popular terms of priorities, this moral and philosophical enterprise ought to be our top national priority.

Since he wrote, the decline of revolutionary fervor in the Soviet Union has lessened the external threat to America. The Soviet Union may now look like a sick society because of its "spiritual void," its sluggish bureaucracy, and in particular its kind of tyranny, as its leaders have been cracking down on writers bold enough to point out its political and moral shortcomings. By contrast America may now look healthier because it has to some extent been engaged in an examination of our collective conscience. Although unpopular, its tradition of self-questioning and self-criticism is still alive, surviving the complacence of the Nixon administration and the attacks of Spiro Agnew on "effete snobs." This self-criticism is dangerous, of course, and can be excessive in the intellectuals who specialize in it; to repeat, they may weaken too much the faith that Americans need to have in themselves and their democratic institutions, and I suppose they have helped to create the "American crisis." Nevertheless the self-criticism seems to me basically salutary, and finally essential to hopes of a healthier society. Even the weakening of the self-confidence that led Lyndon Johnson to launch his war on North Vietnam, Richard Nixon to prolong it by invading Cambodia and setting a historic record by his massive bombardment of all Indochina, might be good for us. Likewise our failure in Vietnam could be good for us if—despite Nixon's efforts—most Americans come to realize that it was a moral as well as military and diplomatic failure. Recalling Henry Luce's vision of our century as the "American century," I for one am pleased that this kind of bombast is no longer in fashion, in particular because he characteristically assumed that our mission to lead the world was blessed by God—a God who also blessed free private enterprise, or the advertisers in Luce's magazines.

Meanwhile Americans are at least less prone to the hysteria or mass neurosis of the McCarthy era. (Spiro Agnew grew popular as a more elegant kind of McCarthy, reviving the threats to civil liberties, but at the moment he appears to be trying to create a more dignified public image.) And the country can still draw on a reservoir of simple decency, good sense, and good will in ordinary Americans, or even a measure of idealism. Most Americans still approve of the simple democratic sentiment expressed in the common saying that every man ought to have a fair chance—historically a rare sentiment, in view of the ancient and widespread institution of slavery, then of serfdom, and the privileges of the upper class, at the expense of the poor, in the predominantly aristocratic societies of the past. It must therefore be emphasized that most Americans are too little concerned about all the blacks and poor people, and their children, who don't have a fair chance; but for the long run the vitality of the simple sentiment might count for more. In particular the student revolt, despite its excesses, stirred a healthy concern over the state of America, especially its moral failings, among a great many earnest, thoughtful students who were not given to excesses, or specifically to violent tactics. I have been heartened by how many such students I have had in recent years.

But I have misgivings about their prospects. Though it is hard to keep up with the youth these days, since they breed new generations so rapidly, I anticipate the emergence of another "silent generation"—not complacent, like that of the Eisenhower era, but quieted by a sense of impotence. Lately I have noticed a spreading feeling of hopelessness among the earnest, thoughtful youth: a feeling that the "system" was too much for them, and there was nothing they could do about it. The many who were aroused by George McGovern were only the more liable to disillusionment or despair. I feel sorrier for these students because "middle America" or the "center" would no doubt welcome another silent generation, as an end to young trouble-makers. On the surface America today is not so obviously sick as it was in the 'sixties, when the country was torn by bitter, often violent dissension; but now one may fear that there is not enough dissension and unrest, in a country that puts up with so much moral squalor and barbarism.

At the end I repeat that we are a sick society, but how sick seems to me an open question. In Adlai Stevenson's terms, I do not know whether our mainspring is broken beyond repair. In a historical perspective one may find reasons for doubting that it is. The country recovered from the plainer American crisis of the Civil War, and then again of the Great Depression. With the help of constant self-criticism, it has likewise survived its long tradition of corruption, of irresponsible politics in the interests of business, and of failure to live up to its democratic ideals. Still, this is not simply a comforting thought. It means that our sickness is not just a transient fever, but may be grave, even mortal, because it has causes deeply rooted in our tradition, the worst of which is more obviously alive than is "the spirit of '76." And there is less comfort in a longer, wider view of history, in which death has been the common fate of whole civilizations. Then we must look to our own civilization, immediately to its heartland in the West. I used to think that there would always be an England, but now it looks sick too. So do the more obviously corrupt societies of France and Italy. Which of the Western democracies are healthy? Perhaps Holland, Switzerland, and the Scandinavian countries; only there are signs of sickness in Sweden as well. Everywhere affluence has led to more self-indulgence, in a "spiritual void," and to higher rates of mental illness, alcoholism, and suicide. Modern civilization looks sick.

As for America, in my black moods I am tempted to think that it will end with neither a bang nor a whimper but a TV commercial, following the announcement of a big bang, or crash. In my philosophical moods, I recall the observation of some European that America, in the past always supremely self-confident and sure of victory, has at last entered history as it is known to all other peoples—history in which defeat and failure are common. Americans are naturally having trouble getting used to such history, which may therefore seem to them more like a "crisis." But for the long run this novel, sobering experience ought to be good for them—better than their typically naïve, immature optimism in the past, together with their cherished illusion of innocence. Now that many Americans have begun to realize that we are not able to police the whole world, or impose our will on it, they might realize in time that we are not morally fit to lead it either. They might at last appreciate the Christian virtues of humility and compassion, or charity. These might then lead to more faith and hope too, in a spoiled people at last grown mature.

Only this remains for me no more than a hope—not at all a prophecy. I venture it as at most a possibility, not a probability.

IX

The Basic Problems and the
Prospects of Liberalism Today,
with a Reconsideration
of the Hopes of John Dewey

DEWEY'S PROGRAM

Way back in 1935, the heyday of Franklin Roosevelt's New Deal, when John Dewey—an ardent liberal—was still the most influential American philosopher of the day, he posed a challenge to liberals in his *Liberalism and Social Action*. They too, he argued, "suffered from the state of confused uncertainty" that was the universal lot in a world of revolutionary change for which there was "no intellectual and moral preparation," and in which old institutions supported the "lag in mental and moral patterns" that intensified the confusion. Specifically, liberals had failed to come to grips with the problems and especially the possibilities raised by the advance of science and technology. In our day, when the fashion is to belittle Dewey and deplore his influence (especially on education), his liberalism may seem outmoded. In particular his faith in science and technology seems naive, another example of cultural lag. Yet I think his challenge is worth reconsidering, in the light of hopes of a desirable future. Certainly most liberals (and I write as one) are still in a state of "confused uncertainty," and are far from success in translating their traditional ideals into effective political action. It is easy to shoot holes in Dewey's program, but not at all easy to propose feasible alternatives. Having pointed out his limitations and his oversights, one may realize more clearly that the fundamental problems he dwelt on, in terms of "the crisis in democracy," are still with us.

To begin with, I assume that liberals in general would still accept his goal: "A social organization that will make possible effective liberty and opportunity for personal growth in mind and spirit in all individuals." They would also agree that liberalism is "committed to the use of freed intelligence as the method of directing change"—not the method of revolution. Traditionally they have been the staunchest champions of freedom of inquiry, criticism, and peaceful dissent. In practice, however, most do not yet agree with Dewey that liberalism must now become "radical," in the sense of perceiving the necessity of radical, thorough-going change, no longer being content with piecemeal, *ad hoc* reforms (such as Franklin Roosevelt offered). Dewey said flatly that any liberalism that was not radicalism in this sense of literally re-forming society was "irrelevant and doomed"; and some un-happy liberals, aware of the ultimate economic and political fail-ure of the New Deal, now suspect that he was right. Nevertheless he rejected as flatly the Communist brand of radicalism, with its insistence on the necessity of revolution, which at the time was popular with many intellectuals and made converts of some erst-while liberals. The widespread disillusionment with Russian Communism since then makes it unnecessary to review in detail his objections to doctrinaire Marxism. But there remains a diffi-cult problem for all who agree on the need of radical change, such as I myself have periodically stressed.

Dewey made it harder for us by stressing that conservatives who denounced the use of violence were themselves committed

[163]

to the use of coercion and force in resisting any such change. Moreover, he said, it was foolish to regard the state as the only coercive power. Such power was exercised more significantly by "concentrated and organized property interests," identified with capitalism, which conservatives identified with democracy in the name of free private enterprise. Dewey added that at times of crisis in America, with its tradition of violence, coercion always broke out into "open violence." So it would again in our day under the aegis of the champions of Law and Order, with the common brutality of the police, the suppression of even peaceful demonstrations, the murders at Kent State, and so forth—and to the approval of most Americans, as registered in public opinion polls.[1]

Dewey made it still harder for liberals when he refuted the Marxist argument that violence was necessary because the dominant economic class controlled all the agencies of power, from the courts, schools, and press to the police and the army. If so, he argued, it would only prove that the use of force against force so well entrenched was futile. Today it appears that most of the once militant students are disposed to agree with him, but also to despair of any alternative for changing the "system," or overcoming the powers that be by peaceful, democratic means. Dewey noted that Marx at times had admitted the possibility that revolution might not be necessary in England and America. Today one may wonder whether Marx would still entertain this

1. A recent example was the persecution of Fathers Philip and Daniel Berrigan and the rest of the "Harrisburg Seven," who were imprisoned and tried on fantastic charges of a "conspiracy." The actual conspiracy was that of the F.B.I., headed by J. Edgar Hoover, which trumped up the charges and hired a sleazy informer with a criminal record to provide evidence; and Hoover was supported by Attorney General John Mitchell, the right-hand man of President Nixon. Add that the trial of the Harrisburg Seven was typically as stupid as it was vicious, and it does not ease the problem of liberals. Perhaps nothing is harder to combat than stupidity entrenched in power. Witness the popularity of J. Edgar Hoover, who was practically invulnerable because of the common agreement with President Nixon that he was a "great American."

possibility, now that the interests of the dominant economic class are supported by a massive bureaucracy and an all-powerful Department of "Defense" such as he did not anticipate, nor Dewey either. In any case, this is what liberals now have to contend with.

Today many of the young people, who feel that the system of power elites is too much for them, are bent simply on living their own life in their own way—a common kind of individualism that Dewey deplored. So let us consider further the alternative he proposed for liberals (which in my experience is the word for most of our thoughtful, discontented youth today, who would approve the goal he set for America). They had erred, he maintained, by regarding freedom of thought and speech as a merely individual right. Precious as this right is, such freedom is more important as a mode of social action—as conservatives recognized by tolerating it only insofar as it did not menace the *status quo*. Similarly intelligence had been misconstrued as merely the native endowment of individuals, whereas it was most important as a social method. A vast amount of cooperative effort, above all since the scientific and industrial revolutions, had greatly increased the native capacities of people of ordinary intelligence, enabled them to achieve an unprecedented degree of "social and political intelligence." Hence Dewey attacked Marxists who obscured all this cooperative effort by their violent simplifications, making class struggle the key to history, reducing modern society to just two classes, and reducing the relations of these classes to simple hostility. Likewise their insistence on the necessity of revolution obscured the most profound revolution that had already occurred in the history of thought, the rise of modern science.

Hence, too, Dewey's own endless insistence on the necessity of sticking to "the method of intelligence." To him it was essentially scientific method in the sense of being cooperative, experimental, and flexible, in keeping with the liberal spirit. Liberals were properly committed to the use of "freed intelligence" because

[165]

science had freed it, made it a new method, and made possible a fuller realization of the very measure of civilization, "the degree in which the method of cooperative intelligence replaces the method of brute conflict." Class conflict of course remained very real, as Dewey recognized in the conservative opposition. His main point was that the potential goods of science and technology were far from being realized because they had been largely applied by capitalistic institutions, for the sake of private profit, in keeping with the age-old tradition that had always favored the interests of a few above the interests of the many. The central task of liberalism today was accordingly to establish a new social organization that would use the new resources for the greater good of the many too, ideally in the interests of "all individuals."

From this followed the need of radical change, in attitudes and beliefs as well as in institutions. Although the New Deal reforms of the day had moved away from the old *laissez faire* liberalism, they were still far from enough; the cause of liberalism would be lost unless it was "prepared to go further and socialize the forces of production." And the immediate need was organization—a key word for Dewey. "Ideas must be organized," as must individuals who held these ideas; "it is in organization for action that liberals are weak"; in their devotion to liberty and individuality they were still too likely to think that this excluded "organized social effort"; only "organized social reconstruction" could serve the well-being of individuals; and so on.

Well, there has been a vast deal of organization since he wrote, and it is no longer a magical word. Another name for it is "bureaucracy"—a term Dewey never used in these passages. In dwelling on the necessity of organization to assure individual liberty and opportunity for self-realization, he slighted its possible threats to these ideals, the good reasons why old-time liberals might distrust it. Dewey's stated ends were always democratic, liberal, and humane, to my mind unobjectionable. The means he made so much of were highly questionable, beginning with his "method of intelligence." I assume that all sensible men must use something of the kind, but for this reason we must take a hard look at it.

The method of intelligence is not a precise concept, of course, and it remained loose when Dewey called it "scientific." Neither is there any one such method; reactionaries, conservatives, liberals, and radicals may all appeal to intelligence, or what they call "reason." As for "scientific" methods, there are many of these too, and they can be put to whatever uses men have a mind to. They gave us H-bombs and Dr. Edward Teller, who wanted to make still bigger and better ones; I much preferred the contrary views of the late Robert Oppenheimer, for reasons that seemed to me intelligent, but that cannot be called strictly scientific. No more can the term be applied in any rigorous sense in judgment of the social and political experimentation that Dewey wanted. He intensely disliked, for what I considered good democratic reasons, the very bold experiment that the Soviet Union was conducting; but again no one can speak with scientific precision and certainty on the measure of its success or failure—or for that matter the success or failure of American democracy, which remains an experiment.

In particular one may wonder what Dewey would have thought about the multiplication of social and/or behavioral scientists since he wrote. As one who constantly called for more knowledge of social action and behavior, or for what he called the "human and moral sciences," to offset the notorious lag in wisdom and virtue behind the spectacular advance in physical science, he might welcome the host of such scientists in America today; but he might also be embarrassed by them. They have erected scientific method into proud methodologies, which have produced all manner of new techniques, incidentally including more "scientific" ways of manipulating people. These can serve the purposes of any kind of ruler or ruling class, and in America have served

[1 6 7]

commercial and other conservative interests more obviously than the interests of liberals. Few social or political scientists are supporting Dewey's demand for radical change if only because as scientists, once more, they say that they must be "objective," confine themselves to a study of the social "reality," and keep their science "value-free," which still means that in effect they support the *status quo.*

Dewey got on more dubious ground when he criticized dependence upon the method of public discussion in politics, "with only incidental scientific control." Here he fell into an apparent inconsistency, since he had previously celebrated the unprecedented degree of "social and political intelligence" that ordinary people had achieved through cooperative effort. As a good democrat, he naturally granted that the method of public discussion was far better than the arbitrary rule of the past, but he now complained that it meant in practice "reliance upon symbols," and that symbols were then commonly substituted for realities, debauched to influence political action; the inevitable result was propaganda. In other words, he pointed to the notorious abuses of language by politicians and the as notorious limitations of American voters, their grievous shortcomings in "social and political intelligence"—problems that have always plagued American democracy, and have often disheartened liberals. But what are the alternatives to reliance on public discussion? Aside from loose talk about "scientific control," Dewey stressed the need of "systematic origination of comprehensive plans," and "approximation to the use of scientific method of investigation and of the engineering mind in the invention and projection of far-reaching social plans." Since his day we have had plenty of assorted social engineers, systems analysts, and planners, and more social and political scientists in government, but they bring up the basic problem that he evaded: Who is to judge the planners? Who is to control the controllers? Today liberals are troubled in particular by a problem Dewey did not anticipate—the many key decisions, such as to wage war on North Vietnam, that have in fact been made without public discussion, only with the approval of specialists or "experts."

Dewey might have answered that our planners and policy-makers have not been "scientific," but this only brings us back to his much too simple faith in science and technology. While he deplored the abuses of them in the interests of private profit, the plain truth remained that their methods provided no sure way of preventing such abuses, or political abuses either. Neither could science and technology provide any assurance that the knowledge and power they gave man would be devoted to his own liberal, humane ends. In his day they were already serving the purposes of Hitler and Stalin, and since then the abuses of technology in particular have become more marked in America. Technology he defined as "all the intelligent techniques" by which human needs are satisfied, but in practice it includes many techniques that are obviously not intelligent for social purposes (as has been plain enough since the beginning of the Industrial Revolution), with no clear standard but efficiency for some immediate, narrow purpose. He did not anticipate either such problems as pollution.

Most important for liberals today are the questions raised by Dewey's solution, "socializing" the forces of production. He did not make clear at this point how much socialism he wanted, short of the "state socialism" he had attacked. Neither do most liberals today, who tend to be sympathetic to democratic socialism, but also to be wary of a natural tendency that for Dewey was obscured by his faith in organization. Although socializing the forces of production would not necessarily require the huge, oppressive bureaucratic apparatus that the Soviet Union has built up, I assume that in any industrial society it would surely require a large bureaucracy. Then we run into the natural tendencies of bureaucracies to subordinate the public interest to their own vested interests—a danger that is not less but more serious because bureaucrats are now commonly devotees of "intelligent techniques," or the "science" of public administration, and have something of an "engineering" mentality.

Still, liberals have to reckon with the reality of bureaucracy, alike under capitalism and socialism, and the apparent impossibility of doing away with it in an advanced industrial society. (The ideal of anarchism that appealed to Paul Goodman and some others is now more impractical than ever.) Short of Dewey's faith in organization, they of course cannot hope to do without organization for either their immediate or their long-range political purposes, nor can they afford to regard it as necessarily incompatible with individual liberty. They might be heartened by the example of Ralph Nader, who in something like the spirit of Dewey has been stimulating citizens to organize themselves into groups and combat the power too often exercised irresponsibly by corporations, and by federal agencies supporting the interests of business rather than the public interest. Another heartening example is John Gardner's effective organization, Common Cause. In any case, liberals must still face the challenge of Dewey. In maintaining that they must go on, not backward, in this way, he wrote: "Either we take this road or we admit that the problem of social organization in behalf of human liberty and the flowering of human capacities is insoluble." They may not take his way, or they may well have serious doubts, but I assume that few would say flatly that the problem is insoluble. Or if they do, they might as well throw up their hands, drop out of political life, and go their own way as private persons, like the hippies and other drop-outs.

2. THE POSSIBILITIES OF SOCIALISM

As it is, liberals in general continue to speak out, engage in public discussion, and remain more or less active in political life, on the implicit assumption that their cause is not hopeless. They might therefore consider more closely the possibilities of social-ism, Dewey's proposed solution of the problem. For some time after the World War, quite a few liberals welcomed what they called "welfare capitalism," inasmuch as most conservatives were coming around to an acceptance of the "welfare state," once a horrid word to them. Liberals also rejoiced in the growing afflu-ence of America, which they thought was filtering down through-out the society, being more and more widely distributed, and promising to eliminate poverty. Many were then brought to their senses by Michael Harrington's *The Other America*, with its revela-tion of the shocking extent of poverty in the "affluent society." By now statistics have made it clear that since the war the rich have been getting richer, with the aid of income tax laws that favored them, and that not only have the poor been getting poorer, but that many millions of Americans not officially clas-sified as poor were relatively worse off, faring so poorly that they became known as "the deprived Americans." As John Kenneth Galbraith recently observed, "Liberalism has been excessively tender toward the rich."

Since federal, state, and municipal government has come to do so much business, even more than government in "socialist" Sweden, I questioned some years ago whether the terms "capital-ism" and "socialism" were really useful any more. Now I would emphasize the important differences between them, and in par-ticular the serious limitations of capitalism in America today, the wide gap between its rhetoric and reality. The rhetoric features freedom, individualism, equality, justice, and the public welfare —in terms of affluence. The reality is extreme inequality, plain social injustice, excessive power for the few, limited effective freedom for the poor and the "deprived," and little concern for welfare programs. In social welfare legislation America still lags behind western Europe, as it has for a century. The dominant economic class, specifically the controllers of corporate property, exercise great political as well as economic power. They have grown somewhat more tolerant of efforts at social reform, but only so long as their power is not threatened. President Nixon has gone out of his way to grant them special favors, most obviously the oil and automobile industries, but also Lockheed Aircraft, which he rescued by a big government loan. (The "work ethic" that he opposes to the "welfare ethic" evidently does not apply to inefficient corporations.) If he does all this on principle, not merely out of political expedience, that is to say that he remains devoted to what has been called the horse-and-sparrow theory of economics: the way to feed the sparrows is to feed the horses. In any case, many of the sparrows—especially their children—have not been getting enough to eat, even though corporate profits have been soaring again. Other by-products of capitalism in America include common social irresponsibility when not downright corruption, the promotion of a banal way of life by advertising, the alienation of the youth, and public apathy, when not cynicism, the acceptance of dishonesty as normal. I should think that no conscientious, thorough-going liberal could celebrate any longer "welfare capitalism."

But there remain the difficulties posed by the alternative of socialism. First of all, its chances in America still seem to be pretty slim; conservatives have succeeded in making it a bad word, little if any short of "red." I see no real hope that Americans, including the "deprived" ones in the lower middle class, will support so radical a change in their economy and their government, or departure from the American way of life. For liberals there remains the question of how much "socializing" of the economy they want. I assume that most of them (like me) want more, at least to the extent of more and stricter regulation of big business in the public interest. But do they want complete socializing, government ownership and management of all the major industries? As a liberal, I for one remain uncertain. The record of the Labor Party in Britain has not been encouraging, even in its limited socializing. I suppose that the miniscule Socialist Party in America, with no experience in government, could not be counted on to do better. But possibly socialists in America might do better, with the support of liberals, because of the inspiration of the still unsullied idealism of their former leaders, such as the late Norman Thomas, and the growing sophistication of their younger ones today, such as Michael Harrington, who are much aware of the dangers of not only statism but bureaucracy and elitism, a new privileged ruling class that might simply impose its will on workers. They might also profit from the very indifference or hostility of the public, because of which there is no immediate prospect of their winning a national election. If America ever does turn to democratic socialism, it would almost surely be a gradual transition (as Dewey anticipated) during which socialists might hope to learn from both the failures and the successes of socialist governments in Europe, and also from the experimentation urged by Dewey, short of his faith that it would be "scientific." Enough for me if they remain flexible, undogmatic, and humanistic (like Harrington)—or essentially liberal in spirit.

At any rate, I for one would be willing to give them a chance. While remaining too doubtful of the desirability of complete socialism to commit myself to it whole-heartedly, I think that liberals can and should support such approaches to it as efforts to provide more and better public services, especially in health and education, and to assure all Americans the "material security" that Dewey recognized was essential to "effective liberty and opportunity for personal growth"—a security that many millions of people have not in fact enjoyed under "welfare capitalism," much less under the present administration, which is bent on economizing on all but the "defense" program. Michael Harrington observed that even President Nixon's boldest welfare proposal, a guaranteed minimum income, set this income so low that it amounted to institutionalizing poverty; and at that the

President subsequently failed to push this proposal in Congress, where conservative opposition was strong, nor did he play it up in his campaign for re-election.

But then liberals have to face up to practical difficulties. Under our present economic and political system, such "socialistic" measures would require increased taxation—whereas the public is complaining that taxes are already too high. This is one reason for agreeing with Dewey on the need of a radical change in the system, as well as in the values of Americans. Do liberals have comprehensive plans for such a change, other than socialism? I know of none myself; and again I should confess that I don't have one either. As for changing the attitudes and the values of Americans, or the American way of life, I still see no other way than education in the broadest sense, which Dewey recognized as the primary task of liberalism; but this would call for radical changes in our school system too, much more provision for radical criticism of our society, which the powers that be are in no mood to tolerate—nor the public either.

Altogether, I see little chance that liberals will agree on a comprehensive program for social reorganization, if only because as liberals they are a diverse lot who agree on the need of reform, but not on just what or how much reform; they are never so unified as conservatives defending the *status quo,* or the virtues of free private enterprise. I assume that most likely they will continue to work for piecemeal reforms. But at least I should question Dewey's assumption that they would therefore be "irrelevant and doomed." On their historic record they have achieved some lasting reforms, including some in Roosevelt's New Deal, like social security, that are now generally accepted by conservatives; and in time they have also recognized the inadequacy of these reforms, continued to work for further change and to attack the *status quo.* They can at least hope to contribute to a somewhat more desirable future, even if not one that will realize all the ideal potentialities of science and technology, or assure opportunities for the full and free personal growth of *all* individuals. Enough for me if they face up to the fundamental problems stressed by Dewey, and also concealed by his too simple faith in the method of scientific intelligence; though I should add that he too knew that there were no easy or sure-fire solutions, and that "the cause of the liberty of the human spirit, the cause of opportunity of human beings for full development of their powers"—the "precious goods" for which liberalism stood —were precarious, and demanded of their devotees ceaseless energy and courage. Liberals can least afford to believe in the sure-fire solutions promised by either conservatives or radicals.

In short, liberalism in America remains at most a fighting cause —not a radiant promise.

4. THE PROSPECTS OF LIBERALISM

Although liberals were naturally dismayed by the prospect of "four more years" of Richard Nixon, my main concern here is the long-range prospects of liberalism. As with other major issues involving human values, I would not venture anything like a confident prediction that liberals will be running America in the year 2000. I feel more confident that they will remain liable to fears of the futility of their efforts. For in spite of their occasional victories, and today many liberals in Congress, they have never won over the American people to a steady devotion to their basic principles, beginning with the principles stated in the Bill of Rights, to me the most remarkable and precious of our national documents. As I see it, moreover, liberals are by their nature more prone to doubts and admissions of uncertainty than are either conservatives or radicals.[2]

They will remain liable as well to their common failings, notably as "moderate" men given to compromise, since it is impossi-

2. I am unavoidably repeating something of what I have previously written about liberalism, a subject I have discussed in a number of books.

ble to draw a hard-and-fast line between reasonable and flabby compromise. They need to remember that the men who signed the Declaration of Independence were not moderates, but in their day radicals or strictly revolutionaries—a truism that Richard Nixon too forgets when he invokes "the spirit of '76." Historically, and still today primarily, a middle-class attitude, liberalism is more likely to lag behind the time because it may now look middle-aged. So it came to look in Adlai Stevenson—one of my favorite Americans of our time—who excited and inspired young people in 1952 when he ran for President against General Eisenhower, but lost his hold on them in his last years, and already, it appears, has been virtually forgotten, except by some aging liberals.

Still, liberals may also find some comfort in a historical perspective, and reasons for faith in their cause as a fighting cause —not one that is clearly destined to win the future, but that is not certainly doomed to defeat either, at least so long as democracy persists, and that will always be worth fighting for. John Dewey might also serve as a reminder that their worries in recent years over a "crisis" in liberalism are an old story: he was dwelling on this crisis in the heyday of liberalism. So was Herbert Croly a generation before him in *The Promise of American Life* (1909), when what lay ahead was the "New Freedom" of Woodrow Wilson. Although liberals can be as complacent as other people, they are naturally more disposed to go in for soul-searching in a changing world than are conservatives, who are more likely to be absolutely convinced of not only the rightness of their principles (unphilosophical though these may be in America) but the "soundness" of their policies. Many liberals were once given to what now looks like a shallow optimism, but all along they recognized, at least implicitly, the strength of the conservative opposition, and in particular of the perennial tendencies to abuse power and privilege. In recent years their experience in conservative America hardly permits any easy optimism, but has given them a sufficient awareness of the difficulties they face. Since the days of Franklin Roosevelt they have learned that they have much more to fear than fear itself.

First of all, some perspective on their tradition may give liberals clearer ideas of who they are and what they stand for. Adlai Stevenson observed that no liberal could precisely define liberalism without getting into an argument with other liberals, but even so he ventured a definition. It included their traditional faith in the possibility of a better future, because of which they naturally favored social and political reform, but also the basic beliefs "that *people* are all that is important, and that *all* people are equally important." American conservatives may agree with this in theory (Richard Nixon is fond of saying that as President he represents all Americans), but in practice they have long been devoted primarily to the interests of the ruling business class, and therefore consistently opposed all the major social and political reforms introduced in this century. That they now generally accept most of these reforms points to one positive achievement that might hearten liberals—to some extent they succeeded in educating conservatives, as well as the public. (Let us remember that not so long ago Medicare was violently denounced as "socialized medicine.") The basic beliefs stated by Stevenson appear in the social goal proposed by Dewey, which remains basically acceptable to liberals. They also explain why liberals gave up their early devotion to *laissez faire*. Like John Stuart Mill, who began as a champion of *laissez faire*, they recognized that many people were suffering from it—in particular workers, including women and children. Until this century American conservatives opposed legislation designed to protect women and children from the abuses of unregulated private enterprise, or the declared rights of manufacturers to run their business as they pleased. People were less important than the rights of profitmakers.

John Stuart Mill stated other basic tenets of the liberal creed in his classic *On Liberty*, which I think will remain as pertinent as ever in the year 2000. Most obvious is the principle of freedom of thought, speech, and the press, or specifically of inquiry, criticism, and peaceful dissent, which liberals have defended much more consistently than have either conservatives or radicals. Let us now add that this freedom, which Americans still enjoy in spite of government threats to it in recent years and the persistent fear of "un-American" activities, is another reason why we cannot confidently predict the state of the country in the year 2000; for there is no telling what political changes free inquiry and criticism may lead to. Mill also pointed to the reasons why liberals are naturally prone to uneasiness and doubts about their policies. In maintaining that society had no right to silence any opinion, even if it were held by only one man, he declared that no man, party, or society could ever rightly claim infallibility. In our time Harry Ashmore has spelled out the implications of Mill's argument. Citing the observation of Justice Holmes, "To have doubted one's own first principles is the mark of a civilized man," he added that it was specifically the mark of the liberal: "Thinking, in his view, requires a degree of detachment, of self-doubt, even of self-irony, all of which are conspicuous elements in the liberal style, and conspicuously absent in that of the radical. The liberal's habit of skepticism, and his concession that his own human limitations embody the possibility of error, apply even in the most weighty considerations of life and death." Needless to say, this has not been the style of all liberals, since they too can be dogmatic; but at least it comes more naturally to liberals, it has been common enough, and today it is more conspicuous by contrast with the style of Richard Nixon. Perhaps the best example in our time was the style of Adlai Stevenson.

Stevenson was especially admirable because with his humility, "self-doubt," and "self-irony" he maintained firm principles. Among them was a belief common to liberals, or at least implicit in their thought, that democracy is not just another system of government but is based on moral principles, such as equity, social justice, the recognition of human dignity, and the belief that *"all* people are equally important." From these principles, as well as from the belief in freedom, follow the common liberal virtues of tolerance and civility, admirably exemplified by Stevenson. Granted that liberals of course have no monopoly on these virtues, I repeat that traditionally they erected tolerance into a principle, clearly essential to the preservation of freedom of thought, speech, and press, and that they have defended it more firmly and consistently than have either conservatives or radicals, who have shown less respect for the rights of those with whom they disagree.

Conservatism remains a necessary principle in society and government, no less in an age of rapid change—at least when it is thoughtful or reasoned, not merely a mask for class interest or economic privilege, a means of protecting the interests only of *some* people. But liberalism too is an essential principle, above all in a democracy. There is always a need of effort to safeguard basic rights, to defend freedom, to attack social injustice, to curb the abuses of power and privilege, and really to *promote* the public welfare. I see no reason to believe that there will be less need in the year 2000, or that the *status quo* at that time will be so admirable that conservatism will be the proper order of the day, even if it becomes more philosophical than it now is, or bids fair to be.

To recognize a need, however, is of course no assurance that it will be met—any more than will be our plain need of more wisdom and virtue, which all past societies needed. But liberals may at least believe that thanks to their efforts, past and present, their kind will still be alive and kicking in the year 2000. For all their failings, they have been by no means so ineffectual as some of them are now inclined to lament. However inadequate their piecemeal reforms, I repeat that these include some lasting reforms, enough to encourage continued effort. If mere reform will no longer do, it might prepare the way for more radical change, since Americans have learned to accept considerable change, beginning with Roosevelt's New Deal. In particular, liberals may claim much of the credit for the freedom that Americans still enjoy, even if most people do not properly appreciate it, nor the prolonged, arduous effort that has been necessary to preserve it. Young Americans, who will have something to say about what their country will be like in the year 2000, are more disposed than most of their parents were to continue this effort, and now to extend it.

So I repeat my conclusion in my own appeal to the youth, "that for the long run—what the youth above all have to bank on, despite their natural anxiety and impatience—the liberal creed represents our best hope, even though it can offer no absolute truths, no guaranteed solutions, no promises of utopia; or rather just because it offers nothing of this—only a humane faith that we must hope is still reasonable." Today I would add that liberals can at least contribute, and can be expected to go on contributing, to the social criticism, in both formal education and public discussion, that has become more necessary than ever before, in view of all our "crises," and that is indispensable to hopes of a desirable future. At this point I venture to be dogmatic. The present state of America is not intolerable, but neither does it warrant any complacence about our prospects. I say flatly that the popularity of easy promises of a "new prosperity," with "a lasting peace for our generation," both to be achieved without any sacrifice of the American way of life, give more reason for alarm.

X

The Future of Communication

As usual, our futurologists are most confident when predicting the technological innovations to be expected in communication. In general, we can expect a continuation of the "revolution" that began with the development of electrical communication through the telegraph and the telephone, and was speeded up by the development of electronics, which gave us radio, television, and computers. Thus John R. Pierce, a scientist who works in the Bell Telephone Laboratories and joined the Commission on the Year 2000, anticipates the spread of cable television at home, which will offer small cities not only better signals but as many channels as are available in the big cities; the much increased use of communication satellites, which will make television more available to the developing countries all over the world; computers that will be able to read aloud intelligibly, answering all kinds of questions asked from a distance; picturephone service, or person-to-person television, and perhaps pocket telephones; and altogether the creation of "an entirely new environment in which life will again be different"—though in what way he cannot say.

My own concern here is a fundamental question he does not take up: Will people be able to communicate more effectively in this new environment? Will they be able to digest all the information they get from computers—considering that they are already swamped by information, much of it superficial when not irrelevant? Will they understand better all the messages they receive in both private and public life? For example from television, which Pierce calls "the greatest unifying force ever to work upon men"? Unifying them in what ways, or on the basis of what attitudes and beliefs? Such questions I cannot answer positively either, also as usual; but in speculating one can at least try to ask the fundamental questions, which as always are the right questions even though—or just because—they cannot be given conclusive answers. So I might remark that the invention of the telephone was an obvious boon, for not only the conduct of business but the maintenance of personal relations in private life; but then ask, what about the level of the conversations held over it? Might not the personal correspondence by mail that it made unnecessary be more thoughtful and civilized? Or how much of a boon is the possibility of exchanging banalities over thousands of miles instead of over the backyard fence? Given pocket telephones, might not banality become still more common?

Specifically, my main concern is a thesis stated in a chapter on language in my *Children of Frankenstein:*

> Modern technology, governed by the ideals of efficiency and rationality, rests upon the machine, which has acquired an admirable precision, and upon elaborate organization, which requires clarity in communication. With science, it has helped to make "definite" one of the key terms of our age. As characteristically our society is now training students in "communication skills," the fashionable new technical name for what used to be called speaking and writing. It has also organized the new science of linguistics, which has developed so rapidly that we know far more about the nature, structure, and operation of language than men ever did in the past, and so might hope to use it more efficiently. Yet language has suffered grievously in our society—and suffered most conspicuously in the qualities valued for our technological purposes. Never before has it been so limp, bloated, muddy, and imprecise as it now is in much common usage. By the rulers of society it has often been used most efficiently for irrational purposes. For commercial purposes it has been systematically corrupted and debased. For ostensibly scientific purposes it has been overlaid with technical

jargon that gives only the illusion of clarity and precision. And at best our many diverse specialists are finding it ever harder to communicate to the rest of us, or with one another. Briefly, the state of language reflects all the basic disorders in our world. Too often we don't speak the same language; or when we do, it is too likely to be an uncivilized language.

Now the question is, will the uses of language be more or less civil in the future? In the terms of Igor Stravinsky's unkind definition of linguists as men who know everything about language except how to use it, developments in technology will enable men to use it more extensively, but will they know any better how to use it? Or in the terms of the new media for "mass communication," especially television, will this do more to unify men in civilized ways, for rational, humane purposes? I assume that our distinctive problems of communication today will become even more important in the presumably still more complex society and interdependent world of the future.[1]

I begin with questions about communication in private life, or the maintenance of personal relations. (In the fashionable jargon of our day, these are generally called "interpersonal" relations, but I have yet to learn what meaning—if any—is added by the "inter"; in my simplicity I assume that such relations have to be between people.) Because a good command of language is obviously helpful for such purposes, I repeat an elementary observation that a shy, relatively inarticulate person may nevertheless communicate effectively by tone of voice, facial expression, smiles, and other signs of feeling, whereas a bright, fluent talker

1. I have discussed these problems in a paper I contributed to an international symposium on Communication and the Human Condition, on which I am also drawing here. In its terms, the disorders in language are one reason why the condition of modern man is commonly described as a "predicament." Because I concentrated on the uses of language—as I shall again do here—I noted at the outset that we should keep in mind the importance of nonverbal communication in the fine arts, including such matters as expressive or significant form, the kind of meaning expressed even in the "purest" art of music, and the whole realm of such symbolical meanings explored by Suzanne Langer in *Philosophy in a New Key*.

may bore or irritate others by talking too much or too compla-cently; and that in general fluency counts for less in maintaining satisfying human relations than do qualities of personality, dispo-sition, and character. But this raises the question whether people in the future will be more troubled or less troubled by the pecu-liar problems of modern man. First we need to consider these problems as we know them today.

Now, as a historian I think our difficulties are to some extent commonly exaggerated, and are not always as peculiar as they are made out to be. At the first International Symposium on Com-munication, Professor Winston Weathers read a paper on the concern of T.S.Eliot with what he called "the breakdown of com-munication," exemplified by Eliot's pathetic lines "That is not what I meant at all, That is not it at all." It seems to me that this and other examples he gave from Eliot of the difficulties and the failures of communication were of a kind that have always trou-bled thoughtful, sensitive people, and I have expressed doubts that they trouble ordinary people any more than they did in the past. I would now add, however, that possibly they do, in view especially of Rollo May's observation about how much people suffer from feelings of impotence and personal insignificance. I suppose they are likely to suffer more from such feelings in the even more massive and complex society of the future.

Yet I would still question the assumption that failures of com-munication in private life have become more common or more serious, and therefore would still stress first of all that we do not know and cannot know much about the talk of the common people in the past, because we seldom hear their voice until we approach the modern world. Mostly illiterate, they didn't write the books, of course, and they seldom entered serious literature except as minor or comic characters. In Europe they ceased to be ignored only to be stigmatized in the last century as "the masses," connoting "rabble" or "mob." This should remind us that however impotent they may feel, they have at least enjoyed more respect, as well as freedom and opportunity, since the rise of democracy. In America politicians may have a low opinion of the intelligence of ordinary Americans, which in practice they often insult, but since the Age of Jackson none have dared to attack openly the "common people" as did some early Federalists who opposed universal suffrage. No more do intellectuals who deplore their tastes advocate a return to an aristocratic social order, which one may suspect many really prefer—in particular those who romanticize the Middle Ages, the Old South, or other periods in the predominantly aristocratic past. (T.S.Eliot was one of the few who made no bones about his preference for aristocracy.) They talk freely of a mass society and a mass culture, but not of the masses in the traditional European sense.

Another popular theme that may call for some discount is the "alienation" of modern man—from nature, from his work, from his society, and from himself—an alienation that Erich Fromm has said is "almost total," and that would presumably hamper or warp communication. This implies a significant change from the human condition in the past; so I would again remark that we cannot be sure about how ordinary people in the past felt about their lot, which with most was poverty and toil. "Alienation" also implies norms of the "natural" life for man, of mental health, and of the "real" or "true" self that generally are not too clear, still less as "scientific" as psychologists and sociologists may assume. Even so it seems clear enough that many people in America today are alienated in some important respects. In the big industrial cities they are alienated from nature, as is also indicated by the brutal disrespect of Americans for the natural environment; and I suppose communication might suffer from insensitivity and the loss of a rich source of metaphor, or of feelings of kinship with life in the natural world; though let us remember that there are still nature-lovers among us, or at least people who like gardening. Many Americans are more clearly alienated from their mechanical work on assembly lines, which has not been humanized much by the belated concern of some business executives with "human relations"; these relations usually remain superficial when not artificial. As for alienation from their society, the widespread feelings of impotence suggest something of the kind, as does the common distrust of their government. But I still doubt that they are as alienated from their fellows as they are reputed to be by Fromm and others—their fellows, that is, in the sense of the people they associate and talk with in daily life. In this respect their condition in America still seems to me ambiguous, and likely to become more so in the future.

On the one hand, personal relations may suffer from the loss of a sense of community in the big cities, or "metropolitan areas," and also in the impersonal organizations or bureaucracies that many people work for. On the other hand, people have learned to communicate more readily with many different kinds of people—in school, store, factory, office, and the new neighborhoods they keep moving to—and in general they manage to carry on decent relations with them. The trouble remains that these relations are mostly superficial, less warm and satisfying than they can be in real communities. The question remains whether the mobility of Americans—the freedom to move to new homes and neighborhoods they like better—compensates for this loss. From my own experience, as one who has enjoyed living in four different cities or towns, and as a youth escaping the confines of Main Street, where community could be oppressive, I am disposed to think that it may compensate. Others may of course feel differently. In view of all the stereotypes about our standardized mass society, I would suggest chiefly that readers check up on them by consulting their own experience.

As ambiguous, I think, is another popular theme, the reputed loss of personal identity, which offhand would obviously tend to make communication difficult. Among other things, it would impede the development of personality and a personal *style*, which may be as important in private as in public life, not to mention literature; for in a real sense style—beyond mere fluency—is the man. This theme is coupled with complaints about the atomized city masses, the faceless crowds that the individual now confronts or gets lost in, and again the common feelings of personal insignificance. It has been said that when John and Bill talk, six persons are involved: Bill's idea of John, John's idea of John, and the "real" John, and ditto with Bill. There would seem to be still more chance of failures in communication if John and Bill don't have a clear idea of who they are. Or might it not be eased if neither has a set idea, which is likely to be a conceited one? Might they not profit or learn more from what they both say? (As E.M. Forster's lady remarked, "How can I tell what I think until I hear what I say?"—a remark that may apply to all of us at times; or at least we may all be affected by what we say—affected more than is the person we are talking with.) At any rate, most of the people I have dealings with in daily life—almost all of them friendly people whom I tend to like—do not appear to suffer from a loss of personal identity; they seem to know who they are and where they stand in society. My impression is that their common attitude might be summed up as follows: "I am a postman, and I don't always like the job, but it's a respectable one, and anyway I deliver my mail conscientiously and enjoy talking with the people I serve." And though I know little or nothing about what is going on in their minds, Daniel Bell implied that Americans in general have enough sense of personal identity to retain a measure of independence when he observed that sociologists can no longer predict so confidently the attitudes and behavior of people on the basis of their class, their occupation, their religion, their sex, and other such traditional indicators. If they are "role-players"—what some other sociologists reduce them to—it appears that they are still more than that, or at least to some extent choose their roles.

It is most obviously the youth who suffer from an "identity crisis," and this, once more, because of their historically rare opportunity to decide for themselves what kinds of persons to become (or roles to play). Add that they don't understand themselves well enough to understand other people—as most people don't, by psychiatric standards—and then ask: Did people understand themselves better in the past? On this score people do not clearly have more difficulty in communicating intelligently and intimately, or approaching the ideal of communion, than they used to. In the future they should have less difficulty because of the diffusion of psychiatric knowledge and sophistication, which at present is generally superficial.

Meanwhile the youth point to another change by the freedom with which they discuss sex and use the once tabooed four-letter words. This could at first be obnoxious because it was too self-conscious, often ostentatious and defiant (as in the Dirty Speech movement at Berkeley), and it still involves too much fashionable obscenity, which has deprived once earthy or lusty words of any real meaning. (Jerry Rubin offered a disgusting example in his chapter "Fuck God.") But I find that my students now use the words in class quite naturally and unself-consciously, especially in their free discussions of sexual relations. This new freedom of speech seems to be basically healthy, preferable to the conventional reticences of the past, which involved as much hypocrisy as refinement, and contributed to the common ignorance about sex. It may be only another passing fashion, and provoke a revulsion—an old story in the history of fashion; but I think the new fashion is likely to persist, and in the future to lead to a more genuine sophistication. My students are more mature than were the youth of my generation, and when they grow older I doubt that they could behave like Victorians, or teach their children the pretenses of innocence.

Meanwhile, however, the youth also bring up another really peculiar problem of communication today—the generation gap. Granted that there has often been some such gap, with some conflict between the generations, it is clearly wider today than

[188]

ever before. The youth have their own vocabulary, reflecting their own culture, which I find it hard to keep up with even though I have taken a basically sympathetic interest in their revolt. Much that "turns them on" is less novel and spontaneous than they think, but anyway it leaves most of their elders cold when not repelled. And though I assume that much in their counter-culture is highly perishable, and that the best of it will cease to repel all but the most conservative of their elders, I also assume that the generation gap will remain wide because of the pace of change. When our youth settle down (as perhaps even Jerry Rubin may in time), they will have to deal with new generations, who like as not will have different interests and values, be perhaps more receptive to change, or perhaps still more hostile to the reign of technology and its compulsions, but in any case will be given to attitudes likely to raise difficulties in communication. Already many of my students have reported some dismay over the attitudes of their adolescent brothers and sisters.

The youth point as well to a broader, more basic problem with which I have been much concerned both as a writer and a teacher —the lack of a common culture. This I should first repeat is not strictly a peculiar problem, since in the aristocratic societies of the past the upper class and the masses of poor, largely illiterate people were sharply separated, and except perhaps for religion did not share a common culture. (Even in religion St. Thomas Aquinas was obviously not for the peasant or the man on the street.) But there is more apparent need of such a culture since the rise of democracy, in which by now almost all people are nominally literate, and all are voters. In America personal relations too have been complicated by such characteristically native distinctions as highbrow and lowbrow, egghead and hardheaded businessman. If we try to speak the same language, we are soon likely to realize that we don't and can't. As for the future, there has been much talk in recent years of a "culture explosion" because Americans have been showing more interest in the arts and buying more "good" books in paperback editions; but I see no prospects of a really common culture in the society as a whole. Traditional or "high" culture remains widely separated from popular or mass culture, which seems much more likely to thrive. There also remain the obvious differences in levels of understanding and appreciation, because of which people reading the same book, or attending the same performance or exhibition, are not having the same experience, even when they all think it is pleasurable. Nevertheless I think teachers and writers could contribute more to the development of a more nearly common culture. Since intellectuals tend to be fastidious, even about the tastes of earnest "middlebrows," they need to be reminded that it is possible for reputable or even great writers to address a popular audience, as Dickens, Mark Twain, and Tolstoy demonstrated, not to mention Shakespeare and Cervantes before them. I have confessed to a possible bias in favor of the educated general reader, who is commonly a middlebrow, because he has got most of my books into paperback editions, and bought a lot of copies; but I would still insist that as a type he is a very important fellow, on whom we must depend if there is to be any hope of improving communication in our society, or raising the general level of its culture.

As a "general" reader he is important as well because of a further complication, that nominally well-educated people may also lack a common culture, and have difficulty in communicating with one another, because of their specialized interests. Here we encounter the gulf between the "two cultures," the sciences and the humanities, with their different vocabularies and ways of looking at man and the world; and despite all the publicity it has got, the gulf remains wide. But the problem is further complicated by the trouble specialists in either of the two cultures may have communicating with one another too, since both cultures embrace many different subjects with different vocabularies. College students majoring in some behavioral science may know as little about the philosophy of science, or the revolution in modern physics, as do majors in literature; and neither may have an adequate knowledge of history or the philosophy of history. Add the many professional schools, such as engineering, agriculture, business administration, and home economics, and one can speak as fairly of twenty-two cultures. The universities are making some effort to bridge some of the various gulfs, for example by what are technically known as "interdisciplinary" courses, but there remains a strong trend toward still narrower and more intensive specialization, alike in the sciences, the humanities, and professional subjects. Graduate students in particular don't speak the same language.[2] I assume that in the future the various gulfs are likely to be still wider and more numerous; though again teachers could do more to bridge them, as could scholarly writers by paying more heed to the general reader.

Meanwhile the problem of communication has been aggravated by the growing popularity of unnecessary technical jargon. It is most notorious in the social or behavioral sciences, whose practitioners perhaps most need the illusion that it is "scientific." So far from being precise, it is here often a ponderous, somewhat obscure statement of an elementary idea. A typical example I have cited is this: "Chimpanzee selection of larger sizes of food pieces in a direct choice situation is mediated by visual size perception." I assume this means what any child knows, that hungry animals naturally go for what look to them like the bigger chunks of food. Another example I cited because I can't make any sense out of it: "The strength of the valence on the percept of, say, a given food will be a function of the general need-push for food activated by the given controlling matrix plus

2. I am often depressed by the abstracts of Ph.D. dissertations that keep streaming over my desk from all over my university. Many of them I cannot understand, and most of those that I can are on more or less trivial subjects.

the degree of cathexis to the particular variety of food as determined by the shape of the generalization fork." Not knowing what this means, or caring enough to get it translated, I can only repeat that scientists are supposedly aspiring to clarity and precision.

Since much jargon has entered ordinary language and become habitual—especially in the official language of bureaucracy—I suppose that most people can now understand it well enough, or at least think they can, and that in the future it may become even more popular. Nevertheless it still seems to be a disease of language, one of the worst in the history of communication, and more infectious because it confirms the prevailing tendency to smother concrete realities under abstractions, and bury people under them, as workers are still dehumanized by being regarded merely as "labor." While it has spread all over the academic community, which is now fond of "areas," "levels," "processes," "reactions," "motivations," "orientations," etc., and among futurologists has made people useful chiefly as means of "input" and "feedback," it has become especially popular with educationists, or specialists in what they call "the educational process," who train our teachers.

So the jargon brings up the basic problems of education, the obvious means to improving communication (or what today may be called "communication behavior" or "the communication process"). Our schools notoriously do a poor job in teaching English, specifically teaching students to read, talk, and write well. They succeed most obviously in killing the natural pleasure that children take in self-expression; by the time our young people reach college, most of them find writing a painful business—though the pain is also due to the kind of theme subjects they are usually assigned. As for talk, our high schools and colleges offer courses in "speech," but these usually train them in speech for formal or ceremonial occasions, not in talk for the purposes of informal discussion, conversation, or the conduct of personal

[192]

relations. And I have complained that nowhere, in either school or college, do most students get a basic training in the nature of language, its various uses, including poetic, scientific, and mathematical, and in particular in the common abuses of language, by admen, publicity men, and politicians. Education for the future might well begin, and certainly should include, a good basic course of this kind; but whether it will remains an open question. The talk today is much more about the "technological revolution" in education, and in particular "information technology," the prospects of increasing use of computers for processing data, storing, retrieving, and transmitting information. While information of course has its uses, our plainer need is more or better understanding, or more intelligent use of information, with more discrimination about its relevance and significance—a task that may be made more difficult as we go on piling up mountains of data.

As for language again, my impression remains that talk in suburbia is less expressive than the homelier talk of simple people in the past, or certainly than the dialect of Negroes in their ghettos, condemned by most schoolteachers as "incorrect." Among the reasons for what strikes me (perhaps somewhat unfairly) as the common banality of popular speech are dulled sensibilities, the addiction to jargon, the influence of the mass media, with their addiction to cliché, the schooling that brands colloquial English—the spoken language—as an inferior kind of English not to be taught, the trends to uniformity, and all the mechanical routines in an industrial society that insulate people from the everlasting homely realities. By contrast I was much impressed by the expressiveness, sometimes the eloquence, of the talk of the poor Mexican family that Oscar Lewis recorded in *The Children of Sanchez.* This reminded me of a pithy statement of a simple African hunter that also helps to explain why popular speech in America is so often less expressive. The difference between the white man and the black man in Africa, he remarked,

[193]

is that the white man *has,* the black man *is.* Since Americans in the future are pretty sure to have still more, teachers of English might try to drive home this simple lesson. Quite a few are in effect trying to do something like this in their teaching of literature and writing.[3]

A more obviously important practical problem, however, is the common abuses of language, which have become systematic and high-powered. They involve the modern development of propaganda, in both business and government, designed not to inform people but to manipulate or exploit them. In government this is most conspicuous in the Communist world, but it is apparent enough in America too, in the spot political commercials in campaigns, the manipulation of public opinion, and the creation of "public images," as in the "selling of the President" by cynical merchandisers in Richard Nixon's campaign of 1968. In business, propaganda is better known as advertising, but also takes the form of "public relations." And business has promoted something of the kind for personal relations, in many manuals or advertised courses on how to develop a winning or forceful personality. The "classic" of this kind, I suppose, is still Dale Carnegie's *How to Win Friends and Influence People,* which has sold

3. In an Anglo-American Seminar on the Teaching of English held a few years ago (whose discussions I reported in a book *The Uses of English*) there was general agreement that one of its main objectives ought to be the personal development of students, helping them not only to express but to know themselves better, and to develop minds of their own. Although the participants in the seminar periodically worried over the question whether our society really wanted such independent young people, they were themselves teachers, engaged in some such effort, and they reported some encouraging developments. In my experience, there has been some improvement in the teaching of English in recent years, in part because English departments in universities have been showing more interest in conferring with highschool teachers and trying to assist them; so I think there is reason to hope for better teaching in the future—*if* our society is willing to spend more on its schools. Only that is a large *if.* As it is, English teachers in our city schools may have as many as 150 students a day—five classes of thirty students each—and can hardly give them much individual attention, which is needed in any effort to assist their personal development and self-expression.

millions of copies and now appears in school libraries too. All these manuals alike reduce communication to a set of techniques or tricks, which are no doubt useful to salesmen, and perhaps to people lacking self-confidence or hounded by a pathetic desire to be popular; but by the same token they tend to trivialize and debase human relations, in effect to depersonalize them by substituting formulas for a truly personal style. How much influence they have on people I do not know, though I suppose it may be considerable because their producers do a thriving business. In any case they are worth mentioning again as another example of the driving tendencies of a commercialized society to exploit decent sentiment as well as pathetic hopes and fears—tendencies that most Americans have grown so accustomed to that they accept them as normal, or "just human nature." Since there is little apparent popular resistance to all the commercial rackets, I assume that they will most likely continue to flourish in the future.

Hence I conclude that education for the future should stress much more the *ethics* of communication, especially in public life, but in all uses of language, in personal relations too. In business and politics the serious trouble is that irresponsible or dishonest uses of language have grown not only more systematic but respectable, as just ways of being "smart" or successful. So they may be too in private life, as means of influencing people, without the hard effort to do so by becoming more of a real person, instead of flaunting a synthetic "personality," and by developing more sensitivity, especially moral sensitivity. In view of the apparent insensitivity of Americans to plainly irresponsible or dishonest uses of language, I cannot be confident that communication in the future will be more ethical.

As obviously important is the related problem of mass communication, the culmination of the "communications revolution." As John Pierce remarks, mass communication is a one-way affair, from the few to the many, but he does not ask the pertinent question—Who are these few, and what are their purposes? The answer in America is of course that the mass media, in particular the newest, most popular medium of television, are owned by corporations and managed directly in the interests of private profit, not necessarily the public welfare.[4] Here I shall consider only television, presumably the most influential of the media. Although studies of its influence have only begun (for example some by the Communications Institute of the Hebrew University of Jerusalem), political leaders everywhere have agreed in considering it an effective instrument of propaganda. President Nixon has complained of the criticism of him by liberal newsmen, but he has made the most of the immense advantage that television has given him; he can command a vast audience whenever he wants to address the public, *make* the news, or show off on his travels, and he has also been able to spend millions of dollars on it in his election campaigns. Businessmen in America have likewise testified that it is the most effective instrument for their propaganda by flooding it with commercials. I think—or hope—that it may be less effective for the purposes of propaganda than is commonly assumed, since there is evidence that much viewing of television is casual, as are the opinions formed by it; but I do not doubt that it has considerable influence.

In my opinion, the networks are on the whole doing a fairly reputable job in reporting the news—except for the increasing number of commercials they have been introducing, not only before and after but throughout their programs. These trivialize the news and break up the programs into fragments, making it

4. Old-timers have mostly forgotten by now that when radio came in, Herbert Hoover—the great champion of free private enterprise or "rugged individualism"—nevertheless said that of course so powerful an instrument for public education and public good should not be turned over to private interests. But of course it was in a commercial society, with little opposition; and when television came in, there was no longer any question about so obviously profitable a business, which would enable private interests to sit comfortably on their fat dividends.

[196]

impossible for the best reporters and commentators to develop a subject thoroughly, and enable people to *understand* the news. Only old-timers can appreciate—as I hope many of them still do —the days when the best newsmen on radio, such as Edward R. Murrow and Elmer Davis, were given fifteen uninterrupted minutes to speak their piece without distraction. As it is today, television is the major source of news for most Americans, and they remain poorly informed. Studies indicate that they fail to make sense out of much of the news they hear about; and though this may be due to their apathy or their limited powers of understanding and retention, it is also due in part to the fragmented programs, which accentuate the unfortunate custom of the rapidfire news bulletin, a scatter of the *latest* news, with little or no background material.

The television networks perform more dubiously in their role as the chief purveyors of mass culture—a new kind in history, differing from the popular or folk culture of the past as a synthetic product, manufactured by professionals for an immense audience, which does not talk back or participate in it. Here I suppose that we still have to reckon with the thesis of Marshall McLuhan, his remorselessly repetitious insistence (in print) that "the medium is the message," not the content, and that the new all-embracing sensory medium of television—visual, auditory, tactile—is not only outmoding print culture but solving the basic problem of communication by tribalizing people again, unifying mankind, bringing the world together in a "global village" because everywhere it has the same cool but deep, benign effect on people, above all the young. While I take for granted that the medium makes a real difference, as new media have all through recorded history, (though I should confess that I get no "tactile" sensations from television that I am aware of), I remain more concerned about the obtrusive content, not only of all the propaganda, including the blatant messages of the incessant commercials, but of the staple entertainment provided by television in

America, in particular the vulgar or violent content of soap operas, thrillers, and Westerns, with their childish message that the good guys always beat the bad guys, and their more dangerous message that violence and lawlessness are quite all right when indulged in by good guys (such as President Nixon's favorite, John Wayne). Grant the standard defense of the networks that they are only giving the public what it wants, and it follows that the American people do not look like a mature, responsible, civilized people, much less the great people they like to think they are, in "this great country of ours."

At the moment, moreover, it is this vulgar kind of message that is supposedly unifying mankind. Elihu Katz of the Hebrew University of Jerusalem has pointed out the difficulties of poor countries that decide to go to the trouble and expense of introducing television. An African country, say, decides to do so in order to unite its tribal peoples, revive its native culture, and keep up with the world. To produce a program is costly, however, and it lacks the necessary trained technicians and experienced talent, whereas it can buy a popular American program for only a few hundred dollars; so it takes the easy way out. Likewise it cannot afford to build up an adequate, properly equipped news staff and send them around the world to televise what is going on; so it buys its news programs from London or New York. All this is substantially what happened even in prosperous, sophisticated Israel. The upshot is that people all over the world are staring at *Bonanza, I Love Lucy,* and *Mission Impossible.* To what effect, who knows? But I doubt that it is the uniform, benign effect described by McLuhan. A report of the Communications Institute in Jerusalem raises a question even about *Sesame Street,* much admired as an imaginative program for children, in particular the "culturally deprived." The report notes that it has recently been introduced in Israel, but that a lively debate is going on about the appropriateness of the program for its children, and children in other societies.

[198]

Katz and his colleagues in the Communications Institute distinguish between mass communication and "public communication," the latter dealing primarily with problems of relations between bureaucracies and their publics. Of these problems they are making some studies, involving various kinds of officials (including, for example, the police), which I should think would be potentially fruitful. Certainly the problems of this kind of public communication will remain important in the future, since bureaucracy is sure to persist and likely to grow or proliferate. I should also think that there is a real chance that relations between officials and the public will be improved, with the help of such studies, at least if the public is permitted to participate more in policy-making—though in America this remains another large *if*. As it is, a notorious excess of "classified" material denies the American people even "the right to know," a right specified in the Freedom of Information Act of 1967. While the Pentagon is the worst offender, the White House has been a serious one too. And though newsmen have protested against the unnecessary secrecy, the directors of the television networks—always inclined to be timid about "controversial" subjects—have not insisted on this right, especially since the Nixon administration began threatening and intimidating them.

About the future of mass communication I am more dubious. If cable television is indeed the wave of the future, as John Pierce believes, the chances are that it will only make available to more people the same kind of programs that Americans are now offered, with too many commercials. If communication satellites make television more available to the poor countries, the question remains what kind of programs they will relay, and these countries will still face the problem of preparing or introducing programs suited to the interests and the needs of their own people, especially their youth. And I remain concerned in particular with an ethical problem that has been accentuated by the improved communication between the world's religions—the

[199]

plain need in America of a better understanding of the rest of the world, and of more concern for the interests of mankind, which might lead to a more humane foreign policy and more generous aid to the poor countries.

"The world is too much with us," Wordsworth complained long ago; but I repeat that in this view it is not with us enough, for reasons suggested in his following line: "Getting and spending we lay waste our powers." Television could obviously contribute to a better understanding of other peoples, and of the conditions of life in One World—give a more vivid sense of these conditions, I assume, than could any other medium. The networks have indeed been trying to do something like this in some programs, and may do it incidentally in some of their reporting of foreign news. But chiefly they continue to distract or delude the public by endless entertainment, while their commercials incessantly exhort Americans to get and spend still more. Those who take seriously the insistence of scientists on the need of a national austerity program cannot expect any help from the big networks.

Nor do I see any reason to believe that they will change their basic policy in the future. The Public Broadcasting Service might offer some promise, but as I write, the Nixon administration is killing this hope, immediately by weeding out "controversial" programs, i.e., those that have involved some criticism of its policies. Defenders of public TV have expressed the fear that the administration is bent on transforming it into a propaganda agency, or creating a "Nixon Network." It may survive "four more years," but at the moment it scarcely offers a bright hope. No more do the kept newsmen on the White House staff.

Altogether, I doubt that communication in the "new environment" created by electronics will become more civil or civilized.

XI

Perspectives from Mexico on the "Developing" Countries, and on Over-developed America

"PROGRESS" AND THE G N P

Because Mexico has earned its reputation as one of the most progressive of the Latin-American countries, it may best illustrate both the limits and the costs of the "progress" to which undeveloped countries all over the world are now aspiring. And the persistence of some of its traditional ways of life may make clearer by contrast the price that Americans have paid for their way of life.

To begin with, Mexico can rightly boast that since its revolution of 1910 it has had no military dictator but has maintained a stable democracy; while it has had in effect a one-party government, since the government party always wins in national elections, this party at least permits an active opposition and a free press. The country also boasts of a steady economic growth, which as measured by GNP has for thirty years been maintained at a rate of almost seven percent, and lately has made its peso a sounder currency than the once almighty dollar. Futurologists who speculate on the possibility of major powers emerging from the developing nations have included Mexico as a likely candidate. Already it is listed among the twenty richest countries in the world.

Yet to American visitors it still looks like a poor country. Much of it is barren; it has no great fertile plains comparable to those of our Middle West. The signs of poverty are unmistakable in the pueblos all over the land, and in the towns and cities too once one gets off the main avenues. As in the United States, the proud figures of the GNP conceal the important questions: Where has the increased national wealth been going? How equitably is it being shared? Is it being devoted to promoting the public welfare?

As one who since 1938 has spent many summers in Mexico, I know that there has been a distinct improvement in the general standard of living. The government has built or improved many roads, brought electricity to many pueblos. It has also built many schools all over the country, especially in pueblos that had never had one before. For workers it has provided social security, with better medical care. The government appears to be as proud as the people are of the Mexican Revolution, which like the original revolution that won the country's independence from Spain was a social as well as political revolution (unlike those in most other Latin-American countries); the government is still making some effort to carry through social reforms, such as land redistribution, which by American standards are "socialistic." And a growing middle class contributes to both the stability and the prosperity of the country.

Still, there remains a wide gap—as all over Latin America, most obviously in wealthy Brazil—between the many poor and the wealthy upper class. Mexico is also typical of Latin-American countries (or for that matter Catholic countries in Europe too) in that its wealthy people do not pay their proportionate share in income taxes. Even conservative Mexico City newspapers have complained that as typically its millionaires do not donate money to its universities, or to other philanthropies on behalf of the public. (It was Protestant tradition that gave the United States its Carnegie, Rockefeller, and Ford Foundations.) While proclaiming ideals of social justice, the government makes little serious effort to enforce anything like heavy taxation of the rich, the chief beneficiaries from the national prosperity.

Another anomaly obscured by the GNP is the distinctively modern problem of widespread unemployment, which is besetting almost all the "developing" countries. This seldom troubled pre-industrial societies, for to meet their typical problems of scarcity they could always do with more food and other goods, and so could more easily find jobs for workers. Mexico now has many more unemployed people—some forty percent of its labor force—than it had before its technological development. One reason is that in spite of the redistribution of much land, it has more landless peasants than ever. Another reason is that many more women now want jobs—jobs that they might not strictly need, but naturally want in order to buy some of the new material goods that have become available. And all such problems are aggravated by the population explosion. Although Mexico has one of the highest birth rates in the world, the government remains indisposed to promote birth control, if only because the Catholic hierarchy is still opposed to it, and the fast growing population is too much for social welfare programs to keep up with. In spite of all the new schools, for example, there are numerically more illiterates in Mexico than ever. Edmundo Flores, a professor of agricultural economics in the national university (on whom I have relied for my statistics), has noted sadly that "more children are *not* going to school every year."

In other respects too Mexico is handicapped by deep-rooted traditions. Political corruption—a common story in poor countries everywhere—remains routine; ordinary Mexicans take for granted that all *políticos* are grafters. One may have to pay a bribe to judges or minor officials to get their necessary approval of quite legal transactions. Professor Flores adds that the corrup-

[203]

tion has been "democratized"—"now everybody has access to it."

Altogether, he concludes, "Mexico's problem today looks virtually unsolvable." Its prospects, like those of other Latin American countries, he thinks are "grim, grim, grim!"

As I write, the President of Mexico is Luis Echeverría. He sounds like a highly intelligent liberal, seriously concerned about social justice and social welfare. But while he has pointed with pride to the economic growth and technological development of the country during his administration, he has also aligned Mexico with the Third World, with the cause of the needy, underdeveloped countries, which some day may cause America trouble. Thus in welcoming President Nixon's agreement with Moscow because it eased the tensions between the super-powers, he complained that it concerned only their own interests, and the public announcement of it said nothing about the interests and the needs of the Third World, or of their obligations to the Third World. Echeverría has likewise complained of America's neglect of the Latin-American countries, in particular of its growing protectionism. In the United Nations he proposed that its Charter of Human Rights be supplemented by a Charter of the Economic Rights and Duties of States, and he has made it clear that he has in mind the rights of the Third World, the duties of the major powers. In all this he was sounding high democratic principles, I assume in all sincerity; but he was also tacitly admitting that in some respects Mexico is still a needy, underdeveloped country.

He accordingly might remind us of its historic fate as a neighbor of the United States. Mexico has had to live in the shadow of the giant to the north, a foreign power it regarded with mixed feelings of fear, resentment, envy, and admiration.[1] Educated

1. Octavio Paz dwells on this theme in the Fall 1972 issue of *Daedalus,* devoted to the topic "How Others See the United States." In a Preface to the issue the editor suggests that "what Mexico has been condemned to live with from the beginning is fast becoming a nearly universal phenomenon." Americans are now

Mexicans are generally proud of their independence and their national identity, their distinctive character and culture; but now that their country has been caught up in the seemingly irresistible trend to modernization, this has accentuated its tendency to imitate us too, sometimes unthinkingly. A prime example is its capital, where its basic problems are concentrated, and aggravated. Mexico City calls for some separate consideration because it typifies the combination of underdevelopment and overdevelopment that afflicts many other capitals in the Third World today, especially in countries that on the surface have made the most progress.

2. MEXICO CITY AS SYMBOL

When I first visited Mexico City in 1938, it was an attractive old city, with a population of about a million and a half. Today it has more than eight million people. It has also grown much more up-to-date by American standards, and for noise, traffic congestion, and smog it now vies with the worst of our cities. Nevertheless it is continuing to grow fast as poor people from the countryside keep flocking to it in search of better jobs and a more exciting life; it is the mecca of ambitious young people in particular. The estimates of what its population will be in the year 2000 are astronomical—or catastrophic. As it is right now, the government is unable to make decent provision for its too many residents.

In his State of the Nation report in 1972, President Echeverría seemed proud when he observed that only thirty years ago Mexico was a predominantly agricultural country of some twenty million inhabitants, but that by the end of this decade it will be

---

aware that the United States "has become more accessible to the rest of the world, and more vulnerable," but they are less aware of how we have got all over the world, and how other countries have to reckon with our purposes and methods, or to put up with us—as Mexico has always had to do, often unhappily.

one of the ten most highly populated nations in the world. He acknowledged, however, that this rapid growth had created more complex problems. In Mexico City these problems center on the by-products or the costs of its growth.

The government has taken some steps to reduce pollution and congestion. Its most notable achievement is the construction of a handsome, clean, quiet subway, with attractive entrances to stations, which not only puts to shame the subways of New York but impresses me more than the ornate Moscow subway that Russians are so proud of. But the government has yet to solve the problem of providing decent housing and jobs for all the new-comers. The signs of poverty are nowhere more conspicuous than in some districts of Mexico City. In *The Children of Sanchez*, Oscar Lewis concluded that Mexico owed much of its stability to the capacity of its poor people for endurance, but he added that unless its increasing wealth were shared more equitably, he thought they might begin to cause trouble. It now appears that they are growing less patient in their endurance, or less resigned to poverty and misery. Professor Flores reports that the children of Sanchez are now on the warpath, tensions are high, Mexicans are angry with one another, and all over there is a mood of discouragement.

In another respect that is important to me as an erstwhile city-lover, modernizing has not been becoming to the appearance of Mexico City—as is also true of most capitals in the developing countries. Except in a few districts it has lost much of its distinctive character and charm. Among the victims of its progress is its Paseo de la Reforma, which once struck me as one of the handsomest boulevards in the world. In recent years many of the old trees lining it were cut down in order to provide more parking space for automobiles, and the remaining trees have suffered from the smog. Likewise many of the fine old residences along it have been torn down to make way for commercial buildings. Today the Paseo is an ordinary commercial avenue, often congested, with enough faded elegance to make it fit for a Hilton Hotel, but not to reward people who still like to explore old cities, or just to stroll or *"pasear."*

Such possibly sentimental considerations, which I prefer to think of as philosophical, lead me to reflections on old ways of life that I have long known in the town of Taxco, and am sorry to think are probably doomed by the trend to modernization.

3. THE OLD TOWN OF TAXCO: SOME PERSONAL NOTES

In 1940, when I settled down in Taxco for most of the year, it was already a tourist town, one of the most popular in Mexico. It owed its fame immediately to William Spratling, an American designer from New Orleans, who had settled down in it toward 1930 and started training some of its young men in the art of working in silver, for which Taxco became known. He also induced the Mexican government to declare it a "national monument," as a lovely example of an old colonial town, and to decree that all new construction should blend with its colonial style. For lovers of architecture its principal attraction is its eighteenth-century Santa Prisca cathedral-church, a splendid example of Mexican baroque or churriguerresque; when approaching the town from afar, one sees first the ornate, pinkish towers of Santa Prisca. With its many cobblestone streets and alleys winding crookedly up and down the mountainside on which it is built, Taxco is almost too blatantly picturesque, as if it had been designed just for the sake of picture postcards or calendar art. And as a mountain town, about a mile above sea level, it offers the further attractions of magnificent scenery all about, and an equable sunny year-round climate, never hot and never cold, with perpetual bloom of flowers.

Since 1940 Taxco has accordingly prospered. Its population has grown from about seven to more than forty thousand, including too many poor people, but in general the townspeople are better off than they had been. For Taxco illustrates the real goods that can come with modernizing. Almost all homes now have running water and electricity, once luxuries enjoyed by a small minority. Trucks pick up daily the garbage that people used to dump into the *barrancas,* or deep ravines, where it supported many grunting pigs but also bred swarms of flies. Whereas there had been only one trained doctor, there are now quite a number; some of them work in the Social Security center, a new establishment that includes a hospital, a service lacking in 1940. Children in particular have benefited from the improved medical service; I used to see almost daily funeral processions bearing little pink or blue caskets, but this spectacle has become much rarer. Children can likewise hope for adequate schooling. Instead of one primary school, too small to accommodate more than a minority of them, the town now has enough schools, including secondary schools, to take care of most of its youngsters.

As usual, however, modernizing has not enhanced the charm of Taxco, in particular because its main industry is tourism (one of the major supports of the Mexican economy). Its too many silver shops—now more than a hundred, almost all selling imitative work—contribute to the invariable aura of commercialism; its main thoroughfare and plaza are often congested with too many automobiles and trucks, smelling of gasoline fumes; its fancy new or enlarged hotels hardly suggest an old colonial town. Neither does a new cement market building, which so far from blending with the colonial style lacks any style whatever. Like government in most of the developing countries, the local government is concerned chiefly with appearances—the appearances of modernity, that is, not charm. One who knew Taxco in 1940 is unlikely to rejoice in what prosperity has done to a "national monument." He may notice as well the incidental costs of real improvements, such as running water in the home. In the old days women came to the local fountains early in the morning, usually carrying a pitcher on their head, looking very stately, and then started the day with lively chatter. This scene is no more—for me only a fading memory.

Yet Taxco is still an old town, and not just a tourist resort. It is quite different from most popular Acapulco, a Mexican Miami on the Pacific coast to the south of it—the destination of most of the tourists who stop off in Taxco, too often only to be herded into its silver shops by guides on organized tours (who get a rake-off of 20% on whatever their sheep buy). The more perceptive tourists may linger in Taxco because of its charms as a distinctively Mexican town. And as one who knew it in 1940, and has spent many summers in it over the years since then, of late much of the year, I can appreciate more how much of its traditional life it has retained beneath its changed appearances. The old ways of life that I still enjoy there—my main theme at this point—afford another perspective on the costs of economic development or modernizing. Americans have already paid these costs, which I suppose are basically unavoidable. But not altogether so, for some city-planners are trying to cut the costs, or to recover some of the values of old ways.

To begin with, Taxco is still a real *community*, something that Americans are seeking but cannot hope to find in the huge metropolis, or "metropolitan area," in which most of them live. Its traditional communal life is centered in the *zócalo*, the main plaza in the heart of the town, on one side of which rise the towers of the Santa Prisca church that still dominate the town, since in its growth it has chiefly spread over the mountainside above or below the plaza. This remains a civic center, not a business district, such as serves as the "heart" of American towns. A magnet for both young and old, and on Sunday evenings for the whole family, all dressed up, it is especially animated on Sundays, for religion in Taxco is no mere pious formality but is woven into the life of the community. (The townspeople were typically untroubled when Pope Paul demoted Santa Prisca from the Catholic calendar, along with other purely mythical saints, for such tech-

[209]

nicalities mean as little to them as does the nature of the Trinity
and its internal relations; and besides, saints who never lived can
be as good as real ones at working wonders, including cures, for
their worshippers.) Old-timers may lament the passing of one old
custom, the young men and girls who on Sunday evenings used
to stroll around the plaza in separate files, one clockwise, one
counter-clockwise; but at least the young people seem to enjoy
themselves no less as they mingle, chatter, and stroll more informally. For them, as for the parents holding babies and the children who romp about the bandstand, it may still be the great
occasion of the week. And the plaza is likewise often the scene of
the many fiestas, in honor of the saints or the Virgin in one of her
manifestations, that keep alive the sense of tradition and community.

One of my chief pleasures during my stays in Taxco is a ritual
daily stroll to the plaza at noon, to relax over a tequila or so in
an open balcony bar facing Santa Prisca. From here I gaze at its
pink towers, usually outlined against a brilliant blue sky, and at
the animated life of the plaza. My pleasure was deepened when
I belatedly realized that I never think of strolling to the main
square in the center of my home town, a small city in Indiana,
which some years ago was honored by being designated an "All-
American" city. As with other such cities, its center is an ordinary
business district, with no pleasant place to sit and look on, and
little worth looking at anyway—least of all on Sundays. The gay-
est day of the week in Taxco, this is at home the dullest, for
Indiana preserves the grim Protestant Sabbath. (I suppose that
only a few ethnic communities in the United States preserve the
medieval tradition of holy day as holiday.)

On weekends Indians from pueblos in the vicinity stream
through the *zócalo* to the market below. This has the animation
and color of native markets all over the world, but is also distinctively Mexican. On weekends the cobblestone alley leading down
to it from the plaza is lined with little piles of tomatoes, chiles,

beans, herbs, avocados, limes, oranges, and whatever other fruit and vegetables are in season—all more attractive because nothing is wrapped in cellophane. Pottery and basketware in the lower reaches of the market are reminders that many of the articles sold in it, as in shops around town, are handmade. Even apart from all the work in silver, the fine old handicraft tradition is still very much alive in Taxco.

It contributes to my pleasure in my daily strolls along the crooked thoroughfare that leads from the main highway to the plaza. Like most of the streets in Taxco, this rewards a stroller with much more variety and color than does Main Street, or the pleasant residential streets I walk at home. The old traffic of burros loaded with charcoal, firewood, or cornstalks has dwindled, but still provides an occasional splash of local color. Always my strolls are enlivened by exchanges of greetings with little grocers, shopkeepers, artisans, postmen—many more such people than I meet in daily life at home. With the grocers and artisans I enjoy the sort of personal relations and services I remember enjoying in my boyhood, but that are disappearing in our land of supermarkets and shopping centers.

Well, how much of this pleasant old way of life can be recovered in America today? Some of its values are plainly irrecoverable, for example the sense of old tradition lacking in most all-American cities; tradition cannot be fabricated or imported. But Americans might at least reconsider their habit of tearing down perfectly good old buildings, usually to make way for commercial enterprises; as someone tried to remind them, they still go to Europe to see all the old buildings that weren't torn down. The sense of community in small cities, and some neighborhoods of big ones, might be enlivened by more festivals or other such occasions for communal gaiety. Something like civic centers might be created by building more pedestrian malls, with sidewalk cafes to relax in. (As it is, the civic centers that some big cities have built are monumental showpieces, not places for the

[211]

citizenry to relax or revel in.) Small cities might supplement their supermarkets by something like native markets, with produce supplied by farmers in the vicinity, especially because of the current vogue of organic farming. These markets might also encourage a revival of handicrafts. All such possibilities might be promoted if Americans simply learned more respect for traditional ways of life, or more awareness of the costs of their mindless rage for modernity and growth, including what is too often their top civic priority—providing more parking space for automobiles.

Lest I seem sentimental, I should add that Taxco, reputed to be one of the friendliest and happiest towns in Mexico, is therefore not representative, but that even so its traditional life has its seamy side. Over the gay weekends there are many sodden drunks too, others who flash knives or pull out pistols in cantina brawls—an old Mexican custom that continues to give the country a much higher homicide rate even than the United States, with its long tradition of violence. A related custom is wife-beating, which appears to be as common in the region as it was in the Middle Ages, when the law gave men the right to beat their wives. What the law is in Taxco I do not know, but I do know that the administration of justice can be an indecent farce, as it too often is in Mexico. One Sunday morning in the market a man pulled out a gun, and in cold blood shot to death a likable little fish peddler to whom he owed money. He was not jailed, or even brought to trial, because he had friends among the local *políticos*. He simply fled.

And even the relaxed way of life in Taxco, with leisurely dinners and siestas, which can be most gracious and certainly is more civilized than life in a "short-order" culture, can also be exasperating when one has important or urgent business to transact in this land of mañana. Then one may appreciate the "unnatural" or "inhuman" habits of regularity and punctuality that people have acquired in our industrial society.

Still, I would give the last word to the charms of life in Taxco. And with more feeling because this word may become ancient history within a generation, because of the prospects of further "development" in the town. Now I think chiefly of what lies in store for its young people.

4. THE PROSPECTS OF THE YOUTH

My chief informant about what goes on beneath the surface of life in Taxco is a vendor of water-colors named Celestino, an uncommonly thoughtful and earnest man in his thirties. When I asked him, for example, whether the Taxqueños still really believed in their old-time religion, or were just going through the traditional motions, he assured me that the great majority do believe. He granted, however, that there has been some falling off in piety among the younger people. From my observation, he himself is representative of the changes among the better educated of them. He says that he doesn't really believe in religion —but he doesn't disbelieve either.

There are good reasons for his qualified skepticism. One is that religion in Taxco is associated much more with festivity than with fear, even though the people still believe in demons and Satan. Celestino seems quite free from any fear that he may go to hell because of his doubts or his neglect of religious duties. For that matter, the many pious Taxqueños who literally believe in hell do not appear to live in fear of it, any more—let us add—than Christian Americans do, in their more evident complacence. (On a poll some years ago a surprisingly large majority of Americans said they still believed in a literal hell, but some 90% of these also indicated that they did not take seriously the possibility that they themselves might go there.) Thus piety in Taxco has never demanded a scrupulous respect for the holy sacrament of matrimony, nor a fear of the mortal sin of fornication; in the old days at least half of its children were illegitimate. A more attractive

[213]

sign of freedom from religious fear is the annual Day of the Dead, when all the spirits of the dead return to Taxco.

On this day the whole town streams to the local cemetery to strew the graves with flowers, in the evening to place lighted candles on them. Special confections are made for the occasion, many in ingenious shapes of animals with all their bones showing and of death's-heads; these are placed on altars in the home, together perhaps with some tequila, as a kind of feast for the dead. Evidently none of the spirits come from hell, all are happy on this day. Celestino may no longer believe literally in the happiness of the spirits, but he does appreciate the piety of the occasion, the comforting human meaning it has for all the living, who know that they are going to die and can expect such attentions.

Similarly with the many ancient superstitions that survive, as might be expected in a town that began entering the modern world only a generation ago. Again Celestino tells me that the great majority of the Taxqueños take them seriously, and that he himself neither believes nor disbelieves. And again he has some excuse for not being simply skeptical. It includes the reason why a belief in magic has been prevalent all through history, and still is over most of the world: usually the magic works—the patient gets well, the rains come, the crops grow. But a particular reason is that the magic in Taxco is typically for the most part not black magic, and its superstitions usually arouse little fear.

One exception is the prehistoric, world-wide belief in the evil eye. There are still witches in town who give the evil eye to people, especially children, with whom it is likely to be fatal. Celestino tells me, however, that there are now fewer such witches, I suppose because all but the poorest people have learned to take their ailing children to the doctor. He knows too that there are good witches who help out the townspeople in emergencies. One has become famous for her apparent powers of extrasensory perception.

At any rate, Americans as a people have no reason to ridicule the superstitions of Taxco, or the half-beliefs of Celestino. Although nominally much better educated, in a supposedly scientific age, a great many of them still cling to ancient superstitions about the number 13, ladders, black cats, etc.—not to mention their common belief in the magical efficacy of prayer. Let us remember that during a prolonged drought some summers ago the churches in the great city of New York prayed for rain; and let me add that the long candlelight processions winding through Taxco for the same purpose usually get prompter results. Here superstitions seem more "normal," like other old traditions. Celestino has more respect for such tradition, more awareness of the genial human purposes it may serve—and of the greater need of the many poor for belief in the efficacy of prayer.

This brings up a particular religious attraction of Taxco—the many patron saints who took over the wonder-working duties of the Aztec gods before them, but are disposed to give their worshippers more personal attention, heed their appeals in times of illness or other trouble. They are fallible, of course, as all gods have been all through history, else the human race would never have suffered so much; but usually they respond to appeals—their worshippers get over their troubles. Although Taxqueños are presumably less dependent on their saints now that they can go to doctors, doctors are fallible too, as well as expensive for the poor. The saints are still very much alive and on duty often enough. So is the Virgin in one of her merciful manifestations that have made her more attractive than God, since she is not given to wrath, and doesn't bother her head—any more than the saints do—over the sexual frailties of Taxqueños.

To my knowledge, however, Taxco has produced no folk saints of its own, such as I have read about in other regions of Mexico. These were simple men and women who experienced a "call" from God or Christ, acquired marvelous powers of curing, exercised these powers chiefly on behalf of poor people without charging for their services, and attracted a large following of worshippers. Taxco has its *curanderos,* but I have never heard of one who had a religious call; they appear to be simply masters of the traditional lore of healing. The most beloved in my time was a gentle, kindly old man, saintly enough, who in spite of his frailty would at any time go up and down the mountainside, with his bag of ointments and herbs, to relieve people in distress. An American resident, for whom he promptly took care of a badly smashed hand, told me that he was especially good at setting bones and relieving aching muscles. After his death another American resident found a *curandero* who as promptly relieved the miseries he was suffering from back trouble; although the man was at the time busy harvesting his corn, he responded at once to the American's call for help and came to his home. My friend was more grateful because he knew that most of our much more prosperous doctors at home are no longer willing to pay house calls.

These *curanderos* were not exploiting superstition among the local people either, but I suppose that many of their poor patients may have believed that they had magical powers, and thereby were more readily cured. Because of the growing sophistication of the young, one might expect that the old superstitions—religious and otherwise—will in time fade away. I am inclined to doubt it, in view of the attitudes of Americans. At least it would take a long time in Taxco—more than a generation. Meanwhile Celestino is in this respect perhaps more fortunate than are the young people of America; in his semi-skepticism he is better able to appreciate the best in both the old and the new.

In other respects, however, he is less fortunate. When he once told me that he wanted to have a lot of children, he listened thoughtfully as usual when I pointed out the problems that Mexico was facing—especially in education—because of its high rate of births, and we had a long discussion of birth control. Now he says he wants no more than the three children he has, but adds that he will have some difficulty in persuading his wife. A woman from the pueblos, she takes for granted that a woman's main

[2 1 6]

function is bearing children. The young women of Taxco are showing increasing interest in birth control, but they too will have to contend against old tradition, supported by their Catholic Church.

Celestino's problem is complicated because he is very proud of his family, and ambitious for his sons. He is a sturdy, hard-working man, whom I see every day in the plaza carrying on his shoulder a heavy portfolio of water-colors, which he flips open as he approaches tourists to display some of his wares. Usually they wave him off. So he spends the whole day, week in and week out, toting his portfolio, encountering chiefly a discouraging in-difference. Although on some days he does good business, there are many more—especially during the long months between the big summer and winter tourist seasons—when he does little or none. Yet his manner is always cheerful. When asked how busi-ness is, he invariably smiles and says *"regular."* When I suggest that this means "irregular," he cheerfully agrees—and keeps smiling. With the help of his affable manner and fluent English, which he learned by himself, he makes out on the whole well enough to achieve something like middle-class status in Taxco. (He is head of the local union of street-vendors, formed to pro-tect them from shop-owners who want to keep them out of the plaza.) He has been able to buy on the installment plan, the most favored status symbol, a television set, paying exorbitant charges that more than double its cost—standard practice in Mexico. For him it is a means to education too, a wider acquaintance with the outside world; so it furthers his ambitions for his sons. But these ambitions raise further problems. The trials of his trade that he sometimes confesses to have given me more insight into both the aspirations of the rising middle class in Mexico, especially the younger generation, and the difficulties they face in a country that has been "developing" fast, but not fast enough to meet all the rising expectations of its people.

The water colors that Celestino sells are the work of local

painters. Mostly they are gaudy representations of local scenes; the staples include views of the towers of Santa Prisca, and of picturesque streets or nooks with masses of purple bougainvillea. Knowing that this calendar art appeals chiefly to tourists with poor taste, he himself began to paint, with increasing pleasure. His water colors are in a simple impressionistic style, rendering something of the distinctive feel of Mexican life without too obvious exploitation of its color; they reveal some natural talent. Although he has no apparent illusions about potential fame, he would like to go to an art school in Mexico City. But that is beyond his means.

Chiefly he wants to give a good education to his little boys whom he is so proud of. It is unlikely, however, that he will be able to do more than put them through secondary school. On his present income he could not afford to put them through a university; although the government is beginning to provide more scholarships, a college education is as yet a privilege reserved for a small minority of Mexico's youth. If they have energy and talent they may manage to come up in the world, as their father did, and as Mexico has done, but it is still not a land rich in opportunity for the sons of the unprivileged.

I have similar questions about the prospects of my neighbor's children, with whom I am much better acquainted, in particular two pretty little girls, aged eleven and twelve, named Carilu and Araceli. Their names are not common Mexican names; their parents chose them because they heard them on television and liked the sound of them. But even so I think of Carilu and Araceli as representative of the children of Taxco, at least those of the lower middle class. They are the oldest of five children of my immediate neighbor, a tailor who works all day in his home, from early morning until after nightfall. (The workmen of Taxco are typically hard-working, not at all like the Mexican peon as commonly pictured—dozing under a tree, face covered by a sombrero.) In apartments adjoining his, live his two brothers with their families, which include four more children. All the youngsters play together in a little dirt yard in front of their home, on which my balcony looks down. I became acquainted with them a couple of years ago when I began giving them presents of candy on Sundays. The girls trotted out with pride their two words of English: *"Mucho* thank you." The little ones at first cried happily only *"Viene el gringo!"* All still seem delighted by my weekly present even though it amounts only to a small bag of candy for each family. I make a point of keeping my presents modest.

For what at once impressed me about the children was how unspoiled they were, and how happy with very little. Although they have a few relatively expensive toys, mostly they amuse themselves with the simplest aids, often with none at all, playing games or devising some make-believe of their own. I never see them moping or sulking. With one exception I very rarely hear them cry either. The exception is my neighbor's youngest child, who sometimes throws tantrums and cries loudly, to the evident embarrassment of both her sisters and her parents.

The children of the upper middle class often seem as disposed to bawl or whine as American children. But my neighbor's youngsters have been brought up in the traditional ways, which still prevail among the older families. Just what the parents' methods are I do not know. My neighbors clearly treat their children with affection, but as a matter of course. They give no sign of the anxieties of American parents who have come to regard child-rearing as a peculiar problem. If they punish them it is evidently not by spanking, for I never hear any but the youngest one bawling. Reprimands apparently do not take the form of yelling at the children either, for this is another sound I do not hear. At any rate, the training appears to be very successful as far as it goes. The children seem well-mannered and well-behaved without being at all repressed. The girls cheerfully do their share in cleaning house, porch, and yard—assuming their natural role in a closely knit family.

The parents' training is in a way eased, however, by an intimacy that an American middle-class family would find trying. My neighbor's family of seven live in but a few rooms; there is a minimum of privacy (as let us remember there was in the homes of most ordinary people all through history until our day). Carilu and Araceli are approaching puberty, and what then? If some arrangement will presumably be made for their dressing and undressing in privacy, they can hardly dream of having a room of their own. Meanwhile I wonder how the family spends its evenings. I never hear sounds of a television set to match the antennae on the roof, perhaps set up just in anticipation. Though I doubt that they own any books, their living quarters are not suited for reading anyway. They have neither armchairs, desks, nor lamps, only naked electric-light bulbs. All I know for sure is that Carilu and Araceli—as well as their father—are pleased by the comics I pass on from the Mexico City newspapers, which they do not buy. I assume that they know little about the goings-on in the great outside world.

As far as it goes, I said, the training of the children appears to be very successful—especially when one considers the too many pampered children in America, who at a tender age begin learning to become ardent consumers. Now I should add that the training does not go far enough to do much by way of developing their minds. My neighbors may do something about this too, since they clearly have some ambition to improve their status or their lot, but from all appearances they depend primarily on the school. And of this too the girls seem to be typical products.

Their school is located directly below my house, close enough for me to hear something of what goes on in it. It holds three separate sessions a day, morning, afternoon, and evening, the two latter for older youngsters. Every morning the girls go tripping off happily to school, wearing the simple dark red dress that is the prescribed uniform of their school, carrying plastic bags loaded with school books. They mystified me by also carrying an old broom back and forth every day, until Carilu explained that it was the class broom, and that she brought it home because the older boys in the afternoon might steal it. They tell me that they like school very much. The younger boys who go to school make the same report, which appears to be the general feeling among the youngsters of Taxco. Judging by all the happy noise I hear now and then, between classes or in rest periods, they have a good time in school.

Still, I wonder about this too. From all I have heard about the schools, they have the common faults of American schools, and in some ways seem worse. The pupils learn by rote through set exercises, or the same mechanical routines. Occasionally I hear them reciting in unison, their teachers addressing them like orators (who in Mexico rarely display humor or fancy). Once Araceli came home carrying proudly a hideous little gilt statue—a prize she had just won for her recitation. The children have some opportunity to express themselves in art or handicraft projects, but little in class discussions, even in the upper grades. Although some teachers no doubt encourage some measure of self-expression, there appears to be in general even less emphasis than in American schools on developing their powers of independent, critical judgment—what to my mind ought to be a primary aim of democratic education, especially in a developing country.

Why, then, is there so little apparent dissatisfaction with the schools of Taxco? Although I can only conjecture, some reasons seem clear enough, and might apply to all developing countries. In the first place, people are likely to be more grateful than Americans for any kind of education, since only a generation ago Taxco was unable to provide one for many of its children. Graduation from the sixth grade is a highly ceremonious occasion, the more so because it is still unknown in many if not most pueblos. The children apparently are also more docile than most American youngsters. They may get more real pleasure from learning and acquiring basic skills because of the lack of educational materials in their homes, and as they grow up they have a livelier sense of the practical value of an education. They may take pleasure too in their simple school uniforms, which give them a feeling of identity, without an oppressive sense of discipline; the uniforms have a democratic quality that an American can better appreciate, since they discourage the competition in stylishness that begins too early with too many of our youngsters, especially the girls. And in Mexico, still proud of its Revolution, all this may stir a livelier patriotic feeling for *La República*. On national holidays the children are pleased to march in parades in distinctive costumes, to the sounds of drums and trumpets provided by the older boys, who may begin practicing weeks in advance. Mexico is democratic enough so that the many parades do not seem like a mode of regimentation, as they were in Germany when Hitler set the youth to marching in uniforms.

Problems lie ahead, however. Although there is no clear sign of a youth revolt in Taxco, some of the teen-age boys are taking to hippie styles in hair, dress, and manner, and have grown noisy and ill-mannered. On the whole they are obviously becoming less docile. University students in Mexico have grown distinctly rebellious, like students all over the world, and something of their spirit may be expected to seep down into secondary-school students, in the small towns too. All this has as yet had little apparent effect on the older girls of Taxco, but they also face problems. And so may Carilu and Araceli, contented though they now are.

They are evidently good students by Mexican standards, as indicated by Araceli's prize for recitation and Carilu's honorary role as custodian of the school broom, and they strike me as fairly bright girls. Hence I assume that they will go on to secondary school, even though entrance to it is difficult because there are many more applicants than can be admitted by the Taxco schools. If so, then what? Few of the young girls appear to aspire to an independent career, and I doubt that many are yet troubled by an identity crisis, which now seems to be *de rigueur* in America;

but some want to become teachers, many more to become typists or secretaries. My neighbor's girls talk of becoming secretaries, but whatever his ambitions for them, they might be better off if they developed none beyond the still normal one of becoming wives and mothers. For Taxco provides by no means enough suitable positions for secondary school graduates. More and more of them are leaving for Mexico City. And I should expect that the excitements of the big city will not compensate indefinitely for the trials of life in it, especially the smog, which must be especially disagreeable for people accustomed to the fresh air of Taxco.

Meanwhile Carilu and Araceli remain eager, happy little girls, exemplifying the possible advantages of childhood in Taxco. Their father is well enough off to provide for their normal needs, such as an occasional new dress, which are not yet needs created by TV commercials and magazines addressed to teenagers. I cannot imagine their drawing up a shopping list like that of an American twelve-year-old girl: "Water pistol, bra, permanent." There is no telling what they will be like when they grow up, and I suppose it would be inhuman to discourage their ambitions, which may include the dream of visiting America—i.e., Hollywood and New York. Yet I hope for their sake that they will remain in Taxco. Some of those who have left for better jobs, in Mexico City or Acapulco, have discovered that they missed the pleasures of communal life that they took for granted here. If this life may eventually be doomed, it should at least last for some time yet. Or so I hope, rather wistfully.

XII

Another Essay on Man, with Some Further Speculations about What Americans Will Be Like in the Year 2000

THE PROBLEM OF HUMAN NATURE

Although we may anticipate that people in the future will have a somewhat different way of life from ours, I assume that they will have the same basic needs, due to basically the same "human nature." But this brings up another elementary question of meaning: What is human nature? Offhand, we all know because it is our own nature, or at least we talk about it freely enough; people commonly explain behavior by saying that it is "just human nature." With a little thought, however, we may realize that we don't really know what we're talking about. Anything that human beings do is necessarily human, but they do all kinds of things, for all kinds of reasons—"human" in this sense means no more than being a member of the so-called human race. In ordinary discourse it may mean only customary behavior, in our own society; and this may include behavior that to other peoples seems unnatural. Or consider the common saying that you can't change human nature—human nature is always and everywhere the same. People who say this usually mean that man is incurably selfish, egotistical, aggressive, or something else disagreeable, characteristic of the damned human race; and I suppose we might all agree that on earth you can't make an angel of man. Yet he clearly has some admirable potentialities too, including a capacity for unselfish behavior, which are also an expression of his nature. So it may be said that you can't make him just an obedient slave or a robot, as some rulers may wish to, and that you can't take away his basic, distinctive tendency to believe that some behavior is wrong, or to desire justice, even though his notions about right and wrong may obviously be fallible. And in a long view of his history his nature *has* changed somewhat. Although we know little about the thought and feeling of prehistoric cavemen, their nature was presumably rather different in some respects from that of educated, civilized people today.

So let us consider the dictum of Alexander Pope: "The proper study of mankind is man." Obviously, one might say. Man has long been a basic concern in literature, philosophy, and religion. But the obvious trouble is that we encounter innumerable different opinions about the nature of man, what is good for him and what he is good for. Typically, moreover, these opinions reflect the interests and values of a particular society or culture. They obscure or confuse the issue of a basic, essential human nature, just what it means to be "human."[1]

1. Today, I should add, some women may bristle at the traditional terms "mankind" and "man" because of the women's lib movement. At public lectures I have been reproached for using these terms, told that I should substitute "humankind." This seems to me an awkward term, however, and I find it difficult to give up the traditional terms, in particular because I often cite past writers who naturally used them; historians have to talk about the idea of mankind in history. So I should remark mildly that "mankind" and "man" have always included women, that I do not regard them as inferior to men, and that they may now tend to be hypersensitive, too disposed to see male conceit everywhere; but let them substitute "humankind" if they want to. Then I venture to add that the problem of just what is human nature is complicated because the physiological differences between men and women, and the division of labor these led to in marriage (including the fact that even liberated women still cannot assign child-bearing to

Such confusion over the nature of man has been deepened now that he has come to be studied scientifically. Biologists, psychologists, sociologists, and anthropologists give different reports of him, nothing like a unified view. They are farther from such a view because as specialists they typically deal with segments or selected aspects of man and his behavior, what has been called "piece work"—not with the whole man, nor necessarily the essentials of "human nature." I have put the term in quotation marks because some scientists have tacitly or even explicitly denied that there is any such thing; they declare that man is merely a product of his society or culture, which can mold his alleged nature in countless different ways, produce as many different natures. Many other scientists shy away from the question what is human nature because of the reigning positivism. They declare that it is a philosophical, not a scientific question, because it cannot be answered positively; it is too "fuzzy." Some go further and declare that it is therefore a "meaningless" question, or even regard "human nature" as a myth.[2]

Now, I am assuming that there is such a thing as human nature, which I shall henceforth refer to without apologetic quotation marks. It is a very large and complex subject, and the problem of defining it is as difficult, for reasons I shall go into presently. It nevertheless seems to me obviously a very important question, even supremely important, now that the traditional answers given by Christianity have lost their authority among the educated. I am quite willing to call it a philosophical question (and therefore regret that it is generally evaded in modern analytic philosophy, especially logical positivism), but I would add that science can throw and has thrown much light on it. If even so we cannot give a conclusive answer, we can at least raise pertinent

men) have meant some possible differences in their nature.

2. These and other answers are reported in *The Human Nature Industry,* by Ward Cannel and Jane Macklin, who posed the question to a number of eminent scientists.

questions that may be stimulating and illuminating. And the basic question seems to be unavoidable for all of us—both scientists and humanists—who share some common concerns. One is the concern with the interests of "mankind" in One World, and with "human rights." Another is all the talk about the "human condition," both the permanent conditions of man's life and the condition of contemporary man, now commonly described as a "predicament." This brings up again the popular theme of the "alienation" of modern man, with its implications of not only a significant change in his condition but assumptions that his life has become "unnatural" in some ways. Likewise the common complaints about the "dehumanizing" tendencies in our technological society imply some notions about what it means to be human, and call for clearer notions than we usually get. Many writers share my own concern with the neglect of basic human values in our society, which are presumably rooted in human nature. As a historian I have stressed that it is hard to talk of a "natural life" for man, a creature who on his record is remarkably adaptable; for he began as a hunter living in caves, with the discovery of agriculture took to the sedentary peasant life of the village, with the rise of civilization moved to the city, a quite different artificial world of his own, and with the rise of industrialism adapted himself to a radically new kind of society. But as a critic of this society I have also stressed my belief that his life today can in some respects be legitimately called unnatural, or in other words unsuited to his basic nature. And so with many specific concerns, such as the problems of communication and the problems of city planners. They all involve the question of what people are like, basically. Likewise in daily life all people perforce carry on with notions about what other people are like, notions that commonly imply some assumptions about human nature. Add that these notions may be erroneous, and it only emphasizes our unfortunate ignorance about ourselves—properly the most important of our interests.

[227]

Today the educated commonly assume that the question is what people *have become* like. Here we run into the most obvious difficulty in defining human nature: man is unquestionably molded by his culture. All along, beginning in the millennia during which he lived in caves and acquired the habit of cooking his food (according to Claude Levi-Strauss, a landmark in the transition from nature to culture), he developed an amazing diversity of cultures, which alike seemed natural to the people brought up in them. His nature therefore became largely a second nature, and his basic needs included acquired needs. Ever since his discovery of agriculture, his cultural evolution has been much more important than his biological evolution. With the rise of civilization he began more consciously to cultivate human nature, in an effort to realize its best potentialities, notably in ancient Greece and Confucian China. At the same time, man still has basically the same set of genes that he had many thousands of years ago. The question, then, is what in his nature is determined by culture, and what by his genes, or heredity—what is basic, common to all cultures; and on this our scientific authorities disagree. Other difficulties include the old story of "the inhumanity of man to man"; apparently such inhumanity, which has grown frightful in our day, is basically natural to man, or all too human. The growing but still ineffectual protests against it point to another difficulty—not only cultural but individual differences, beginning with the biological fact that man is the most highly individualized of animals. The Western tradition of individualism, which has given the individual more opportunities, incentives, and rights than he enjoyed in any other civilization, has in our time led to still another difficulty, the "identity crisis," most obvious in young people. To repeat, they have to decide what their "real" or "true" self is, and what kinds of persons they want to become. Many have been seeking a more "natural" life than the conventional American way of life today, and have further complicated the problem of the natural life by experimenting in different lifestyles, usually to the dismay of their elders. Hippies are only the most obvious example. But they have behind them a long tradition of primitivism, dating at least as far back as the Cynics in ancient Greece, the example of Diogenes in his barrel. Long before Rousseau the idea that civilized life is artificial, or an imposition on human nature, has seemed natural to many men, especially to city-dwellers.

2. SOME ELEMENTARY TRUTHS

These and other difficulties will continue to crop up as we look into the problem of human nature. But it is now time to stress that we have much positive knowledge about man, and that agreement is possible on at least some elementary statements about him.

To begin with, man is an animal. He may or may not have an immortal soul, but he certainly has some needs common to other animals. As certainly he has some different potentialities from all other animals, due in particular to his brainpower, or power of conscious choice. (I repeat that even B. F. Skinner, who in effect denies this power, exercises it in conditioning his rats.) He belongs to a unique biological species, which has given itself the possibly conceited name of *Homo Sapiens*. In the Age of Enlightenment, with its faith in reason, he was pleased to consider himself a rational animal. Now that we are much aware of how prone he is to irrational behavior it is necessary to repeat that he is nevertheless distinctive in his capacity for rational, responsible behavior, and his insistence on ideas of right and wrong. Then we may add that his power of conscious choice is also the source of his distinctive problems, always including the depressing truth that no other animal, or "brute," is as brutal as man can be, or as foolish.

Very early in his history, at any rate, man began chipping flints and becoming a tool-making animal. As such he would have a remarkable history, culminating in the marvelous—and awful—powers of modern technology. Quite early he became a symbol-making animal too, developing the extra-ordinary instrument of language. Other animals can communicate effectively, sometimes in remarkable ways.[3] But only man has elaborated a language with symbols that made possible the development of literature, learning, logic, abstract thought, and finally modern science. By the same token, as usual, language has also made possible faultier communication than that of other animals, who have a surer instinct for recognizing signals. As ambiguous have been man's distinctive achievements as a culture-building animal, whose environment became primarily man-made; his culture determined the meaning and the uses of the natural environment he perforce lived in—and today it threatens to make his whole environment unfit for human habitation. Through culture man in time realized all his distinctive potentialities, and became able—as no other animal is—to transmit all his acquired knowledge, arts, and skills to his young. By culture he was also imprisoned; his ideas about the natural world might become foolish or even preposterous, his nature might be warped, his basic needs left unsatisfied, his customary behavior made apparently "inhuman"—above all in ostensibly civilized societies.

Now to go back to the beginning, man has some plain enough biological needs, including the need of not only physical but psychological security. They lead to the living truth in the platitudes about our "common humanity." Despite all the loose rhetorical talk about it, we all do have some common needs and common desires, notably the desire to enjoy our life, which is made more poignant by our common fate, "the pathos of mortality"; of all animals man alone has grown conscious of the fact that

3. We have lately learned that dolphins have an audible symbolic language. Although chimpanzees, unlike parrots, cannot be taught to say words, experimenters have succeeded in teaching them a kind of sign language, something like that used by deaf people.

he is bound to die. This helps to explain another distinctive characteristic of his nature—his common respect for his dead. As far back as Neanderthal man we find him burying his dead ceremonially. The chunks of meat and the weapons that Neanderthal man buried with them suggest that he had some notion of an after-life, such as virtually all known peoples have had; but if so, we cannot assume that he dreamed of a happy hunting ground. On the historic record, peoples have had very different notions of the life to come, some of them (like the Greek Hades) depressing, others simply gruesome (and none more so than the Christian Hell). The chunks of meat and the weapons might be only signs that Neanderthal man respected his dead—as do people today who have no belief in a life to come, but may bury the dead in their best clothes. The respect may be warmer, or sadder, because our life on earth is the only one we can be really sure of.

Here we have another clue to an understanding of human nature—the universals of culture. Anthropologists long stressed the fantastic diversity of cultures, with its implication of not only the relativity of values but the seemingly almost unlimited plasticity of man. Of late, however, some anthropologists have been giving more attention to the uniformities underlying the diversity. George Murdock, for example, has drawn up a list of seventy-two universals found in all human cultures. They include such genial customs as hospitality, feasting, joking, greetings, and gift-giving, which suggest that man is not so selfish and nasty as he is often made out to be. And Ralph Linton has even found some universal ethical principles, belying the prevalent assumption that morals are only *mores*.

I would stress in particular a simple fact that has been obscured by the commonplaces about the relativity of morals—the fact that all known societies, past and present, have had moral codes. All have insisted on basic ideas of ought and ought not. All have prescribed duties. None has encouraged the seemingly natural impulse to consider only one's own sweet pleasure. There are of course always people—especially in civilized societies—who violate the code or break the social rules. But it is more significant that most people obey the rules most of the time, and that almost all have accepted the idea of duties. If they may naturally find some of their duties disagreeable, they may as naturally take pride and pleasure in performing others. In any case, only abnormal people reject all idea of ought and ought not.

The universality of moral codes is not at all surprising, inasmuch as they are a plain requirement of social life. This points to another basic truth about man, that he is a social animal, who as far back as we can see him—in his caves—lived in groups, just as other animals lived in herds, packs, or flocks. Nowhere do we see him in the "state of nature" as pictured by Hobbes, an endless war of all against all. He early had to cooperate with his fellows as a big-game hunter, and then more extensively as a farmer in the village, still more so as a city-dweller, who could no longer be self-sufficient, alone take care of his basic needs of food, shelter, and security. The natural sociality of man should be plain enough, but it has been obscured by the current fashion of stressing his natural agressiveness, which has behind it the long Western tradition—from Hobbes down through Freud, in an increasingly competitive society—of stress on his selfishness and egotism, his lust for power, and in general his unsocial or anti-social impulses, which by Freud's time were regarded as "instincts." Needless to add, he does plainly have such impulses or tendencies, but as natural is his loyalty to his group or tribe, for which he has always been willing to fight and die. His aggressiveness has been most apparent in his relations with outsiders, who with the rise of civilization came to be known as foreigners, or in war as enemies. But civilization was the culmination of a natural tendency that was obscured by the stress in early Darwinism on the struggle for survival, with loose talk about the survival of the fittest. During his long evolution man survived and came up in the world not so much by a struggle with his fellows

as by cooperation with them. Like all organized competition today, war itself was possible only because of cooperation.

To stress the natural sociality of man is accordingly not to
idealize him, or revert to the simple idea of his natural goodness.
Say that he is not essentially a wolf, still less a lone wolf, and one
must add that too often he looks more like a sheep. In America
today other words for his tendency to cooperate and obey are
togetherness and conformism. The rebel against society and convention has been a rare type historically, and generally was not
admired in his day. Often he was punished, just as Jesus was
crucified.

Decorative art, one of the universals of culture noted by Murdock, points to another significant truth about man, that in the
course of his evolution he somehow acquired an aesthetic sense.
Like some other universals (such as joking) its value for human
survival, or the reason why it was developed by natural selection,
may be unclear, but at any rate an aesthetic sense clearly became
an element in the hereditary equipment of man, or his human
nature. We can note it in the artifacts of prehistoric men, in the
art of all societies (however different their conceptions of
beauty), and in the talk and behavior of all children today; they
don't have to be taught that many things are pretty, and have a
natural fondness for drawing or making things that seem to them
pretty. When they grow up in America today, a commercial society that has created so much ugliness, while also cheapening
ideas about prettiness, their aesthetic sense may be dulled; but
if so they are deprived. I repeat that aesthetic values are much
more important than "practical" Americans are likely to think.

These values point to another hoary platitude, that man cannot
live on bread alone. Literary and religious people who rejoice in
this idea may need to be reminded that first of all he needs bread,
"the staff of life," and that hundreds of millions of people over
the world today don't get enough to eat; yet man plainly does
have real spiritual needs. As I have said, they are not necessarily

[233]

religious needs in the traditional sense; though this is an open question; beliefs about supernatural beings or powers are so old and widespread that they may be a real need for human well-being. Enough for me, once more, that there unquestionably is a spirit in man that seeks truth, beauty, and goodness. Later I shall return to the reasons for believing that the American way of life, with the common devotion to a high material standard of living, is spiritually unsatisfying, and however natural it seems to most Americans, it is in a real sense unnatural, or at least if fails to satisfy some basic needs of man.

Other universals of culture raise interesting questions. One, for example, is the institution of marriage. Why is it universal? Although it has a plain connection with the sexual instinct, this leads naturally only to copulation, and may threaten marriage because it also leads to adultery. A more apparent reason for marriage is another universal, the family. Societies have different kinds of family arrangements, but everywhere we find the family. The reason for this seems to me clear enough—the need of caring for the young. While other animals also care for their young, the need is most conspicuous with human beings because of the prolonged helplessness of the human infant, and all it has to learn. Some people today argue that it would be better to have the state bring up children (as ancient Sparta did), but most people resist the idea, on the grounds that parents naturally give their children more of the affection they need.[4]

A broader universal is some kind of regulation of sexual behav-

4. It should be noted, however, that while mother love is common and natural enough, this instinct can be suppressed. Infanticide was a common practice in Hellenistic Greece and in Rome; girl babies in particular were often put to death. And though we don't know how mothers felt about it, because we don't hear their voices, an appalling number of infants in America today are killed by parents, or even tortured, as by burning their flesh with cigarettes or breaking their bones. Students of the problem have estimated that more children under five years old are killed by abusive parents than die from disease. Nothing I know of in past history is more horrible than this; the most barbarous people at least didn't torture infants. Here is another incidental sign of a sick society.

[254]

ior, including specifically the prohibition everywhere of rape, at least within the group. Some societies permit more sexual freedom than others, especially in premarital relations, but no known society has permitted complete sexual freedom, or promiscuity. This may seem rather strange, since men know that the impulse to promiscuity—God help us—is common enough. Although no student of the problem, I suppose that the ban may be due to a recognition of a basic human need of companionship, if not love. Ralph Linton observed that in societies that permit premarital relations it is assumed that these will lead eventually to permanent matings, and that everywhere—even though separation or divorce may be easy—the accepted ideal of marriage is a lifelong union. One apparent reason for this ideal, beyond the need of companionship, is again the proper care of children, the duties of parents, which, like their rights, Linton observed "are always culturally defined and enforced by ethical sanctions."

The question remains to what extent such universals of culture are genetically or biologically determined, by natural selection, and to what extent culturally determined through experience. About this we cannot be sure, but I think it makes little difference. At least the universals point to uniformities and permanencies in the human condition. The diversities in culture also come down to different ways of dealing with the basic facts of man's life everywhere—such facts as sex, the needs of subsistence, the common fate of mortality, and again the reality of spiritual needs. And at least we can dispose of some common fallacious beliefs, due to our culture. Thus most white racists in America assume that feelings about color are instinctive. As the common saying goes, would you like your daughter to marry a black man?— implying an instinctive revulsion against the idea. In fact, feeling about color has been rare in history. Although people everywhere tended to regard themselves as superior to other peoples, they seldom based their claims to superiority on the color of their skin. Racism in America is plainly due to its long ugly tradition of treating black people as inferiors, even to denying their humanity.[5]

Somewhat more complex is the issue raised by the common American assumption that people have an "acquisitive instinct," because of which the most powerful motives are economic motives. Property rights are indeed a universal of culture—though chiefly in the sense of such personal possessions as ornaments, tools, and utensils. But the drive to acquire ever more possessions is not found in all cultures. The ambition to get rich, which in the Middle Ages was called the deadly sin of avarice or greed, in America came to be regarded as quite normal, even honorable when it was dignified as free private enterprise, the heart of the American Way. So today the profit motive is still honored as the mainspring of our economy. One problem of non-Western countries aspiring to economic growth is that their people have to learn to acquire a proper "acquisitive instinct." Americans might consider the story of the peasants of Java, who our economists took for granted would bring more coconuts to market when their price went up. Actually the peasants brought fewer to market, for a quite sensible reason: they had only a few simple needs, and if they could satisfy them with less work, so much the better. They were not yet hounded by admen, whose business is to create artificial new needs—a strictly unnatural affliction that has become an essential part of the American way of life.

This is more of a problem because acquired needs, which in a rational view may look quite unnecessary, are nevertheless real needs. In America today they include many that are obviously foolish, and contribute to the discontents of a people that is

5. As a visiting professor at the University of Istanbul, in the days long ago when Americans were still popular, I learned that my sympathetic Turkish students simply could not understand our treatment of the Negroes. They were more mystified, as well as horrified, when an officer in our Mediterranean fleet in port cracked a bottle over the head of a black man who was escorting a Turkish girl because they regarded Negroes as especially handsome types of male.

apparently not enjoying very much its unprecedentedly high standard of living. But they also include some honorable needs. In my effort to write a history of freedom, I was forced to question our traditional assumption that man has not only a natural right to freedom but a natural passion for it; for in the early civilizations, and most later ones, the masses of common people displayed no such passion; even though they were often oppressed, they seldom rebelled. The historical record supports rather the argument of Dostoyevsky's Grand Inquisitor, that man needs first of all bread, and then "miracle, mystery, and authority"—the authority of priests and of monarchs, often divinely appointed and endowed with a right to rule despotically, which people everywhere accepted. Then I could add that on his record, and by his nature, man nevertheless has potentialities for freedom, which he realized in some societies; among other things, he naturally does not like to be enslaved or imprisoned, even though he might then enjoy the security that psychologists now tell us is his primary need, more apparent than his need of freedom. I concluded that once people had come to enjoy freedom, they would not willingly relinquish it. The responsibilities of freedom may indeed be too heavy a burden for most men, as the Grand Inquisitor argued; many Americans seem prone to the tendencies noted by Erich Fromm in his *Escape From Freedom;* yet I assume that with most people this acquired need has become a basic need. Many Americans are demanding more freedom, most obviously women and young people.

Other difficulties about human nature are aggravated unnecessarily by what seems to me the plain "not-but" fallacy. Robert Ardrey, for example, has sought to restore the respectability of the concept of "instincts," which anthropologists had discredited, and he argues plausibly that some habits or traits that man acquired during his long evolution persist because they have become instinctive; but then he concludes: "We act as we do for reasons of our evolutionary past, not our cultural present." The

[237]

truth seems to me clearly "both-and" instead of "not"—and with both to an extent strictly unknown. For one may question the specific instincts that Ardrey stressed in his *Territorial Imperative.* Thus he states, "Man is a predator whose natural instinct is to kill with a weapon." If so, I am myself strictly unnatural, for I have never had an impulse to kill with a weapon; at worst I have only gone fishing, not even hunting. But I do not feel at all queer or inhuman because I have known many people who never displayed an instinct to kill with a weapon, and like me never bought a lethal weapon. I also know that some societies have been much less predatory, or more peaceful, than others. Ashley Montague noted that although Ardrey assumes that man shares with other animals the instinct to defend territory, some animals nearest to him on the evolutionary ladder, such as the gorilla, the orangutan, and the intelligent chimpanzee, are neither territorial nor "killers," and display aggression only when threatened. (The fierce-looking gorilla is easily intimidated.) I should add that Ardrey later dwelt on population genetics, with its implications of the primary importance of group survival, which might suppress aggressive behavior that would aid only the individual.[6] The imperatives of group survival help to explain why the tendency to cooperate—whether cultural or instinctive, or both— has been more marked in the history of man, and essential to his survival, than the tendency to exterminate his fellows.

3. SOME QUESTIONS ABOUT IMPLICATIONS FOR MAN TODAY

I suppose there is no question about the reality of the interests of "mankind," now that we are all in the same boat or spaceship.

6. Thus wolves instinctively do *not* fight to the death. When the defeated wolf lies down and exposes its throat, the victor leaves it alone instead of tearing open its throat. One could wish that "civilized" men would learn from the wolf not to fight to the death in their organized warfare, now with mechanized, monstrously unnatural weapons.

The only question is whether man can learn to develop an effective enough concern for these interests, whether through religion or education. The obvious difficulty is that the natural sociality that led to loyalty to the group or tribe has applied only to the in-group, as did the universal ethical principles found in all societies, including the condemnation of murder; outsiders remained fair game—killing them was not murder but might be authorized, even given the loftiest sanction, as it was by the God of ancient Israel for the sake of his "chosen people." In time men learned a loyalty to a much larger group, the nation, but now nationalism —long the ruling religion in the Western world—is the plainest obstacle to putting first the interests of mankind, instead of "my country." A further complication is that allegiance to the country may be a necessary step toward a larger allegiance, any sufficient sense of mankind. One may wonder, for example, whether some African peoples, who have not yet acquired a live sense of their nation but think chiefly of the interests of their tribe, can be expected to get on to the idea of mankind and its overriding interests.

Similar difficulties are raised by the idea of "human rights." Once a revolutionary doctrine, it is now enshrined in the Charter of the United Nations, and universally accepted—in theory. It may be grounded in our common humanity, the idea that all people should have some elementary rights simply by virtue of their humanity, or their claims as our fellow men. In common practice, however, nations notoriously fail to respect such rights. Thus America, whose founders declared that all men are endowed with "inalienable" rights to life, liberty, and the pursuit of happiness, long denied these rights to the Negroes it enslaved, and lately in effect denied any human rights to the Vietnamese peasants on whom we dropped bombs and napalm. Then a further difficulty is defining just what human rights are or ought to be in a changing world. We might all now agree that human beings ought not to be tortured, not to say tortured to death, as

[239]

many "heretics" were in the Middle Ages; though let us remember not only that torture was common practice in Hitler's concentration camps and Stalin's prisons, but that our napalm horribly burned people. (I remember too vividly a picture in *Life* magazine of a naked little Vietnamese boy stumbling down a road, crying —he had been hit by our napalm.) At best, the rights to life and liberty are not strictly inalienable, since they are denied to criminals; though now many people are questioning the ancient tradition of capital punishment.

On the other hand, some ancient rights are being questioned, notably the right to have as many children as one pleases. In affluent America scientists who are calling for a national austerity program are questioning the rights of Americans to pursue their happiness by consuming as much as they please, maintaining their high standard of living at the expense of the rest of mankind. But affluence has also made possible the declaration of new human rights. One is the right to decent medical care, which has grown too expensive for many poor people to afford. Another is the assurance of all the basic necessities of life, through such proposals as a guaranteed minimum income. The rising demands of a right to a job, in a country plagued by unemployment, might be offset by a demand that mothers on welfare rolls not be required to get a job outside the home. (As it is, President Nixon has attacked what he calls the "welfare ethic," insisted on the need of restoring the old "work ethic"; he appears to think that the traditional duty of mothers to take care of the home and the children is not work.)

Modern technology has likewise forced some new issues. One is the right to privacy, now threatened by government surveillance, with the help of wire-tapping, bugging, and super-snooping devices. In a supposedly free country, this may now be regarded as one of the most precious rights, no longer taken for granted. Somewhat more novel is the right to die when and as one pleases. Though this has long been denied by laws against

[240]

suicide, it now involves the rights of people to resist the traditional effort of doctors to prolong life at almost any cost, today by such means as endless blood transfusions, and in nursing homes by tending helpless, hopelessly senile people, even human vegetables. The families of such unfortunates might claim the right of euthanasia.

Less debatable, I think, are the dehumanizing tendencies of modern technology. Human beings are not suited, biologically or psychologically, to the mechanical, repetitive work that many have to perform.[7] The man-made environment today—noisy, crowded, polluted—suggests more plainly that people are not infinitely adaptable, to any kind of environment; though they may get used to it, they obviously suffer from it, even if to an extent unknown. Then one may wonder whether, in a revolutionary world, they can adapt themselves indefinitely to incessant, rapid change. Many are failing to do so adequately now, as indicated by the prevalence of tension, anxiety, and neurosis.

Hence one may complain of the dehumanizing tendencies too in the study of man, especially psychology. In an essay on "A Philosophy of Psychology: The Need for a Mature Science of Human Nature," the psychologist Abraham Maslow stressed how little we know for certain about people, how supremely important therefore the study of psychology is, and how sadly orthodox psychologists are failing to rise to this exciting challenge, because of narrow, unphilosophical, immature notions about science. He dwelt specifically on "the contrast between our knowledge of psychological sickness and our wholly inadequate attention to psychological health." He called for more attention to the "good life experiences," including the "peak experiences" of love, beauty, and creativity, or what people are like at their best—

7. I have read of a recent experiment in a chemical plant, where women had the job of spotting faulty capsules on a conveyor belt. Pigeons were trained to do the job—and proved better at it than the women. Not, of course, because they were brighter; the job was simply better suited to a birdbrain.

obviously important matters that psychologists shied away from because of a fear of not being precise or "scientific." (Maslow remarked incidentally that he couldn't find the word "love" indexed in any of the psychology books on his shelves, even those on marriage.) In general he argued that psychology should be more humanistic and philosophical, more concerned about the problems of humanity instead of the problems of the guild. As it was, the professionals tended to be at once too arrogant about their little knowledge and too timid to stray off the beaten path, to get involved with disreputable people like poets and artists who don't have a Ph.D. in psychology. Maslow lamented that most students came into the field with natural humanistic interests, but were then scared off from them, even made ashamed of them as fuzzy or unscientific.

His concern with good experiences that enrich the meaning of life, make it more worth while, and foster growth brings me back to the reasons for believing that the conventional American way of life, with its gospel of a high material standard of living, may be called unnatural. It is still possible, of course, for Americans to enjoy even "peak experiences," but they are distracted by the strictly artificial needs created by admen. Add that these become real needs, and that people get a real pleasure from satisfying them, the behavior of Americans suggests that this pleasure is not enriching their life or fostering growth. It is offset by the discontents that the admen are forever promoting, and at best it is not satisfying the basic spiritual needs of man. Like Maslow, I believe that people have a natural desire to grow and to realize their potentialities—to wonder and philosophize, to satisfy their curiosity, to enjoy beauty, to be creative, not merely to buy and consume, or to "adjust." My judgment of the American way of life remains debatable, needless to add, in particular because people all over the world envy our standard of living. Nevertheless I insist that the questions I have raised are the most important ones, which Americans ought to be pondering and debating

—more than most of them are. And then I should add that the common envy abroad of our standard of living does not prove its naturalness for modern man, for the envious are unlikely to realize the costs of the American way of life.

At any rate, I am led to my next topic, what Americans will be like in the future, for the immediate prospects are that they will have a superabundance of material goods, a still higher standard of living to enjoy, or to fail really to enjoy; at least if the rest of the world permits them to go on wallowing in their goods and squandering the earth's natural resources.

4. PEOPLE IN THE YEAR 2000

Although one cannot be sure what Americans will be like in that year 2000, one can venture some assumptions with a fair degree of confidence. To repeat, I assume that their human nature will remain basically the same. Biologists inspired by the hope of guiding or controlling human evolution, through genetic surgery or engineering, and with more widespread use of artificial insemination, will no doubt keep working to realize these possibilities; but at best it would take generations, or even centuries, to alter significantly man's hereditary constitution. Hence Americans in the next generation will retain basically the same capacities for enjoying and for suffering, as frail, fallible mortals. A few zealots today are indeed crusading against death as an intolerable indignity, proclaiming man's right to immortality on earth, but I know of no scientific authority for their belief that death can be done away with. It appears likely that Americans will live much longer than we do today, perhaps to the age of a hundred or more, with such aids as organ regeneration and transplantation, and means of reducing or postponing senility; but they will still know the pathos of mortality.

I also assume that life in the year 2000 will to a considerable extent be more of the same. Americans will still be trying to adapt

[243]

themselves to incessant, rapid change, since there is no prospect whatever of our calling a halt to the drive of our science and technology, much less of scrapping our knowledge and power. By the same token they will live in a still more massive, complex technological society, Although they should be more aware that their economic growth cannot continue indefinitely because of the depletion of the earth's finite natural resources, they might have available new sources of energy, such as solar energy, and in any case they will meanwhile almost surely have a still grosser national product to boast of or to deplore, inasmuch as there is no prospect either of the nation's adopting an austerity program, which the public is no more prepared to accept than are business and government. Americans will therefore still face the same odd problem of how to live well with abundance and affluence, which among other things would mean doing without many trivial, superfluous, or meretricious goods. With this they are pretty sure to inherit some of our specific problems, including such grave ones as the urban crisis and the environmental crisis. Not to mention the further problems that our futurologists anticipate, on the basis of what the nation is doing or failing to do right now, in particular what the men engaged in research and development are up to.

Since I know that I almost certainly will not live to see that year 2000, when my unknown grandchildren will be young, I wonder first of all what they will think of our age today. Will they look back on it with a shudder as a benighted age, full of horrors? Or will they look back on it wistfully as a time when life was simpler, and so presumably more wholesome or "natural"? Or will they look back on it at all? Our ever-fleeting present will be their past, and they might still share the delusion of many Americans today that the past is something dead and done with, even though they will be creatures of it just as we are today. I cannot know what they will think. All I feel sure of is that they will not be impressed by the high standard of living that Americans now boast of, nor awed by our technological feats, which their engineers will be able to surpass. (They may sneer, for example, at our vaunted "conquest of space"—the little space between our planet and the moon.)

From here on I can only speculate, sometimes with assurance about changes confidently anticipated by our futurologists, but always with uncertainty about how Americans will respond to these changes. Thus in general they may become more adaptable, through long experience of change, and suffer less from "future shock." On the other hand, they will still be subject to strains, perhaps more tensions than Americans now have to cope with. They may live in a less polluted environment, since we are now taking some steps to reduce pollution; but I suppose that really fresh air—not to mention fragrant air (such as I remember wistfully from my boyhood)—will remain a luxury. For Americans will also be living in a more crowded country, with still more automobiles. They are likely to be affected as well by the problems created by a more crowded planet, their little spaceship teeming with people.

Specifically, most Americans will most likely continue to live in or about our big cities, which are continuing to deteriorate, but which only prosperous people can afford to escape. Inasmuch as there is as yet no sign that government will launch the mighty, costly national effort it would take to clean up and restore the cities, make life in them more tolerable, I assume that they will probably be in worse shape in the year 2000. Los Angeles, the self-styled city of the future, inspired someone to say: "I have seen the future, and it doesn't work." At best our forecasters anticipate the growth of monstrous urban agglomerates to which they have given such suitably ugly names as Boswash (a sprawl extending from Boston to Washington). Elsewhere I have speculated that these will preserve some pleasing remnants of old towns and countryside, but that still more landscape and city-scape will have been destroyed by bulldozers; they will almost

[245]

certainly be threaded by highways, with cloverleafs every mile or so, for the sake of the untamed automobile; and at best they hold out no promise of a rich civic life, or a stimulating urban environment (such as I enjoyed when a young man in New York—a city that today I cannot stand).

This brings up my own main concern—the state of American culture in the year 2000. Daniel Bell has observed that developments in culture, or changes in values, are the hardest to forecast. Nevertheless Herman Kahn, our foremost futurologist, seems fairly confident about some immediate trends. In his latest work, *Things to Come: Thinking About the 70's and 80's* (written in collaboration with B. Bruce-Briggs, a colleague in the Hudson Institute, our foremost think-tank of futurologists), he anticipates an increasingly "sensate" culture, by which he means empirical, secular, humanistic, pragmatic, rational, and utilitarian, but also epicurean or hedonistic. Since he anticipates as well the continued growth of bourgeois, bureaucratic elites, I can only wonder: What will the ruling values of Americans be in the year 2000? Their living faith? Their lifestyle?

The current trends would lead me to expect a continued devotion to the conventional middle-class American way of life—except for the plain signs that it is spiritually unsatisfying. Conceivably Americans might seek more satisfaction of spiritual needs that I think they still have in spite of their materialism. In particular I think of the youth who are rebelling against the American way and experimenting with different lifestyles. But here the difficulty is that their so-called counterculture is not clearly a portent of the future. It involves much mere fashion or fad, which we can expect will be as passing as the fashions of yesteryear. It also involves much self-indulgence, most obviously in their drug culture, which even their sympathetic elders may deplore, and must hope is a passing fashion. In any case, I cannot know what they will be like when—or if—they mature. As one who is disposed to sympathize with their revolt, in particular because it has stirred up many thoughtful, earnest students who are neither wild-eyed radicals nor hedonists, I think that they will probably settle down and assume the responsibilities of adulthood and parenthood, though not—at least I hope—the American obligation to be first and last faithful, ardent consumers; but I cannot be sure.

Meanwhile the youth point to some more specific questions, such as the now popular demand for "liberation"—most vociferously by women, but also by homosexuals, pleased to think of themselves as "gay people," and other assorted rebels against convention or tradition. The chances are, I think, that they will achieve more liberation, well before the year 2000, as young people on the campus already have, at least in their social life. But there remains a troublesome question. Although I am disposed to regard the current demand for liberation as basically healthy, it involves some foolish posturing (in my experience homosexuals are not really gayer than other men), and in particular it often has a schizophrenic aspect as an exclusive insistence upon one's own personal demands, or as the popular saying now has it, upon what one owes oneself. It may come down to a liberation from all social constraints and responsibilities. I suppose that once these rebels against convention or tradition are liberated, and no longer have to posture, they are likely to settle down and assume their normal responsibilities; but again I cannot feel sure. The current trends to self-indulgence are pretty strong, and with increasing affluence and material abundance are likely to get stronger. At best Americans will have still greater need of the perennial wisdom of self-direction and self-mastery.

This brings me back to the problems of "alienation." I suppose that in their big cities Americans will remain more or less alienated from nature, despite the growth of suburbs and the persistence of lawns in Boswash. As things are going, the chances are that there will be still more commercial blight on the landscape, in "God's own junkyard," unless a "sensate" culture develops much more concern about educating and pleasing the senses

[247]

than seems likely under the prevailing rule of commercial values in our "pragmatic" land of neon and billboards.

Alienation from work may be eased by automation, but I assume that there will remain much mechanical work, in factory and office—work in which people cannot express or fulfill themselves. By the year 2000, however, more Americans should have a chance to realize their potentialities. Futurologists generally anticipate that there will be more professional or intellectual work in the society of the future, and this can be satisfying for its own sake, not merely a means of making a living. Professional people may therefore be expected to work longer hours than factory workers (as I have been doing all my life), yet not feel aggrieved.

Meanwhile automation points to an interesting question, and then to another odd problem. Because of improved technology, the work-week is being reduced, and by the year 2000 it may involve only half as many hours as workers now put in, perhaps even fewer. Herman Kahn and Anthony Weiner therefore anticipate that the value and necessity of work will be downgraded; they have said that "the man whose missionary zeal for work takes priority over all other values will be looked on as an unfortunate, perhaps even a harmful and destructive neurotic." In other words, the Protestant ethic will be no more, and Americans in the future might have to look up the term in their dictionaries. If so, however, there would have to be a considerable change in their attitude, for today they are complaining bitterly of the "welfare loafers" or "cheaters" whom they accuse of not wanting to work, and they are suspicious of such proposals as a guaranteed minimum income because they feel that only hard-working people deserve public support. By the year 2000 Americans may have learned to adapt themselves more readily to changed conditions of life, and may suffer less from the confusions and contradictions of cultural lag; but it will be difficult to eradicate such deep-rooted attitudes.

As it is, many men on relief suffer because they share these attitudes; they find it hard to maintain their self-respect unless they are breadwinners. The actual problem in America today is not getting rid of the loafers but finding jobs for the millions of unemployed who want to work. And since America has had millions of unemployed even when its economy was booming, my guess is that it will still be facing this whole problem in the year 2000—unless the economy is radically overhauled, a possibility that now seems to me highly unlikely. "Radical" remains one of the most horrid words in our land of revolutionary change.

An odder problem today is the problem of leisure—and the clear prospect of much more leisure because of a shorter workweek. Through the long ages of toil leisure was naturally regarded as a blessing, and it was never a problem for ordinary people because they had traditional, communal ways of enjoying their free time, through sport, song, dance, and festival. Americans still play games, enjoy picnics, go fishing, and have hobbies, but too many of them find it a problem how to spend all their free time or "empty hours," which too often remain empty. Most of them depend on the mechanical entertainment provided by the mass media, especially television, which is clearly here to stay. This serves as a distraction from their mechanical work, but is no more a means of expressing or fulfilling themselves; it is not recreation in the original sense of the word—a means to re-creation—but more a means of running away from themselves, or simply escaping boredom. While they think they enjoy the endless entertainment they spend so much of their time lapping up, day after day, on their record it is not deeply satisfying. Americans have made even so worldly a philosopher as Bertrand Russell look naive. In *In Praise of Idleness* (1932) he wrote that in a world where no one is compelled to work for more than four hours a day, "there will be happiness and a joy of life, instead of frayed nerves, weariness, and dyspepsia. . . . Since men will not be tired in their spare time, they will not demand only such amusements as are passive and vapid." Americans today hardly

[249]

look or behave as if they were approaching so joyous a state.

So the question is: Will they be more joyous in the year 2000, when many may be working little if any more than the four hours a day Russell dreamed of? Will they make more satisfying use of all their free time, which they are due to have more of? Will they depend less on passive or vapid television entertainment? I am inclined to doubt that most of them will. Leisure will be still more of a problem—unless our schools do much more to educate people for a wise use of it (according to Aristotle, a primary purpose of education). A possible exception will be the many Americans who will have gone to college, where they should be able to develop the intellectual or artistic interests that can make free time the blessing it ought to be; but I say only "possible" because of the current stress on professional training, in not only technical subjects but the humanities. Now I think in particular of retired people, who face the problem of filling the whole day, years on end, and many of whom lack the interests that could ease the problem. Many are unhappy because they are now *forced* to retire at an earlier age than in the past, and this growing trend seems likely to become stronger, especially because experience and skills may be antiquated by the latest developments in technology, a kind of premature obsolescence that is afflicting more and more men.[8]

These various obstacles to full self-realization recall another common refrain in the complaints about the alienation of modern man—that people are now alienated "from themselves." This

8. As an aging academic who was free to make my own choice, I feel sorry for even middle-aged men in the business world when I hear of the common refrain in the Help Wanted columns, especially advertisements of opportunities in middle management: "Men over forty need not apply." To think that men approaching only forty must begin to worry about their future! They ought to be vigorous enough at that age, but I suppose that by the year 2000 competition among managers might demand still more youthfulness. This might also assure an ability to endure the "rat-race" that businessmen now complain of, and that is plainly hard on their human nature, even though they in general have a properly developed "acquisitive instinct."

in turn leads to another of my own major concerns over the years —the Western tradition of individualism, because of which always unique individuals became self-conscious individual*ists,* and personal freedom came to be regarded as a natural *right.*

In America the issues were confused by the gospel of economic or "rugged" individualism, the glorification of free private enterprise and its rights. Today this gospel is strictly archaic. Rugged invidualism has become meaningless to most people, underlings in factories and offices, in an economy dominated by big corporations. Only the men at the top of these corporations can act like rugged individualists—as too many have been doing. Even some conservatives have come to recognize that big businessmen can no longer be granted their traditional right freely to exploit, squander, and pollute for the sake of private profit, at the expense of the public welfare. In a technological society, due to grow still more complex, private and public interests can no longer be separated as sharply as they traditionally have been.

But this development complicates as well the quite different kind of individualism I have supported, the kind upheld by John Stuart Mill in his classic *On Liberty*—the ideal of free and full personal development, to the end of having a life and a mind of one's own, pursuing one's own good in one's own way. The American gospel of economic individualism, with its primary if not exclusive devotion to business, tended to warp and impoverish individuality, and so led, not too paradoxically, to the conformism for which Americans have become notorious, a lack of enterprise and independence in thought, and a lack of pride in the sense of genuine self-respect. As I have already suggested, however, there may now have to be more restrictions on personal freedom in private life too; private and public interests can no longer be separated sharply either in such matters as breeding as many children as one pleases.

More troublesome are other reservations about Mill's gospel of individualism. He tended to slight the deep human need of community, or a sense of belonging. In our kind of society it has become clearer that the self-conscious individual may be a solitary person, feel lonely, isolated, or alienated. For all his rights and opportunities, such as men rarely if ever enjoyed in the past, he may suffer more as well from feelings of personal insignificance than did men in the past, who had a definite social status, however lonely. (Even the village idiot could feel at home.) And the costs of individuality may well be higher in the still more massive society of the future, with still bigger—and lonelier—crowds.

Nevertheless I still think that personal freedom is worth the costs. So too with the opportunities of young people for self-determination, even though they create the problem of an "identity crisis" that rarely troubled young people in the past, since with most of them their social status and personal identity were predetermined; only the privileged and the most ambitious could decide what kind of person they wanted to become. Basically I still adhere to Mill's ideal of having a life of one's own, within the limits imposed by social responsibilities, and above all the ideal of having a mind of one's own. This has become more important because of all the notorious pressures against the individual—the massive tendencies to regimentation and depersonalization, the social and business pressures to conformism, strengthened by the mass media, and lately the growing threats to privacy and personal freedom by government surveillance, all the data about people that may be stored and retrieved by computers. Hence I adhere as well to the dictum of Socrates, "The unexamined life is not worth living." Granted that most people throughout history have always lived such a life, accepting without question the bulk of the customs or conventions of their society, and that their conformity could promote simple decency, the Socratic ideal has also become more essential now that most Americans are educated enough to think for themselves, and most nevertheless accept unthinkingly the American way of life, despite the evi-

[252]

dence that it is not conducive to the happiness they are forever seeking by buying and consuming. Not to mention that natural, decent conformity has been transformed into a compulsive kind of conform*ism*, which in effect makes the unexamined life almost *de rigueur*. At least basic criticism of the American Way is commonly regarded as subversive, an un-American activity.

Then again the question: What will people be like in this respect in the year 2000? I assume that almost certainly they will have to contend against the same basic pressures against the individual. Most likely they will have more reason to worry over insidious threats to privacy and personal freedom. Herman Kahn, among other futurologists, confidently anticipates improved techniques for the surveillance, manipulation, and control of people. Inasmuch as present techniques are sufficiently effective to keep most Americans from worrying enough over threats to their rights, there is reason to believe that most will be even more docile in the future.

Yet I think that many Americans, at least, may have greater powers of resistance and self-assertion because of the strong counter-tendencies today, beginning with the spreading awareness of the pressures against the individual and his rights to independence, and the growing alarm over them. Other signs of resistance include the student revolt, the demonstrations in Washington, and the calls for participatory democracy. How effective these will be remains to be seen, but at least the best in the Western tradition of individualism is still alive. And I think that young people in particular will have as many choices in self-expression, self-realization, and self-determination as they now have, and perhaps more. If so, what they make of their opportunities will remain up to them. Then one may add that they will have to assume the responsibility of their choices, face the constant possibility of making some choices that they will later regret; at best, the grass will remain greener on the other side of the fence. And like many people today in our fast-changing world, amidst a wealth of opportunities and novelties, they may suffer because they are *forced* to make more choices than people were in the past. As they age, they may hanker more for a stability and security they are unlikely ever to know because of the dynamism of our technology, and in our cities the impermanence of surroundings. I see no prospect that our industrial cities will mellow with age, or that Boswash will either.

Finally, I take it that Americans in the year 2000 will still be interested in futurology, and have specialists looking ahead and trying to plan for the year 2100, even though it will lack the portentous significance of a beginning of a new milennium, or the end of an old one. To me the most important consideration is the spirit in which people will look ahead, the question whether they will *care* more about the future than most Americans now do. As it is, Americans may be dazzled by the popular visions of new wonders to come, but they either are too apathetic, bored by the American way of life, or are grumbling too much about the taxes they have to pay for the privilege of their high standard of living, really to care much about the immediate future in which their children will grow up; so they are mostly unwilling to pay more even for better schools. Their basic unconcern is due as well to a lack of a sense of the past, and a lack of reverence for our rich cultural heritage, especially from the distant past. I can only hope that in the next generation Americans will care more about the future. I cannot be confident that they will, if only because their heritage from our generation will scarcely be an inspiration; more obviously they will inherit the messes that we are failing to clean up. The chief reason for hope, as I see it, is again the many good earnest, thoughtful students who are concerned about the state of America today. They represent the best in our heritage from the American past, no less because they don't talk glibly about "the spirit of '76." In time they might offer new visions of better possibilities, beyond a "new prosperity," or a future gleaming with gadgets. If so, God bless them; or maybe God help them; that is if there be a God, which I don't know either.

XIII

A Personal Postscript

As an old man, Bertrand Russell remarked that he was fortunate in his late Victorian heritage because he grew up in an age that was dominated by hope rather than fear. In America I too grew up intellectually in an age that was still hopeful. Most of the serious American writers and thinkers in the period between the World Wars were highly critical of America, but they were typically upholders of the liberal tradition, not alienated from our society, and few wrote as if our social and political ills were incurable. When most alarmed by the urgency of our problems, as James Harvey Robinson sounded in *The Mind in the Making*, they still seemed basically confident; Robinson plainly had high hopes of his "new history," just as John Dewey did of his "method of intelligence." Most ordinary Americans likewise remained as hopeful as Americans had been all through their history. Even after the shock of the Great Depression—and those were very bad days indeed—most of them (including me) responded to the breezy challenge of Franklin D. Roosevelt: "We have nothing to fear but fear itself." When the war clouds gathered and burst, they had more reason for fear, but still did not really worry about our future; after the shock of Pearl Harbor they remained typically confident that America would win, as always. Intellectuals in particular were more united in a fighting cause, too convinced of the evil of Hitlerism to despise or despair of America.

Today, needless to add, their spirit is rather different. Our age is hardly dominated by hope. As for me, I have in this work conscientiously pointed out some reasons for hope—but somewhat too conscientiously, because I am not really hopeful about our future. At times I suspect that I ought to be more so, since we certainly need to retain hope. But I also suspect that I am not really fearful enough either, if only because I am pretty well off myself. Despite all the complaints of intellectuals about our mass society and its mass culture, I know from my own experience that America has in recent decades provided them with richer opportunities, and more lavish support, than ever before. Literary people have been pleased to call our age the Age of Anxiety—rather too pleased, I think, because they often appear to regard anxiety, like "alienation," as a kind of badge of distinction, and to wear it on their sleeve; while they also imply that never before have people suffered so from anxiety, forgetting the brute anxieties of the poor—the great majority of mankind throughout history— and the uncounted millions who starved to death during the periodic famines. At any rate, I do not boast that I don't suffer from anxiety. Lacking both a hopeful spirit and deep fear, I suspect too that—like many intellectuals these days—I am disposed to be merely querulous, as I keep harping on themes grown too familiar.

For this reason, however, I have tried hard to maintain a balanced view of our condition and our prospects. In this effort, which in the past was much easier for me, it has been a help that I have enjoyed life in our extraordinary age, despite all its horrors and its terrors, and have never wished that I had been born in an earlier age. At the same time, it has helped that I am cheerfully resigned to the thought that I shall not live to see the year 2000. For this reason too I can contemplate our prospects more or less philosophically, without intruding personal hopes, anxieties, or complaints.

Finally, I am comforted by the knowledge that thoughtful readers can always be trusted to discount or supplement my views, and that all along I have stressed the ambiguities and the uncertainties that give them ample opportunity to do so. For me this compensates for my inability to end on a high note, with either a radiant vision or a resonant statement of faith.

Index

Carnegie, Dale, 194
Castro, Fidel, 31, 133
China, xiv, xviii, 22, 131, 137; ancient, 45, 46, 59, 69, 128
Christianity, 117, 120–23, 127, 128, 129, 133–35, 136, 139, 140
Cold War, 12, 16, 17, 92
Communication, basic problems of, 182–84, 190–91, 192–93
Communism, 132–33, 157, 163. *See also* Karl Marx, Soviet Union
Computers, 6, 181, 193, 252
Confucius, 138, 140, 152
Cox, Harvey, 133
Crises, xvi, 138, 180; urban, xvii, xviii, 4, 22, 154, 205–6, 244, 245; environmental, 8, 14, 18, 25, 26, 53, 77–80, 244; American, 142–43, 146, 151, 154, 156, 157, 160, 161
Croly, Herbert, 154–55, 176
Culture, problems of today, 189–91, 197–98
Cyclical theory of history, 35–36

Darwinism, 232
DDT, 79, 80
Democracy, growth of, 40; present state of in America, 41–42, 140, 144, 145, 185. *See also* American way of life.
Descartes, René, 94
de Tocqueville, Alexis, 39–40
Dewey, John, 58, 162–70, 173, 175, 176, 177, 256
Dostoyevsky, Feodor, 237
Drug addiction, 86–88, 142
Dubos, René, 26, 46, 59, 77–78, 89

Eccles, John, 84, 93
Echeverría, Luis, 204, 205–6
Economic growth, goal of, 16–19, 37, 80, 209; problems created by, 19–21, 22, 23–24, 53, 80, 81, 90, 243–44. *See also* GNP.
Economics, 81–82
Eisenhower, Dwight, 15, 44n., 92, 137n., 148, 157, 159, 176
Eliot, T.S., 184, 185
Ellul, Jacques, 83
England, 160, 164, 172
Erlich, Paul and Anna, 18n.
Europe, western, xv, 10, 133, 160, 171

Fisher, David H., 41
Flores, Edmundo, 203–4
Forrester, Jay, 6–7
Forster, E. M., 187
Freud, Sigmund, 5, 91, 123, 132
Fromm, Erich, 185, 237
Futurology, growth of, 5–6; limitations of as a "science", 7–9, 12, 38, 44; need of, xiii, 13, 52

Galbraith, J. Kenneth, 171
Gandhi, 139
Garaudy, Roger, 134–35
Gardner, John, 66, 170
Gellman, Murray, 73
Geophysics, 77
Gideonse, Harry, 62n.
Gigantism, problems of, 80–81, 82, 93
Ginsberg, Allen, 69
Girardi, Giulio, 134, 136
GNP, 10, 19–20, 53, 81, 143, 144, 201, 202, 203. *See also* Economic growth

Goethe, Johann Wolfgang von, 63, 69
Goldsmith, Edward, 79
Goodman, Paul, 55, 170
Graham, Billy, 123, 135, 139
Greece, ancient, 41, 45, 46, 59, 73, 83, 97, 128, 130, 140, 143, 231, 234

Hacker, Andrew, 36
Handlin, Oscar, xvi
Harrington, Michael, 171, 173
Heard, Gerald, 119
Hedonism, xv, 63, 155, 246–47
Hegel, Georg, 32, 33, 35, 36, 58
Heisenberg, Werner, 73, 124
Hiroshima, 18, 42, 92
History, need of studying, xv, 27, 45, 52; dangers of as taught in schools, 27–28, 37; philosophy of, 33, 136; possible contributions to futurology, 38–40
Hitler, Adolf, 82, 92, 95, 105, 131, 169, 222, 240
Hobbes, T., 232
Holmes, Justice, 178
Hoover, Herbert, 196n.
Hoover, J. Edgar, 164n.
Human nature, relations to culture, 46, 58, 59, 212, 224, 225, 228, 230, 235–36; changes in, 58–59, 225, 228; reality of, 58, 59, 67, 224–25, 227, 229–38, 243; problems of defining, 83, 224–29
Humanism, religious, 116, 129–30, 136, 137
Humanities, values of, 28, 51–52, 54–55, 56, 57, 60–61, 65, 73, 91, 111; limitations of, 28–29, 61
Hutchins, Robert, 24, 30, 31

Huxley, Aldous, 3, 24, 39, 54, 105, 114
Huxley, Julian, 137

Ideology, growth of, 130–31; meanings of, 131n.
Imperialism, American, 15, 16, 204–5n.
India, ancient, 14, 41, 45, 46
Individualism, 103, 110, 146, 165, 171, 251–52, 253

James, William, 93, 130
Japan, xiv, xv, 18, 21, 39
Johnson, Lyndon B., 44–45, 152, 158
Jouvenel, Bertrand de, 7

Kafka, Franz, 122
Kahn, Herman, 5, 6, 48, 52, 53, 145, 246, 248, 253
Kant, Immanuel, 91, 98
Katz, Elihu, 198–99
Kennedy, John F., 16, 139
Kierkegaard, Soren, 129
Kissinger, Henry, 156–57

Langer, Suzanne, 74, 183n.
Language, abuses of, 194, 195
Lapp, Ralph, 44
Lawrence, D.H., 61, 69, 74
Leisure, problems of, 249–50
Lenin, Nikolai, 105, 134n.
Levi, Albert, 91
Levi-Strauss, Claude, 228
Lewis, Oscar, 193, 206
Lincoln, Abraham, 146
Linton, Ralph, 231, 235
Los Angeles, 22, 245

Watson, John B., 105, 108, 112
Watts, Alan, 84
Weathers, Winston, 84
Weber, Max, 29
Wells, H.G., 4
White, Lynn, Jr., 47
Whitman, Walt, 148–49, 150
Wiener, Anthony, 5, 6, 52, 248

World War II, 12, 92, 140, 256
Wurmser, Leon, 87–88

Youth, advantages of modern, 54, 57, 187, 253; problems of modern, 57, 187, 253–54; prospects of, 189